LÉON DENIS

# Joan of Arc Medium

HER VOICES, HER VISIONS, HER PREMONITIONS
HER PRESENT VIEWS EXPRESSED
IN HER OWN MESSAGES

ACCORDING TO THE 1926 EDITION

LÉON DENIS

# Joan of Arc Medium

HER VOICES, HER VISIONS, HER PREMONITIONS
HER PRESENT VIEWS EXPRESSED
IN HER OWN MESSAGES

ACCORDING TO THE 1926 EDITION

*ISBN: 978-1-948109-47-5*
*LCCN: 2025948045*

*Translation: Jussara Pretti Korngold*
*Book design: Diego Henrique Oliveira - Lab Editorial*
*Cover design: Jussara Pretti Korngold / Diego Henrique Oliveira*

*International data for cataloging in publication Denis, Léon, 1846-1927*
*The problem of life and destiny: experimental studies / Léon Denis.*
*Translator: Jussara Pretti Korngold. – New York: United States Spiritist Council, 2025.*

*Original title: JEANNE D'ARC MEDIUM. ses voix, ses visions, ses premonitions ses vues actuelles exprimees en ses propres messages (new rev., augm. ed., 1926).*

*ISBN: 978-1-948109-47-5*
*LCCN: 2025948045*

*1. Mediumship. 2. Spiritism. 3. Spiritualism. I. Title. II. Title.*

*1st edition, 1st print – November 2025*

# Contents

PREFACE .......... 11
INTRODUCTION .......... 13
JOAN OF ARC MEDIUM .......... 25

FIRST PART
LIFE AND MEDIUMSHIP OF JOAN OF ARC .......... 25

I
DOMRÉMY .......... 27

II
THE SITUATION IN 1429 .......... 33

III
CHILDHOOD OF JOAN OF ARC .......... 37

IV
THE MEDIUMSHIP OF JOAN OF ARC;
THE NATURE OF HER VOICES;
ANCIENT AND MODERN ANALOGOUS
PHENOMENA .......... 45

V
VAUCOULEURS .......... 93

VI
CHINON, POITIERS, TOURS .......... 97

VII
ORLÉANS .......... 109

VIII
REIMS .......... 121

IX
COMPIÈGNE. .......... 131

X
ROUEN; THE PRISON .......... 139

XI
ROUEN; THE TRIAL ........................................ 145

XII. – ROUEN; THE EXECUTION ........................... 171

SECOND PART
THE MISSIONS OF JOAN OF ARC ........................... 179

XIII
JOAN OF ARC AND THE IDEA OF THE
FATHERLAND ........................................ 181

XIV
JOAN OF ARC AND THE IDEA OF HUMANITY... 193

XV
JOAN OF ARC AND THE IDEA OF RELIGION...... 201

XVI
JOAN OF ARC AND THE CELTIC IDEAL .............. 227

XVII
JOAN OF ARC AND MODERN SPIRITUALISM..... 249

THE MISSIONS OF JOAN. ....................................... 249

XVIII
PORTRAIT AND CHARACTER OF
JOAN OF ARC ........................................ 271

XIX
MILITARY GENIUS OF JOAN OF ARC .................. 291

XX ........................................ 307

JOAN OF ARC IN THE
TWENTIETH CENTURY; ........................................ 307

HER ADMIRERS; HER DETRACTORS. .................. 307

XXI
JOAN OF ARC ABROAD ........................................ 323

CONCLUSIONS ........................................ 337

# PREFACE

It is with deep reverence and a heart filled with gratitude that I present this translation of Léon Denis' *Joan of Arc, Medium*. For many years, I have carried a profound admiration for Joan—her courage, her purity of heart, her mission of love and sacrifice. Always, in moments of reflection and work, she has remained a source of inspiration to me. It is, in truth, under the silent guidance of her memory that I felt called to render this sublime work accessible to new readers.



Léon Denis, with his luminous vision and unshakable faith, knew how to unveil the spiritual grandeur of Joan of Arc. His words penetrate beyond history, allowing us to glimpse not only the young shepherdess of Domremy, nor only the warrior and martyr, but the eternal soul who continues to illuminate humanity. To translate his testimony is to share in the torch he carried, passing it forward so that her voice may still be heard in our time.

This labor of translation has been more than a literary task—it has been a pilgrimage of the spirit. As I worked, I often felt that Joan herself whispered encouragement, just as she once spoke to inspire her companions in the hour of trial. May the reader, too, hear in these pages the call of her faith, the radiance of her courage, and the tenderness of her love.

It is my hope that this book may bring you closer to Joan, not as a distant figure confined to history, but as a living presence, ever near, who teaches us that even in our darkest hours, the light of the invisible world guides and sustains us.

*With veneration and joy.*
*Jussara Pretti Korngold*

# INTRODUCTION

Never has the memory of Joan of Arc been the subject of controversies as heated and passionate as those that erupted a few years ago around this towering figure of the past. On the one hand, while praising her, some have sought to claim her entirely for themselves, enclosing her personality within the confines of Catholic dogma. On the other hand—through tactics sometimes crude, as with Messrs. Thalamas and Henri Bérenger, and at other times subtle and scholarly, as in the case of Mr. Anatole France, whose exceptional talent gave weight to his arguments—efforts were made to diminish her prestige and reduce her mission to the proportions of a mere historical episode.

Where, then, can we find the truth about Joan's role in history? In our view, it lies neither in the mystical reveries of the devout nor in the overly literal arguments of positivist critics. Neither camp seems to hold the guiding thread that would allow us to navigate through the facts composing the fabric of this extraordinary life. To approach the mystery of Joan of Arc, it seems necessary to study and deeply engage with the psychic sciences; one must have explored the depths of that invisible world—that ocean of life that surrounds us, from which we emerge at birth and into which we return at death.

How could writers whose minds have never risen beyond the circle of earthly contingencies, beyond the narrow horizon of a purely material world, ever hope to understand Joan—when they have never even glimpsed the perspectives of the Beyond?

For the past fifty years, an entire body of facts, manifestations, and discoveries has shed new light on these vast dimensions of existence—long intuited, but until recently known only through vague and uncertain hints. Thanks to careful observation and the methodical study of psychic phenomena, a broad and powerful science is gradually taking form. The universe now reveals itself as a reservoir of unknown forces and incalculable energies. A dizzying infinity opens to human thought—an infinity of realities, forms, and vital powers once hidden from our senses, some of which have now been measured with remarkable precision by recording instruments.



The notion of the supernatural is crumbling; yet vast Nature ceaselessly pushes back the boundaries of its domain, and the possibility of an invisible organic life—richer, more intense than that of humankind—reveals itself, governed by majestic laws. This life, in many cases, intermingles with our own, exerting influences for good or for ill.

Many of the phenomena of the past, once affirmed in the name of faith and dismissed in the name of reason, can now receive a logical, scientific explanation. The extraordinary events that illuminate the life of the Maid of Orléans belong to this category. Their study—facilitated today by the knowledge of identical phenomena observed, classified, and recorded in our own time—alone can shed light on the nature and intervention of the forces that acted within her, around her, and guided her destiny toward a noble end.

The great historians of the nineteenth century—Michelet, Wallon, Quicherat, Henri Martin, Siméon Luce, Joseph Fabre, Vallet de Viriville, Lanéry d'Arc—were unanimous in their praise of Joan, seeing in her a heroic genius, a kind of national messiah.

It was only in the twentieth century that the critical note began to sound, and sometimes with violence. Was it true, as certain Catholic journals claimed, that Mr. Thalamas, a professor at the University, went so far as to call this heroine a *"ribaude"*—a wanton? He denied it. In his book *Jeanne d'Arc: History and Legend* (Paclot & Co., publishers), he remained within the bounds of fair and courteous criticism. His standpoint is that of the materialists: "It is not for us," he writes (p. 41), "who consider genius to be a form of neurosis, to reproach Joan for having projected onto saints the voices of her own conscience."

Yet in his public lectures across France he was often more trenchant. At Tours, on April 29, 1905, speaking under the auspices of the League of Education, he recalled the opinion of Professor Robin of Cempuis, one of his teachers, who believed that Joan of Arc had never existed at all, that her story was nothing more than a myth. Mr. Thalamas, perhaps reluctantly, acknowledged the reality of her life, but he attacked the sources from which her admirers had drawn, striving to diminish her role—though not stooping to insult. She had done little or nothing on her own, he suggested; for instance, the people of Orléans themselves, not Joan, deserved the credit for their deliverance.

Henri Bérenger and other writers echoed these views, and even official teaching seemed, to a degree, to absorb them. In elementary school textbooks, every trace of spiritualism was stripped away from the story of Joan. Her voices disappeared; now it was always "the voice of her conscience" that guided her. The difference is telling.

Anatole France, in his two-volume work—a triumph of art and intelligence—does not go so far. He cannot bring himself to deny the reality of Joan's visions and voices. A graduate of the École des Chartes, he was too well documented to risk denying the evidence. His book is a faithful reconstruction of the age: the appearance of cities, landscapes, and figures of the time is painted with masterly skill, with a delicacy of touch that recalls Renan. And yet, his narrative leaves us cold, even disappointed. His judgments are sometimes distorted by partisanship, and—more gravely—one senses throughout his pages a subtle, penetrating irony, which is no longer history but satire.

In truth, the impartial observer must admit that Joan, exalted by Catholics, has been diminished by freethinkers not so much out of hatred, but out of a spirit of contradiction and opposition toward the former. Thus the heroine, torn between two extremes, becomes a kind of pawn in the hands of rival factions. Both sides exaggerate, and the truth, as almost always, lies between them.

At the heart of the matter is the existence of hidden forces ignored by materialists—powers not supernatural or miraculous, as they claim, but belonging to domains of nature they have not yet explored. Hence their inability to comprehend Joan's mission and the means by which she was able to accomplish it.

They have failed to grasp the immensity of the obstacles that stood in her path. A poor child of eighteen, the daughter of humble peasants, uneducated— "not knowing her A or B," as the Chronicle says—she stood against her own family, against public opinion, against the whole world!

What could she have achieved without that inspiration, without that vision of the Beyond that sustained her?

Imagine this country girl in the presence of great lords, noble ladies, and prelates. At court, in the camps, everywhere—a simple commoner, coming from the depths of the countryside, ignorant of the art of war, speaking with her imperfect accent—she had to face the prejudices of rank and birth, the pride of caste, and later the mockery and brutality of soldiers, accustomed to despising women and unable to accept that a woman could command and direct them. Add to this the distrust of churchmen, who at that time saw in anything abnormal the intervention of the devil; they would not forgive her for acting outside of them, beyond their authority, and this would, above all, be the cause of her downfall.

Picture the unhealthy curiosity of everyone, and especially of the rough soldiers among whom, as a spotless virgin, she was obliged constantly to live: enduring fatigue, exhausting rides, the crushing weight of iron armor, sleeping on the ground under a tent, the long nights of camp life, with the worries and overwhelming concerns of her difficult mission.

During her brief career she overcame all these obstacles, and out of a divided people, torn by factions, demoralized, worn down by famine, plague, and all the miseries of a war lasting nearly a century, she made a victorious nation.

And yet writers of talent, blinded by a psychic and moral blindness—the worst of intellectual infirmities—have tried to explain this by purely material and earthly means. Poor explanations, poor lame arguments that do not withstand the test of facts! Poor shortsighted souls, souls of night, dazzled and disturbed by the light of the Beyond! To them applies the saying of a thinker: *What they know is nothing, and with what they do not know one could create the universe!*



It is a deplorable fact: certain critics of our time feel compelled to belittle, to diminish, to extinguish with frenzy everything great, everything that rises above their own moral incapacity. Wherever a hearth glows, wherever a flame is kindled, they hurry to pour a flood of icy water over that ray, over that torch.

Ah! How Joan, in her ignorance of human affairs but in her profound psychic vision, gave them a magnificent lesson with these words, addressed to the examiners at Poitiers, which apply so well to modern skeptics, to the shallow minds of our time: "I read in a book where there are more things than in yours!" Learn to read in it as well, gentlemen critics, and to acquaint yourselves with these problems; then you will be able to speak with a little more authority about Joan and her work.

Through the great scenes of history one must perceive the souls of nations and heroes. If you know how to love them, these souls will come to you, and they will inspire you. That is the secret of the genius of history. It is what made powerful writers such as Michelet, Henri Martin, and others. They understood the genius of races and times, and the breath of the Beyond runs through their pages. Others—Anatole France, Lavisse and his collaborators—remain dry and cold, despite their talent, because they neither know nor understand the eternal communion that nourishes soul by soul. This communion remains the secret of great artists, thinkers, and poets. Without it, there is no imperishable work.

An abundant source of inspiration flows from the invisible world upon humanity. Close bonds remain between the living and the departed. All souls are united by mysterious threads, and, even here below, the most sensitive vibrate to the rhythm of universal life. Such was the case with our heroine.



Criticism may attack her memory: its efforts will be in vain. The existence of the Virgin of Lorraine, like that of all great predestined beings, is engraved on the eternal granite of history; nothing can weaken its features. She is among those who show most clearly, through the tumultuous tide of events, the sovereign hand that leads the world.

To grasp the meaning of this life, to understand the power that directed it, one must rise to the higher, immanent law that governs the destiny of nations. Beyond earthly contingencies, above the confusion of facts produced by human freedom, one must see the action of an infallible will that overcomes the resistance of individual wills and acts, and brings to fruition the work it pursues. Instead of being lost in the chaos of events, one must embrace them as a whole, discern their hidden connection. Then the pattern, the chain that unites them, appears; their harmony is revealed, while their contradictions fade and merge into a vast plan.

One understands that there exists a latent, invisible energy that radiates over beings, and while allowing each a certain measure of initiative, it envelops and draws all toward the same goal.

It is in the proper balance between individual freedom and the authority of the supreme law that the apparent incoherences of life and history are reconciled and explained, while their deeper meaning and purpose are revealed to the one who knows how to penetrate the inner nature of things. Outside of this sovereign action, there would be nothing but disorder and chaos in the infinite variety of individual efforts and impulses—in short, in the whole work of humankind.

From Domrémy to Reims this action is evident in the epic of the Maid. Then the will of men coincided largely with the aims pursued from above. From the coronation onward, however, ingratitude, malice, the intrigues of courtiers and clerics, and the king's bad will took hold again. In Joan's own words, *"men refused themselves to God."* Selfishness, disorder, and greed obstructed the divine work carried out through Joan and her unseen allies. The work of deliverance became more uncertain, marked by vicissitudes, retreats, and defeats. Yet it continued nonetheless, though its accomplishment would require more years and more painful efforts.

It is, as we have said, solely from the point of view of a new science that we undertake this work. We wish to repeat this, so that our intentions are not misunderstood. In seeking to shed a little light on the life of Joan of Arc, we obey neither personal motives nor political or religious prejudice; we stand as far from anarchists as from reactionaries, equally distant from blind fanatics and from unbelievers.

It is in the name of truth, of moral beauty, and also out of love for the French homeland, that we will try to free the noble figure of the inspired Maid from the shadows that have been heaped around her.

Under the pretext of analysis and free criticism, there exists in our time, as we have said, a deeply regrettable tendency to disparage everything that has been admired through the centuries, to alter and tarnish whatever is pure and without stain.



We regard it as a duty—one incumbent on anyone who, by pen or word, is capable of exercising some influence around them—to uphold, defend, and elevate all that constitutes the greatness of our country: the noble examples it has offered the world, the scenes of beauty that enrich its past and shine over its history.

It is a wrongful act, almost a crime, to seek to weaken the moral heritage, the historical tradition of a people. Is this not, in fact, what gives them strength in difficult times? Is this not where they draw their most virile sentiments in the moment of danger?

The tradition of a people, its history, is the poetry of its life, its consolation in trial, its hope for the future.

Through the bonds it creates among all, we truly feel ourselves to be children of one and the same mother, members of a common homeland.

Thus it is necessary often to recall the great scenes of our national history and to highlight them. It is full of shining lessons, rich in powerful teachings, and in this, perhaps, it surpasses that of other nations. As soon as we explore the past of our race, everywhere, in every age, we see great figures rise up, and these figures speak to us, exhort us. From the depths of the centuries, voices arise that remind us of great memories—memories that, if always present in our minds, would suffice to inspire and illuminate our lives. But the wind of skepticism blows, forgetfulness and indifference set in; the concerns of material life absorb us, and we end up losing sight of what is greatest, most eloquent in the testimony of the past.



Among these memories, there is none more moving, more glorious, than that of this extraordinary young girl, who illuminated the night of the Middle Ages with her radiant appearance, and of whom Henri Martin could say: *"Nothing like it has ever occurred in the history of the world."*

In the name of the past and the future of our race, in the name of the work that still remains for it to accomplish, let us strive to preserve in its entirety all its moral heritage, and let us not hesitate to correct the false judgments that certain writers have put forward in their works. Let us labor to cast out from the soul of the people the intellectual poison that some attempt to spread there, so as to preserve for France that beauty and that strength which will make her great again in hours of peril, and to restore to the national genius all its prestige and brilliance, weakened by so many harmful theories and sophistries.

The war of 1914 silenced vain polemics and sterile criticism. In the midst of the storm, France remembered Joan only to implore her protection, her aid!

It must be acknowledged that in the Catholic world, better than anywhere else, solemn homage has been rendered to Joan. In believing circles she is praised, she is prayed to, after having been beatified. On their side, republican freethinkers have contributed to the establishment of an annual festival in her honor—a national festival, which is at the same time a festival of patriotism. But in one camp as in the other, little success has been had in truly understanding the character of the heroine, in grasping the meaning of her life.

The history of Joan is like an inexhaustible mine of lessons, whose full scope has not been measured, from which not all the benefit has been drawn that could elevate minds and deepen the understanding of the higher laws of the soul and of the universe.



In this life there are depths that can make unprepared minds dizzy; there are facts likely to sow uncertainty and confusion in the thoughts of those who do not possess the necessary data to resolve this vast problem. Hence so many sterile discussions, so many futile controversies. But for the one who has lifted the veil of the invisible world, Joan's life becomes clear, luminous. Everything in her is explained, understood.

Indeed, among those who praise the heroine, how many differing perspectives, how many contradictory judgments! Some seek above all, in her memory, an illustration for their party; others, by a belated glorification, aim to absolve a certain centuries-old institution of the responsibilities that weighed upon it.

There are those who see in Joan's success nothing more than the exaltation of popular and patriotic sentiment.

One may well ask whether, in the praise that rises from all corners of France toward the great inspired one, there are not mixed many selfish motives and interested views. People think of Joan, no doubt, they love Joan, but at the same time, do they not think too much of themselves or of their party? Do they not seek, in this august life, what might flatter their personal feelings, their political opinions, their unavowed ambitions? Very few people, I fear, know how to rise above partisanship, above the interests of caste or class. Very few attempt to penetrate the secret of this existence, and among those who have, none, until now—except in limited cases — has dared to raise his voice and say what he knew, what he saw and understood.

As for myself, if my titles are modest for speaking of Joan of Arc, at least there is one I claim proudly: that of being free from any concern of party, from any desire to please or displease. It is with the full freedom of my thought, in the independence of my conscience, unattached to anything, seeking and desiring nothing but truth, that I approach this great subject, to seek the key to the mystery that hovers over this incomparable destiny.

# JOAN OF ARC MEDIUM

## FIRST PART
## LIFE AND MEDIUMSHIP OF JOAN OF ARC

# I
# DOMRÉMY

*The valley is delightful: a dazzling stream*
*Plays there in the light of day: it is the Meuse.*

*Saint-Yves d'Alveydre*

Son of Lorraine, born like Joan in the valley of the Meuse, my childhood was cradled by the memories she left in the land.

During my youth, I often visited the places where she had lived. I loved to wander beneath the great arches of our Lorraine forests, remnants of the ancient forest of Gaul. Like her, I often listened to the harmonies of the fields and the woods. And I can say that I, too, know the mysterious voices of space—the voices that, in solitude, inspire the thinker and reveal to him eternal truths.

Grown to manhood, I wished to follow, throughout France, the trace of her steps. I retraced, almost stage by stage, that sorrowful journey. I saw the castle of Chinon, where she was received by Charles VII, now nothing but a ruin. I saw, deep in Touraine, the little church of Fierbois, from which she had the sword of Charles Martel brought forth, and the caves of Courtineau where she took refuge during the storm; then Orléans and Reims, and Compiègne, where she was taken prisoner. There was not a place where she had passed that I did not go to meditate, to pray, to weep in silence.

Later, in that city of Rouen, over which her great shadow still hovers, I completed this pilgrimage. Like the Christians who trace step by step the way to Calvary, I followed the sorrowful path that led the great martyr to her punishment.

More recently, I returned to Domrémy. I saw again the humble cottage where she was born; the small room with its narrow window, where her virginal body, destined for the stake, once brushed the walls; the rustic cupboard where she kept her garments; and the very spot where, rapt in ecstasy, she listened to her voices; then the church where she so often prayed.

From there, by the path climbing the hill, I reached the sacred place where she loved to dream; I saw again her father's vineyard, the fairy tree, and the murmuring fountain. The cuckoo sang in the ancient woods; the scent of hawthorn floated in the air; the breeze stirred the foliage and awakened a plaintive sound deep in the thicket. At my feet stretched smiling meadows, dotted with flowers, watered by the winding Meuse.

In the distance, wooded hills and deep ravines succeeded one another as far as the horizon; a penetrating gentleness, a serene peace, hovered over the whole countryside. This, indeed, is the blessed place, suited to meditation; the place where the vague harmonies of heaven mingle with the distant, tranquil murmurs of the earth. O dreamy soul of Joan! Here I seek the impressions that enveloped you, and I find them—overwhelming, profound. They seize my spirit, filling it with poignant rapture. And your entire life, a dazzling epic, unfolds before my mind like a vast panorama, crowned by an apotheosis of flames. For an instant I lived that life, and what my heart felt no human pen could ever describe!

Behind me, like a foreign monument, a discordant note in this symphony of impressions and memories, rise the basilica and the theatrical monument where one sees Joan kneeling at the feet of Saint Michael and two gilded images of saints. The statue of Joan alone, rich in expression, touches, moves, and holds the gaze.

At some distance from Domrémy, on a steep hillside amid the woods, lies the modest chapel of Bermont. Joan went there every week; she followed the path that, from Greux, stretches across the plateau, winds beneath the shade, and passes near the fountain of Saint-Thiébault. She climbed the hill to kneel before the ancient Madonna, whose statue, dating from the eighth century, is still venerated today. I followed this picturesque path, thoughtful, reverent; I walked through those thick woods where birds sing. The whole region is steeped in Celtic memories; our ancestors had erected there an altar of stone. Those sacred fountains, those austere groves, were witnesses to the ceremonies of the Druidic cult. The soul of Gaul still lives and throbs in these places. Doubtless it spoke to Joan's heart, as it still speaks today to the hearts of patriots and enlightened believers.

I went further; I wished to see in the surrounding area all that was part of Joan's life, all that recalls her memory: Vouthon, where her mother was born, and the small village of Burey-la-Côte, which still preserves the home of her uncle Durand Laxart—the one who helped fulfill her mission by taking her to Vaucouleurs, to Sir de Baudricourt. The humble house still stands, with fleur-de-lis emblems decorating its threshold, but it has been turned into a stable. A simple chain holds its door; I loosened it, and at my sight a little goat, nestled in the shadows, uttered its thin, plaintive cry.

I wandered everywhere in that land, intoxicated by the sight of the places that framed Joan's childhood. I walked the narrow valleys branching off from that of the Meuse, hollowed out between the dark woods. I meditated in solitude, in the evening, at the hour when the stars light up the depths of the heavens. I listened to every sound, to every mysterious voice of nature. In those places I felt far from humankind; an invisible world hovered around me.

Then prayer sprang forth from the depths of my being; I invoked Joan's spirit, and at once I felt the support and sweetness of her presence. The air trembled; everything around me seemed illuminated; invisible wings beat in the night; an unknown melody descended from the skies, lulled my senses, and brought tears to my eyes.



And the Angel of France dictated to me words which, at her command, I faithfully set down here:

## MESSAGE OF JOAN

"Your soul is rising and feels in this moment the protection that God bestows upon you.

"With me, may your courage grow, and, as a sincere patriot, love and desire to be useful to this beloved

France, which, from above, as Protectress and as Mother, I always behold with joy.

"Do you not feel within yourself the birth of thoughts of gentle indulgence? Near God, I have learned to forgive; yet these thoughts must not give rise in me to weakness. And, as a divine gift, I find in my heart enough strength to seek, at times, to enlighten those who, out of pride, wish to seize hold of my memory.

"And when, through indulgence, I call down upon them the light of the Creator, of the Father, I feel that God says to me: *'Protect, inspire, but never merge yourself with your executioners. The priests, in recalling your devotion to the homeland, must ask only forgiveness for those whose legacy they have taken up.'*

"A devout and sincere Christian on earth, I feel in the beyond the same impulses, the same desire for prayer. But I want my memory to be free and untainted by calculation; I give my heart, as a remembrance, only to those who see in me nothing more than the humble and pious daughter of God, loving all those who live on this land of France, to whom I seek to inspire sentiments of love, integrity, and strength."

# II
# THE SITUATION IN 1429

*Now France lay in the tomb! Of her glory,*
*What remained? To the West an urn of tears: the*
*Loire: A shadow, to the East the Dauphiné.*

*Saint-Yves d'Alveydre*

What was the situation of France in the fifteenth century, at the moment when Joan of Arc was about to appear upon the great stage of history?

The war against England had lasted for nearly a hundred years. In four successive defeats, the French nobility had been crushed, almost annihilated. From Crécy to Poitiers, and from the fields of Agincourt to those of Verneuil, our chivalry had strewn the ground with their dead. What remained of it was divided into rival factions, whose internal quarrels weakened and devastated France. The Duke of Orléans was assassinated by the hirelings of the Duke of Burgundy, and the latter, a little later, was killed by the Armagnacs. All this took place under the eyes of the enemy, who advanced step by step, invading the provinces of the North, while Guyenne had long since been under his occupation.

After a desperate resistance, during a siege that surpassed in horror all that imagination could conceive of the dreadful, Rouen was forced to surrender. Paris, its population decimated by disease and famine, was in the hands of the English. The Loire beheld them on its banks. Orléans, whose fall would deliver the very heart of France to the foreigner, still resisted—but for how long?

Vast stretches of our country were turned into desert. No more cultivation; villages were abandoned. One saw only brambles and thistles growing unchecked, ruins blackened by fire; everywhere, the marks of war's ravages, desolation, and death. The peasants, in despair, hid in underground shelters; others took refuge in the islands of the Loire or sought asylum in the towns, where they perished of hunger. Often, to escape the soldiery, these wretched people fled into the forests, banded together, and soon became as cruel as the marauding troops from whom they had fled. Wolves prowled around the edges of the cities, entered them at night, and devoured the unburied corpses.

This was, as Joan's voices said to her, *"the great pity that is in the kingdom of France."*

The poor Charles VI, in his madness, signed the Treaty of Troyes, which disinherited his son and made Henry of England heir to his crown. And when, in the basilica of Saint-Denis, over the coffin of the mad king, a herald-at-arms proclaimed Henry of Lancaster King of France and England, the remains of our kings, lying beneath the heavy slabs of their tombs, must have shuddered with shame and sorrow.

The dauphin Charles, dispossessed and mockingly called the *"king of Bourges"*, gave way to discouragement and inertia; he lacked both resources and valor; his counselors secretly negotiated with the enemy. He himself thought of fleeing to Scotland or Castile, renouncing the throne to which, he believed, he might not even have a right, for doubts assailed him concerning the legitimacy of his birth. And nothing more was heard but the lamentable plaint, the cry of agony of a people whom their conquerors were preparing to lay in the tomb. France felt herself lost; she was struck to the heart. A few more defeats, and she would descend into the great silence of death.

What help could be expected, indeed? No earthly power was capable of accomplishing such a prodigy: the resurrection of a people that had surrendered itself. But there is another power, invisible, that watches over the destinies of nations. At the moment when all seemed to collapse, it would bring forth from the bosom of the masses the redeeming aid. Certain omens seemed to herald its coming.



Already, among so many other signs, a visionary, Marie of Avignon, had gone to the king; in her ecstasies, she said, she had seen an armor that heaven was reserving for a young girl destined to save the kingdom[1]. Everywhere, people spoke of the ancient prophecy of Merlin, announcing a virgin deliverer who would come forth from the Bois Chesnu[2].

And then, like a ray from above, in the midst of this night of desolation and misery, Joan appeared.

1 J. FABRE, *Procès de réhabilitation*, t. I, pp. 157-158.
2 J. FABRE, *Procès de réhabilitation*, t. I, pp. 123, 162, 202, 366.

Listen, listen! From the depths of the fields and forests of Lorraine, the gallop of her horse resounded; she was coming; she would revive this despairing people, raise up fallen courage, direct the resistance, and save France from death!

# III
# CHILDHOOD OF JOAN OF ARC

*At the sound of the Angelus ringing,*
*Her heavenly memory vibrates and lives again.*
*Saint-Yves d'Alveydre*

At the foot of the hills that border the Meuse, a few cottages cluster around a modest church; upstream and downstream stretch green meadows watered by the little river with its clear waters. On the slopes, fields and vineyards succeed one another up to the deep forest, rising like a wall along the crest of the hills—a forest full of mysterious murmurs and birdsong, from which, at times, wolves suddenly emerge, terror of the flocks, or armed men, plunderers and devastators, more dangerous than wild beasts.

This is Domrémy, a village until then unknown, but which, through the child born there in 1412, would become famous throughout the world.

To recall the story of that child, of that young girl, is still the best way to refute the arguments of her detractors. This is what we shall do first of all, by focusing especially on the facts that have remained in shadow, some of which have been revealed to us through mediumship.

Numerous works, masterpieces of learning and erudition, have been written about the Maid of Lorraine. Far be it from me to claim to equal them. Yet this book is distinguished by a characteristic feature: it is illuminated here and there by the thought of the heroine herself. Thanks to authentic messages—messages which will be found especially in the second part of this volume—it becomes, as it were, an echo of her own voice and of the voices of the beyond. By this title, it recommends itself to the attention of the reader.

Joan was not of noble birth; the daughter of poor farmers, she spun wool at her mother's side or tended her flock in the meadows of the Meuse, when she was not accompanying her father at the plough[3].

She knew neither how to read nor to write[4]; she was ignorant of all things concerning war. She was a gentle and good child, loved by everyone, especially by the poor and the unfortunate, whom she never failed to help and console. Touching anecdotes are told about her in this regard. She would willingly give up her own bed to some weary pilgrim and spend the night on a bundle of straw, so as to provide rest for old people exhausted by a long journey. She cared for the sick, as in the case of little Simon Musnier, her neighbor, who shivered with fever; placing herself at his bedside, she watched over him during the night.



Dreamful by nature, she loved in the evening to contemplate the star-filled sky, or during the day to follow the gradations of light and shadow. The sound of the wind in the branches or in the reeds, the murmur

3 J. FABRE, *Procès de réhabilitation*, t. I, pp. 80, 106, etc.
4 J. FABRE, *Procès de réhabilitation*, t. II, p. 145.

of springs—all the harmonies of nature delighted her. Yet, above all, she preferred the sound of bells. For her, it was like a greeting from heaven to earth. And when, in the peace of evening, far from the village, in some fold of ground where her flock was sheltered, she heard their silvery notes, their calm and slow vibrations announcing the time of return, she was absorbed into a kind of ecstasy, into a long prayer in which she poured out her whole soul, thirsting for divine things. Despite her poverty, she always found a way to give the village bell-ringer a small gratuity, so that he would prolong the song of the bells beyond the usual time[5].

Filled with the intuition that her coming to earth had a lofty purpose, she plunged in thought into the depths of the invisible, seeking to discern the path she should take. "She was searching for herself," Henri Martin[6] tells us.



While among her companions so many souls remained shut away, as if extinguished in their bodily prison, her whole being opened itself to higher influences. In sleep, her spirit, freed from material bonds, soared into ethereal space; there it perceived the intense radiance, it was renewed in the powerful currents of life and love that reign there; and upon awakening, it retained the intuition of the things glimpsed. Thus, little by little, through such exercises, her psychic faculties awoke and grew. Soon, they would enter into action.

Yet these impressions, these reveries, did not diminish her love of work. Diligent in her tasks, she neglected nothing to satisfy her parents and all those

5 Voir J. FABRE, *Procès de réhabilitation*, t. I, p. 106.
6 *Histoire de France*, t. VI, p. 140.

with whom she had dealings. *"Long live labor!"* she would say later, affirming thereby that work is the best friend of humankind—its support, its counselor in life, its comforter in trial—and that there is no true happiness without it. *"Long live labor!"* was the motto that her family would adopt and have inscribed on their coat of arms when the king ennobled them.

Even in the humble details of Joan's daily life there was manifested a keen sense of duty, sound judgment, and a clear vision of things that set her above all those around her. Already one recognized in her an extraordinary soul, one of those passionate and profound souls who descend to earth to accomplish a great mission. A mysterious influence surrounded her. Voices spoke to her ears and to her heart; invisible beings inspired her, directed all her actions, all her steps. And then those voices gave commands. Imperious orders made themselves heard. She must renounce her peaceful life. Poor child of seventeen, she would have to face the tumult of the camps! And at what time? At that savage time when soldiers were too often little more than bandits. She would leave everything—her village, her father and mother, her flock, all that she loved—to hasten to the aid of dying France. To the good people of Vaucouleurs, who pitied her fate, what would she reply? *"It is for this that I was born!"*

The first vision occurred one summer's day, at the hour of noon. The sky was cloudless, and the sun poured down upon the drowsy earth all the enchantments of its light. Joan was praying in the garden adjoining her father's house, near the church. She heard a voice that said to her: *"Joan, daughter of God, be good and wise; attend the church*[7]*; put your trust in the Lord*[8]*."* She was seized with awe; but, raising her eyes, in a dazzling brightness she saw an angelic figure, which expressed both strength and gentleness, and which was surrounded by radiant forms.

One day, the Spirit—the Archangel Saint Michael and the holy women who accompanied him—spoke to her about the state of the country and revealed to Joan her mission: *"You must go to the aid of the dauphin, so that through you he may recover his kingdom*[9]*."*

At first Joan resisted: *"I am but a poor girl, knowing neither how to ride nor to make war!"*

*"Daughter of God, go; I will be your help,"* the voice replied.

Little by little, her conversations with the Spirits became more frequent; they were never long. The counsels from above are always brief, concise, full of light. Such is evident from her answers at the interrogations in Rouen. *"What doctrine did Saint Michael teach you?"* she was asked. *"Above all things, he said to me: Be a good child, and God will help you*[10]*."*

This is simple and sublime at once, and it sums up the entire law of life. The higher Spirits do not extend themselves in long discourses. Even today, those who can communicate with the higher planes of the Beyond

7 At that time, the Catholic religion was the only one known. This is why the Spirit who presented himself under the name of Saint Michael—entering into the views of the age in order the better to achieve his aim—could not have spoken in any other way. See further on: *Mediumship and the Idea of Religion in Joan of Arc.*

8 HENRI MARTIN, *Histoire de France*, t. VI, p. 142.

9 HENRI MARTIN, *Histoire de France*, t. VI, p. 142.

10 J. FABRE, *Procès de condamnation*, p. 174.

receive little more than short instructions, profound and marked with the stamp of great wisdom. And Joan added: *"Saint Michael taught me to conduct myself well and to attend the church."*

Indeed, for every soul aspiring to goodness, upright conduct, recollection, and prayer are the first conditions of a righteous and pure life.

One day Saint Michael said to her: *"Daughter of God, you will lead the dauphin to Reims, that he may there receive his rightful coronation*[11]*."* Saint Catherine and Saint Margaret repeated to her unceasingly: *"Go, go, we will help you!"*

Thus there was established between Joan and her guides a close relationship. From her "brothers of paradise," she drew the resolution necessary to accomplish her mission; she was wholly imbued with it. France awaited her—she must depart!



At the first light of a winter's day, Joan rose. She prepared her small bundle, her travel stick, and then went to kneel at the bedside where her father and mother were still sleeping, and silently she murmured a tearful farewell. At that painful hour she recalled the worries, the tenderness, the care of her mother, and the concerns of her father, whose brow was already bent with age. She thought of the emptiness her departure would cause, of the sorrow of all those with whom she had until then shared life, joys, and sorrows. But duty commanded; she would not fail in her task.

Farewell, poor parents! Farewell, you who were so often troubled by dreams of your daughter seen in the

---

11 *Procès*, t. I, p. 130.

company of soldiers[12]! She would not conduct herself as you had feared, for she was pure, pure as the spotless lily; her heart knew only one love: that of her country.

*"Farewell, I am going to Vaucouleurs,"* she said as she passed the house of the farmer Gérard, whose family was close to hers. *"Farewell, Mengette,"* she said to her companion. *"Farewell, all of you, with whom I have lived happily until now!"*

There was, however, one dear friend from whom she avoided taking leave: her beloved Hauviette. Such a farewell would have been too moving; Joan might perhaps have felt shaken, and she needed all her courage[13].

She departed for Burey, where one of her uncles lived, in order to go from there to Vaucouleurs and then to France. At seventeen years of age, she set out alone, under the vast sky, on a road strewn with dangers. And Domrémy never saw her again.

12 J. FABRE, *Procès de condamnation*, pp. 142-143.
13 J. Fabre, *Trial of Rehabilitation, Depositions of Six Peasants*.

# IV
# THE MEDIUMSHIP OF JOAN OF ARC; THE NATURE OF HER VOICES; ANCIENT AND MODERN ANALOGOUS PHENOMENA

*Standing, eyes in tears, she listens intently*
*To some messenger from the heavens!*
*Paul Allard*

The phenomena of vision, audition, and premonition that mark the life of Joan of Arc have given rise to the most diverse interpretations. Among historians, some have seen in them nothing more than cases of hallucination; others have gone so far as to speak of hysteria or neurosis. Still others have ascribed to these events a supernatural and miraculous character.

The essential aim of this work is to analyze these phenomena, to demonstrate that they are real and connected to laws long unknown, but whose existence is being revealed, day by day, in a manner ever more striking and precise.

As knowledge of the universe and of the human being expands, the notion of the supernatural recedes and vanishes. It is now understood: nature is one. Yet within its immensity it contains realms, forms of life, that long escaped our senses. And our senses are of the narrowest kind. They allow us to perceive only the coarsest, most elementary aspects of the universe and of life. Their poverty, their insufficiency, was revealed most clearly at the moment when powerful optical instruments—the telescope and the microscope—were invented, widening in every direction the field of our visual perceptions. What did we know of the infinitely small before the construction of magnifying instruments? What did we know of those innumerable existences swarming and stirring around us, and even within us?

And yet, these are but the lowest depths of nature, so to speak—the substratum of life. Above them, planes rise in succession and ascend step by step, upon which existences of ever greater subtlety are graded: more ethereal, more intelligent, still of a human character at certain levels, then angelic at higher ones—belonging always, in their forms if not in their essence, to those imponderable states of matter which science today acknowledges in several aspects: for example, in the radioactivity of bodies, in Roentgen rays, and in the whole set of experiments concerning radiant matter.

Beyond the visible and tangible forms familiar to us, we now know that matter persists under many and varied states, invisible and imponderable. Little by little it refines, transforms itself into force and into light, until it becomes the cosmic ether of the physicists. In all these states, under all these aspects, it is still the substance in which countless organisms are woven—forms of life of unimaginable tenuity. In this ocean of subtle matter, a life intense and vibrant stirs above and around us.

Beyond the narrow circle of our sensations, abysses open; a vast unknown world unfolds, populated with forces and beings we do not perceive, yet who nonetheless take part in our existence, in our joys and our sorrows, and, to some extent, may influence us, may aid us. It is into this immeasurable world that a new science strives to penetrate.

In a lecture delivered at the Institut Général Psychologique some years ago, Dr. Duclaux, director of the Pasteur Institute, expressed himself in these terms: *"This world, filled with influences which we undergo without knowing them, permeated with that quid divinum which we divine without perceiving in detail, is more interesting than the world to which our thought has until now confined itself. Let us endeavor to open it to our investigations: there are immense discoveries to be made there, discoveries from which humanity will benefit."*

And here is the marvelous thing: we ourselves, for the most important part of our being, belong to this invisible world that is revealed daily to attentive observers. In every human being there exists a fluidic form, a subtle, indestructible body, a faithful image of the physical body, of which the latter is only the temporary covering, the coarse sheath. This form has its own senses, more powerful than those of the physical body; the latter are nothing more than their weakened prolongation[14].



14 The existence of this double or phantom of the living is established by innumerable facts and testimonies. It can detach itself from its corporeal envelope during sleep, whether natural or induced, and manifest at a distance. The telepathic cases, the phenomena of doubling, of exteriorization, of apparitions of living persons at locations far from the place where they rest—so often reported by F. Myers, C. Flammarion, Professor Ch. Richet, Doctors Dariex and Maxwell, etc.—are the most evident

The fluidic body is the true seat of our faculties, of our consciousness, of what believers of all ages have called the soul. This is not a vague metaphysical entity, but rather an imperishable center of strength and life, inseparable from its subtle form. It preexisted our birth, and death has no power over it. Beyond the grave, it is found again in the fullness of its intellectual and moral acquisitions. Its destiny is to pursue, through time and space, its evolution toward ever better states, increasingly illuminated by the rays of justice, truth, and eternal beauty. The being, forever perfectible, gathers in its expanded psychic state the fruits of the labors, sacrifices, and trials of all its existences.

Those who lived among us and now continue their evolution in space do not remain indifferent to our sufferings and our tears. From the higher planes of universal life, currents of strength and inspiration constantly flow down to the earth. From there arise the sudden illuminations of genius, the powerful breaths that sweep over the masses in decisive hours; from there also comes support and comfort for those who bend beneath the burden of existence. A mysterious bond links the visible and the invisible. Relations can be established with the Beyond through certain specially gifted persons, in whom the hidden senses of the soul—the psychic senses, those profound faculties dormant in



---

experimental demonstration of it. The reports of the Society for Psychical Research of London, composed of the most eminent scholars of England, are rich in facts of this kind. For more details, see: LÉON DENIS, After Death, "The Perispirit or Fluidic Body," chap. XXI; In the Invisible, "The Spirit and its Form," chap. III – "Exteriorization of the Human Being. The Phantoms of the Living," chap. XII.

every human being—may awaken and come into action even in this life. These intermediaries are those we call mediums.

In the time of Joan of Arc, such things could not be understood. Knowledge of the universe and of the true nature of being was but confused, and in many respects incomplete or erroneous. Yet, for centuries, the human spirit—despite its hesitations and uncertainties—has advanced from conquest to conquest. Today, it begins to spread its wings. Human thought rises, as we have just seen, above the physical world and plunges into the vast regions of the psychic world, where one begins to glimpse the secret of causes, the key to all mysteries, the solution to the great problems of life, death, and destiny.

We have not forgotten the mockery to which these studies were subjected at the beginning, nor how many criticisms are still aimed at those who courageously persevere in these researches and relations with the invisible. But have not many discoveries—even within scientific societies—been ridiculed, only to be later revealed as shining truths? So it will be with the existence of Spirits. One after another, men of science are compelled to admit it, often as the result of experiments originally intended to disprove its very foundation. Sir W. Crookes, the famous English chemist, ranked by his compatriots alongside Newton, was among them. We may also cite Russell Wallace, O. Lodge; Lombroso in Italy; Doctors Paul Gibier and Dariex in France; in Russia, the State Councillor Aksakof; in Germany, Baron du Prel and the astronomer Zöllner[15].



15 We are familiar with the experiments of the illustrious physicist Sir William Crookes, who, for three years, ob-

The serious person who keeps an equal distance from blind credulity and from an equally blind incredulity is compelled to recognize that such manifestations have taken place in all ages. They are found on every page of history, in the sacred books of all peoples—among the seers of India, Egypt, Greece, and Rome, as well as among the mediums of our own day. The prophets of

---

tained materializations of the Spirit *Katie King* in his home under conditions of strict control. Speaking of these manifestations, Crookes declared: *"I do not say that this is possible; I say: this is."*

It has been claimed that W. Crookes later retracted. However, he wrote again to the *Revue scientifique et morale du spiritisme* in Paris (May 1919 issue): *"In response to your request, I see no objection to stating my position regarding what are called psychic phenomena and to reaffirming, just as I did forty years ago when I began my investigation, that I remain faithful to what I wrote and have nothing to retract."*

Oliver Lodge, rector of the University of Birmingham and member of the Royal Academy, wrote: *"I was personally brought to certainty regarding future existence by evidence resting on a purely scientific basis.*

Frederic Myers, professor at Cambridge, whom the official International Congress of Psychology in Paris in 1900 elected honorary president, reached in his admirable book *Human Personality* the conclusion that voices and messages come back to us from beyond the grave. Speaking of the medium Mrs. Thompson, he wrote: *"I believe that most of these messages come from Spirits who temporarily use the organism of mediums in order to give them to us."*

The renowned Professor Lombroso of Turin declared in *La Lettura*: *"The cases of haunted houses, in which, for years, apparitions or noises are reproduced that correspond with the accounts of tragic deaths, and which are observed outside the presence of mediums, argue in favor of the action of the departed."* — *"These often concern uninhabited houses, where such phenomena sometimes occur for several generations and even for centuries."* (See also *Haunted Houses*, C. Flammarion, 1 vol., 1924).

Judea, the Christian apostles, the druidesses of Gaul, the inspired ones of the Cévennes at the time of the Camisard war, all drew their revelations from the same source as our good Lorraine.

Mediumship has always existed, for the human being has always been spirit, and that spirit has, in every age, opened a window into the world inaccessible to our ordinary senses.

Constant, permanent, these manifestations occur in every environment and in every form, from the most common, the crudest—such as table-turning, the transportation of objects without contact, haunted houses—to the most delicate and sublime, such as ecstasy or lofty inspirations, depending on the elevation of the Intelligences involved.

Let us now turn to the study of the phenomena found in abundance in the life of Joan of Arc. It must first be noted that it was thanks to her extraordinary psychic faculties that she was able to gain such rapid ascendancy over both the army and the people. She was regarded as a being endowed with supernatural powers.

That army was nothing more than a motley collection of adventurers and mercenaries driven by the love of plunder. All vices reigned among those undisciplined troops, always on the verge of dispersing. It was in the midst of these coarse soldiers, without restraint and without shame, that a young girl of eighteen was called to live.

Such rough men, who did not even respect the name of God[16], she had to transform into believers—into men ready to sacrifice everything for a noble and holy cause.

She knew how to accomplish this miracle. At first, she was received as an intriguer, as one of those women whom armies often drag along in their wake. But her inspired speech, her austere manners, her sobriety, and the prodigies that soon occurred around her quickly imposed respect upon those crude imaginations.

The army and the people, too, were tempted to regard her as a kind of fairy, a sorceress. She was given the names of those fantastical beings said to haunt springs and woods.

Her task only became more difficult to fulfill. She had to make herself both respected and loved as a leader; through her authority, she had to compel those mercenary soldiers to see in her an image of France, of the homeland she sought to embody.

Through her fulfilled predictions and accomplished deeds, she inspired them with absolute confidence. They came almost to deify her; her presence was, for them, a guarantee of success, a symbol of celestial intervention. Admiring her, becoming attached to her, they proved more faithful to her than to the king and the nobles. At the mere sight of her, all malicious thoughts and feelings were silenced, giving way to veneration. All regarded her as a superhuman being, according to the testimony of her steward, Jean d'Aulon, at the trial[17]. Count Guy de Laval, after seeing her at Selles-sur-Cher in the company

---

16 "If God were a man-at-arms," said La Hire, "He would become a plunderer."

17 J. FABRE, *Procès de réhabilitation*, t. I, pp. 158, 248.

of the king, wrote to his mother on June 8, 1429: *"It is a wholly divine thing to see her and to hear her*[18]*."*

Without hidden assistance, how could a simple peasant girl have acquired such prestige, achieved such victories? What she had learned of war in her youth—the constant alarms of peasants, the devastated villages, the cries of the wounded and dying, the glow of fires—was enough to repel her from the art of arms rather than draw her to it. But she was chosen from on high, to raise France from its downfall and to instill in every soul the notion of homeland. For this, marvelous faculties and powerful aid were granted to her.

Let us examine more closely the nature and scope of Joan's mediumistic faculties.

First, there were those mysterious voices she heard in the silence of the woods as well as in the tumult of battle, in the depths of her prison cell, and even before her judges—voices often accompanied by apparitions, as she herself testified at her trial, during twelve separate interrogations. Then, there were the many cases of premonition—that is, prophecies fulfilled, announcements of events yet to come.

First of all, are these facts authentic? On this point, no doubt is possible. The texts and testimonies are abundant; letters and chronicles confirm them in great number[19].

18 E. LAVISSE, *Histoire de France*, t. IV, p. 55.

19 PERCEVAL DE CAGNY, *Chronicles*, published by H. Moranvillé, Paris, 1902. – JEAN CHARTIER, *Chronicle of Charles VII*. – *Journal of the Siege of Orléans (1428–1429)*, published by P. Charpentier. – *Chronicle of the Maid*. – *Mystery of the Siege of Orléans*, etc.

Above all, there is the trial of Rouen, whose records—drafted by the accused's enemies—bear witness even more strongly in her favor than those of the trial of rehabilitation. In the latter, the same facts are attested under oath by witnesses of her life, testifying before the investigators or before the tribunal[20].

And above all these testimonies, we must place the judgment of one man, a contemporary whose authority is considerable: Quicherat, director of the École des Chartes. He was no mystic or visionary, but a serious, sober man, an eminent historian and critic. After profound research, entirely erudite and based on a scrupulous examination of Joan of Arc's life, he concluded[21]: *"Whether science accepts it or not, her visions must nevertheless be admitted."*

I would add: new science *will* accept them. For all these phenomena, once considered miraculous, are explained today by the laws of mediumship.



Joan was uneducated; her only books were nature and the starry sky. When Pierre de Versailles questioned her at Poitiers about her learning, she replied: *"I do not know A from B."* Several witnesses confirm this in the rehabilitation trial[22]. Yet she undertook the most marvelous work ever accomplished by a woman. To succeed, she displayed rare aptitudes and extraordinary qualities. Illiterate, she confounded and convinced the learned doctors of Poitiers. By her military genius and the skill of her plans, she quickly gained influence over

20 This rehabilitation trial includes, according to A. France, 140 depositions given by 123 witnesses.

21 J. QUICHERAT, *New Insights on the Trial of Joan of Arc*, pp. 60–61.

22 J. FABRE, *Rehabilitation Trial*, vol. I, p. 161; vol. II, p. 145.

captains and soldiers alike. At Rouen, she stood before sixty scholars—casuists skilled in legal and theological subtleties—she thwarted their traps, answered all their objections, and more than once embarrassed them with replies as swift as lightning and as piercing as a blade.

How can such overwhelming superiority be reconciled with her lack of education? Ah! There is another source of teaching besides the science of schools. It was through constant communion with the invisible world, since the age of thirteen when she experienced her first vision, that Joan acquired the light necessary for the accomplishment of her arduous mission. The lessons of our guides from the Beyond are more effective than those of professors, and richer above all in moral revelation.

These paths of knowledge are rarely cultivated by Universities or Churches. Their representatives read little in that *"book of God"* of which Joan spoke, in that great book of the invisible universe from which she had drawn wisdom and light: *"There are in Our Lord's books more than in yours. My Lord has a book in which no clerk has ever read, however learned he may be!"* she declared at Poitiers[23].



By this, she reminds us that the occult and divine worlds possess sources of truth far deeper and richer than those accessible to human effort. These sources open sometimes to the simple, the humble, the ignorant—those marked with God's seal. There, they find elements of knowledge that surpass everything study alone can provide.

---

23 J. FABRE, *Rehabilitation Trial*, vol. I, Deposition of Pasquerel, p. 228.

Human science is rarely without a touch of pride. Its teachings almost always carry the weight of convention, of affectation, of pedantry. They often lack clarity and simplicity. Some works of psychology, for example, are so obscure, complex, and bristling with baroque expressions that they border on the ridiculous. It is almost amusing to see the feats of imagination and intellectual gymnastics to which men like Professor Th. Flournoy and Dr. Grasset resort, in order to construct theories as laughable as they are learned. Truths that come from higher revelation appear, by contrast, as flashes of light: in a few words, through the mouths of the simple, they resolve the most difficult problems.

*"I thank You, O Father," said Christ, "for having revealed to the little ones what You have hidden from the wise.*[24]*"*

Bernardin de Saint-Pierre expresses the same thought: *"To find the truth, one must seek it with a simple heart."* It was with such a simple heart that Joan listened to her voices, that she questioned them in important matters, and, always confident in their wise guidance, she became, under the impulse of higher powers, a marvelous instrument endowed with precious psychic faculties.

Not only did she see and hear wonderfully, but her sense of touch and even her sense of smell were affected by the apparitions that presented themselves to her: *"I touched Saint Catherine when she appeared visibly to me,"* she said. *"Did you kiss or embrace Saint Catherine or Saint Margaret?"* she was asked. *"I embraced them*

24 Luke, X, 21.

*both." "Did they smell sweet?" "It is good to know that they smelled sweet!*[25] "

In another interrogation, she expressed herself in these terms: *"I saw Saint Michael and the angels with the eyes of my body just as well as I see you. And when they left me, I wept, and I would have wished they had taken me away with them.*[26] "

Such is the impression felt by all mediums who glimpse the splendors of space and the radiant beings who live there. They experience a rapture that makes the realities of earth all the sadder and heavier. To have shared, even for an instant, in the life of heaven, and then to fall back heavily into the darkness of our world—what a poignant contrast! It was even more so for Joan, whose exquisite soul, after finding itself for a moment in the milieu that was familiar to her, from which she had come, and having received "great comfort" from it, now saw itself once again faced with the harsh and painful duties that lay upon her.



Few people understand these things. The vulgarities of the earth conceal from them the beauties of that invisible world which surrounds them, in which they move as blindly as one who walks in light without perceiving it. Yet there are delicate souls, beings endowed with subtle senses, for whom the heavy veil of material things is at times torn. Through these openings they glimpse a fragment of that divine world, the realm of true joys, of genuine felicities, where we shall all meet again at death—freer and happier in proportion as we

25 J. FABRE, Trial of Condemnation, p. 187.

26 J. FABRE, Trial of Condemnation, 4th public interrogation, p. 81.

have lived better in thought and heart, have loved more, and suffered more.

It was not only upon these extraordinary facts—these visions and these voices—that Joan's confidence in her friends of the unseen world was based. Reason also demonstrated to her how pure and elevated was the source of her inspirations, for her voices always guided her toward useful action, in the direction of devotion and sacrifice. While some visionaries lose themselves in barren dreams, in Joan's case the psychic phenomena all contributed to the fulfillment of a great work. Hence her unshakable faith: *"I believe as firmly,"* she replied to her judges, *"in the words and deeds of Saint Michael, who appeared to me, as I believe that Our Lord Jesus Christ suffered death and passion for us. And what moves me to believe it is the good counsel, the comfort, and the teachings that he gave me.*[27] *"*



In her sound judgment, it was above all the moral side of these manifestations that constituted, in her eyes, a guarantee and a proof of their authenticity. By their effective advice, their constant support, and the wholesome instructions they gave her, she recognized in her guides true messengers from on high.

During the trial, as in her military actions, her voices advised her on what she should say and do. She turned to them in all difficult situations: *"I asked counsel of the voice about what I should answer, telling it to seek counsel from Our Lord. And the voice said to me: 'Answer boldly. God will help you.*[28] *'"*

---

27 J. FABRE, Trial of Condemnation, p. 176.

28 J. FABRE, Trial of Condemnation, p. 68.

Her judges pressed her on this point: *"How do your saints give you their answers?"* To which Joan replied: *"When I make request to Saint Catherine, then she and Saint Margaret make request to God, and afterward, by God's command, they give me the answer*[29]*."*

Thus, for all who know how to seek the unseen in recollection and prayer, divine thought descends, step by step, from the heights of the heavens to the depths of human conscience. But not all discern it as Joan did.

When her voices were silent, she refused to answer on any important question: *"You shall not have that from me yet; I have not God's permission. I believe I do not tell you fully all that I know. But I have greater fear of failing my voices by saying something that would displease them than I have of answering you."*

Admirable discretion—and one that many men would do well to imitate—when the voices of wisdom and conscience do not bid them to speak[30].

Until the very end of her tragic life, Joan showed deep love for her invisible guides and complete trust in their protection. Even when they seemed to abandon her, after having promised deliverance, she uttered no complaint, no blasphemy. By her own admission, they had told her in prison: *"You will be delivered by great victory.*[31]*"* And instead of deliverance, it was death that came. Her interrogators, who neglected no opportunity to drive her to despair, pressed her on this apparent



29 J. FABRE, Trial of Condemnation, 5° secret interrogation, p. 157.

30 J. FABRE, Trial of Condemnation, 3° inter. public, p. 69.

31 J. FABRE, Trial of Condemnation, p. 159.

betrayal. Joan replied calmly: *"Never have I cursed nor spoken ill of any saint."*

The history of the Maid of Lorraine contains numerous cases of clairvoyance and premonition, which lent her, in the eyes of all, a mysterious power of divination. At times, she seemed to read the future—for example, when she said to the soldier at Chinon who insulted her as she entered the castle: *"Ah! you deny God, and yet you are so near your death!"* That very evening the soldier accidentally drowned[32].

So it was with the Englishman Glasdale, at the assault on the fortress of the Bridge before Orléans. She summoned him to surrender to the King of Heaven, adding: *"I have great pity for your soul!"* At that very moment Glasdale fell, fully armed, into the Loire, where he drowned[33]. Later, at Jargeau, she foresaw the danger threatening the Duke of Alençon, to whose life she had promised to attend: *"Gentle Duke,"* she cried, *"withdraw from where you stand, else that cannon yonder will send you to your death."* The warning was exact, for Lord du Lude, who took the place the duke abandoned, was slain there shortly after[34].

At other times, and most often, Joan herself declared, she was forewarned by her voices. At Vaucouleurs, without ever having seen him, she went straight to Robert de Baudricourt: *"I recognized him,"* she explained, *"thanks to my voice. It said to me: 'That is he[35]!'"* She foretold to him the deliverance of Orléans, the coronation of the

32 J. FABRE, Trial of Rehabilitation t. I, p. 218.
33 J. FABRE, Trial of Rehabilitation, t. I, p. 227.
34 J. FABRE, Trial of Rehabilitation, t. I, p. 179.
35 J. FABRE, Trial of Rehabilitation, p. 58.

king at Reims, and even announced the French defeat at the "Day of the Herrings," at the very moment when it had just occurred[36].

At Chinon, brought into the king's presence, Joan unhesitatingly recognized him among three hundred courtiers in whose midst he had disguised himself: *"When I entered the king's chamber,"* she said, *"I knew him among the others by the counsel of my voice, which revealed him to me.*[37]*"* In a private audience, she even reminded him of the words of a silent prayer he had addressed to God when alone in his oratory.

Her voices told her that the sword of Charles Martel lay buried in the church of Sainte-Catherine-de-Fierbois, and they revealed it to her[38].

It was again the voice that roused her at Orléans when, exhausted with fatigue, she had thrown herself on a bed, unaware of the assault on the fortress of Saint-Loup: *"My counsel has told me to go against the English!"* she cried suddenly. *"Why did you not tell me that the blood of France was being shed?*[39]*"*



Joan knew, because she had been warned by her guides, that she would be wounded by an arrow during the attack on the Tourelles, on May 7, 1429. A letter from the Sire de Rotselaer, chargé d'affaires of Brabant, preserved in the Brussels archives and dated April 22 of the same year—fifteen days before the event—records this prediction and the manner in which it would be

36 *Journal du siège*, p. 48. - *Chronique de la Pucelle*, p. 275.
37 J. FABRE, Trial of Condemnation, pp. 61-62.
38 *Ibid.*, 4th public interrogation, pp. 85-86.
39 J. FABRE, Trial of Rehabilitation, t. I. Deposition of page of Joan, p. 210.

fulfilled. On the eve of battle, Joan again declared: *"Tomorrow, blood shall flow from my body*[40]*."*

On that same day, against all likelihood, she foretold that the triumphant army would re-enter Orléans by the bridge, though it had been broken. And so it was.

Once the city was delivered, Joan pressed the king not to delay the march to Reims, repeating: *"I shall last but a year, Sire, therefore you must make good use of me*[41]*!"*—a clear foreknowledge of her brief career.

She was also warned by her voices of the impending surrender of Troyes; later still, of her coming captivity: *"During Easter week, as I stood on the moat of Melun, it was told me by my voices that I should be taken before Saint John's Day,"* she told her judges at Rouen, *"and I begged them that when I was taken, I might die at once without long torment in prison. And they said to me: 'Accept all with grace. It must be so.' But they did not tell me the hour*[42]*."* On this point, she gave a beautiful reply to her interrogators: *"Had I known the hour, I would not willingly have gone there. Yet I would have done as my voices commanded, whatever might have come of it*[43]*."*



A touching scene is also told from the church at Compiègne: in tears, she said to those around her: *"Good friends and dear children, know that I have been sold and betrayed. Soon I shall be delivered to death. Pray for me*[44]*!"*

In prison, her guides foretold to her, to her great joy, the deliverance of Compiègne[45]. She also had the

---

40 J. FABRE, Trial of Rehabilitation, p. 226.

41 *Ibid.*, t. I. Deposition of the duc d'Alençon, p. 182.

42 J. FABRE, Trial of Condemnation, p. 129.

43 J. FABRE, Trial of Condemnation, p. 130.

44 See HENRI MARTIN, *Histoire de France*, t. VI, p. 228.

45 J. FABRE, Trial of Condemnation, p. 156.

revelation of her tragic end, under a form she did not understand, but which her judges readily grasped: *"What my voices tell me most is that I shall be delivered... They add: 'Accept all with grace; do not trouble yourself about your martyrdom. At last you shall come to the kingdom of Paradise[46].'"*

Often her voices warned her of the secret councils held by captains jealous of her glory, who concealed their deliberations on the conduct of war. But suddenly Joan would appear, already knowing their decisions in advance, and would foil them: *"You have held your council, and I have held mine,"* she told them. *"The counsel of God will be fulfilled, yours will perish[47]."*

Is it not also to the inspirations of her guides that Joan owed those eminent qualities which make the great general—her knowledge of strategy and ballistics, her skill in employing artillery, then a novelty? How else could she have known that the French preferred to advance in open field rather than fight behind walls? And how else could one explain that a simple shepherdess became, in a single day, at eighteen years old, an incomparable commander and consummate tactician?

Thus it is clear: her mediumship took varied forms. Those faculties, dispersed and fragmentary among most subjects today, were united in her, grouped in powerful harmony. Moreover, they were heightened by her great moral worth. The heroine was the interpreter, the agent of that invisible, subtle, ethereal world which extends beyond our own, and whose vibrations, harmonies, and voices certain specially gifted human beings can perceive.



46 J. FABRE, Trial of Condemnation, p. 159.
47 J. FABRE, Trial of Condemnation, t. I, p. 226.

The phenomena that fill Joan's life are linked together and converge toward the same goal. The mission imposed by the higher Entities, whose nature and character we shall later attempt to determine, is clear and precise. It was announced in advance and was fulfilled in its broad outlines. Her whole story bears witness to it. To her judges in Rouen, she said: *"I have come on behalf of God. I have nothing to do here. Send me back to God, from whom I came*[48]*."*

And when, at the stake, the flames surrounded and consumed her flesh, she cried out once more: *"Yes, my voices were from God! My voices did not deceive me!*[49]*"*

Could Joan have lied? Her sincerity, her integrity—manifested in all circumstances—stand as her testimony. A soul so loyal, who accepted every sacrifice rather than renounce France and her king, could not stoop to falsehood. There is such an accent of truth, such conviction in her words, that no one, not even among her most ardent detractors, dared to accuse her of imposture. Anatole France, who certainly does not spare her criticism, wrote: *"What emerges above all from the texts is that she was a saint. She was a saint with all the attributes of sanctity in the fifteenth century. She had visions, and these visions were neither feigned nor fabricated."* And further: *"One cannot suspect her of lying.*[50]*"*

Her loyalty was absolute; to support her statements, she did not, like so many others, resort to excessive words or exaggerated expressions. *"She never swore,"* says a witness at the rehabilitation trial, *"and to affirm*

48 J. FABRE, Trial of Condemnation, p. 66.

49 J. FABRE, Trial of Rehabilitation, t. II, p. 91.

50 ANATOLE FRANCE, *Vie de Jeanne d'Arc*, t. I, pp. 32-39.

*something, she was content to add: 'Sans manque' [Without fail]*[51]*."* These words also appear in the interrogations of the Rouen trial. They carried a special meaning when spoken by her, uttered with that tone of frankness and with that open countenance that were uniquely hers.

From another point of view: was she mistaken? Her good sense, her clarity of mind, her sure judgment, and those flashes of genius that illuminate her life here and there, do not permit us to believe so. Joan was not delusional! Certain critics, however, have thought otherwise. Most physiologists—such as Pierre Janet, Th. Ribot, Dr. Grasset—and alienists like Dr. Lélut, Dr. Calmeil, and others, see in mediumship only one of the forms of hysteria or neurosis. For them, seers are but patients, and Joan of Arc herself does not escape their judgment. More recently, Professor Morselli, in his study *Psychology and Spiritism*, even goes so far as to consider mediums to be weak or unbalanced minds.



It is always easy to label as delusions, hallucinations, or madness those facts that displease us or that we cannot explain. In this, many skeptics believe themselves very wise, when in truth they are merely victims of their own prejudice.

Joan was neither hysterical nor neurotic. She was strong and enjoyed perfect health. Her morals were chaste, and although her beauty was full of charm, her presence inspired respect and even veneration, even among the rough soldiers who shared her life[52]. Three times—at Chinon, at the beginning of her career, at

51 J. FABRE, Trial of Rehabilitation, t. I, p. 78.

52 J. FABRE, Trial of Rehabilitation, t. I. Déposition de Jean de Metz, p. 128. - Déposition de

Poitiers, and at Rouen—she underwent examination by matrons, who attested to her virginity.

She endured the greatest fatigues without weakening. *"It happened that she passed as many as six days under arms,"* wrote Perceval de Boulainvilliers, counselor and chamberlain of Charles VII, on June 21, 1429. And when she was on horseback, she inspired the admiration of her companions-in-arms, by the length of time she could remain mounted without feeling the need to dismount[53]. Her endurance is attested in many depositions. *"She bore herself in such a manner,"* said the knight Thibault d'Armagnac, *"that it would not be possible for any man whatsoever to have shown better conduct in the act of war. All the captains marveled at the hardships and labors she endured*[54]*."*

The same was true of her sobriety: we have many testimonies on this point, from those who saw her only briefly, like Lady Colette, to those who were part of her daily entourage. Her page, Louis de Contes, said: *"Joan was very temperate. Many times, during an entire day, she ate nothing but a piece of bread. I marveled that she ate so little. When she stayed at home, she ate only twice a day*[55]*."*



The marvelous rapidity with which our heroine recovered from her wounds reveals in her a powerful vitality: a few moments, a few days were enough for her, and she returned to the battlefield. After having leapt

---

Bertrand de Poulengy, p. 133. - Déposition de l'écuyer Gobert Thibault, p. 164. Déposition du duc d'Alençon, p. 183. - Déposition de Dunois, p. 201, etc.

53 J. FABRE, Trial of Rehabilitation, t. I, p. 149.

54 J. FABRE, Trial of Rehabilitation, t. I, p. 282.

55 J. FABRE, Trial of Rehabilitation, t. I, pp. 201, 211, 273, 279, etc.

from the tower of Beaurevoir and sustaining serious injuries, she regained health as soon as she was able to take some nourishment. Do such facts indicate a weak or neurotic nature?

And if we pass from her physical qualities to those of the mind, the same conclusion imposes itself. The many phenomena of which Jeanne was the agent, far from disturbing her reason—as is the case with hysterics—seem, on the contrary, to have strengthened it, if we judge by the lucid, clear, decisive, and unexpected answers she gave to her interrogators at Rouen. Her memory remained sound, her judgment intact; she preserved the fullness of her intellectual faculties and her self-mastery.

Dr. G. Dumas, professor at the Sorbonne, in a note published by Anatole France at the end of his second volume, declared that, from the testimonies, he had not succeeded in finding in Joan any of the classical marks of hysteria. He insists at length on the externality of the phenomena, on their objective clarity, on the *"relative independence and authority"* of the inspired one with respect to the *"saints."* It does not seem to him that her visions can be reduced to any pathological type observed experimentally.

"Nul indice," says Andrew Lang[56], "permits us to think that Joan, while she was in communion with her saints, ever found herself 'dissociated,' or unconscious of what surrounded her. On the contrary, we see that, in the terrible scene of her abjuration, she heard at once, with equal clarity, both the voices of her saints and the



56 A. LANG, *la Jeanne d'Arc d'Anatole France*, pp. 126-127.

sermon of her preacher, whose errors she did not hesitate to criticize."

Let us add that she was never obsessed, since her Spirits came only at certain moments, and especially when she called them, whereas obsession is characterized by the constant, inescapable presence of invisible beings.

Joan's voices were always related to her great mission; never were their words childish; they always had their reason for being, they never contradicted one another, nor were they tainted with the erroneous beliefs of the time, which would have been the case had Joan been predisposed to hallucinations. Far from placing faith in fairies, in the virtues of the mandrake, and in a hundred other false ideas of the period, she shows in her interrogations either ignorance of them or the contempt in which she held them[57].



In Joan, there was no selfish sentiment, no pride, such as in hallucinators who, attributing great importance to their small person, see around them only enemies and persecutors. Her every thought, under divine inspiration, was for France and for her king.

The great alienist Brierre de Boismont, who studied the question attentively[58], recognized in Joan a superior intelligence. Yet he qualified the phenomena of which she was the subject as hallucinations, but gave them a physiological and not a pathological character. By this, he meant that these hallucinations did not prevent her from preserving the integrity of her reason; they would be the fruit of a mental exaltation which, however, had

57 J. FABRE, Trial of Condemnation, 3° et 5° public interrogation ; 9° secret interrogation ; act of accusation.

58 BRIERRE DE BOISMONT, *De l'hallucination historique.*

nothing morbid about it. For him, the conception of the guiding idea, a "powerful stimulant," took form as an image in Joan's brain, and in her he admired a soul of the elect, one of those "messengers sent to us from the depths of the mysterious infinite."

Without sharing the view of the celebrated physician of the Salpêtrière as to the determining causes of the phenomena, Doctor Dupouy, who attributed these to the influence of celestial Entities, concluded in the same sense. Only, for him, Joan's hallucinations had the gift of objectifying the angelic personalities who served as her guides. We might adopt this perspective, since we know she regarded her saints as being those whose images adorned the church of Domremy.

But, we ask again: can one truly attribute a hallucinatory character to voices that wake you in deep sleep to warn of present or future events—as was the case at Orléans and during Joan's trial at Rouen? To voices that counsel you to act otherwise than you would wish? During her captivity in the tower of Beaurevoir, the prisoner received many recommendations from her guides, desiring to prevent her from making a mistake; yet they could not stop her from leaping from the top of the tower, and Joan had to repent of it.

To say with Lavisse, Anatole France, and others that the voice Joan heard was that of her conscience seems to us likewise in contradiction with the facts. Everything proves these voices were external. The phenomenon is not subjective, since she was awakened, as we have seen, by her guides' calls, sometimes catching only the end of their discourse[59]. She heard them clearly only in times of silence: *"Le trouble des prisons et les noises de ses gardes*[60] *"* ("the disturbance of the prisons and the quarrels of her guards") prevented her from understanding their words. It is therefore evident that these came from without; noise does not hinder the inner voice, which is perceived in the secret of the soul even in moments of tumult.

Let us conclude, then, by once more recognizing in Jeanne a great medium.

Despite Doctor Morselli[61] and so many others, mediumship is not manifested only in weak spirits or minds inclined to madness. There are talents of great breadth—for example, Petrarch, Pascal, Goethe, Swedenborg, Sardou, and so many others—profound thinkers like Socrates, men imbued with the divine spirit, saints or prophets, who had their moments of mediumship, in whom this faculty, latent within, sometimes revealed itself repeatedly.



Neither the height of intelligence nor the elevation of soul is an impediment to such manifestations. If there are so many mediumistic productions whose form or substance leaves much to be desired, it is because high intelligences and great characters are rare. These qualities were united in Joan of Arc, and this is why her psychic faculties had reached such a degree of power. One may say of the Maid of Orléans that she realized the very ideal of mediumship.

Now, a question arises, a question of the highest importance. Who were the invisible personalities who

---

59 J. FABRE, Trial of Condemnation, p. 68.

60 J. FABRE, Trial of Condemnation, p. 157.

61 *Psychologie et Spiritisme*, par H. MORSELLI.

inspired Joan and guided her? Why saints, angels, archangels? What should we think of this constant intervention of *saint Michel, saint Catherine, saint Marguerite*?

To resolve this problem, one must first analyze the psychology of seers and sensitives, and understand the necessity they are under to attribute to manifestations of the Beyond the forms, names, and appearances suggested to them by their upbringing, the influences they have undergone, the beliefs of the environment and of the time in which they live. Joan of Arc did not escape this law. To express her psychic perceptions, she used the terms, the expressions, the images familiar to her. This is what mediums of all times have done. Depending on the environment, the inhabitants of the invisible world are given names of gods, genii, angels or *daïmons*, spirits, etc.

The invisible Intelligences who intervene manifestly in human affairs themselves find it necessary to enter into the mentality of the subjects to whom they manifest, borrowing the forms and names of illustrious beings known to them, in order to impress them, inspire their trust, and better prepare them for the role assigned to them.

In general, in the Beyond, not as much importance is attached as we do to names and personalities. Grand works are pursued there, and, in order to realize them, means are used that correspond to the state of mind—one could say the state of inferiority and ignorance—of the environments and the times in which these Powers wish to intervene.

It may be objected that these superhuman Powers could have revealed to the Maid of Domremy their true nature by initiating her into a higher, broader knowledge of the invisible world and its laws. But besides the fact that it is very long and very difficult to initiate a human being, even the most gifted, into the laws of higher and infinite life—laws which no one yet embraces in their entirety—such an effort would have gone against the assigned goal. It would have made the conceived work, a work of action, impossible to realize, by creating in the heroine a state of mind and divergences of outlook that would have set her in opposition to the social and religious order under which she was called to act.

If one examines closely Joan's words about her voices, one is struck by a significant fact: the Spirit to whom the name *saint Michel* is attributed never gave his own name[62].

The two other Entities were said to have been designated by *saint Michel* himself, under the names of *saint Catherine* and *saint Marguerite*[63].

Let us recall that the statues of these saints adorned the church of Domremy, where Joan went daily to pray; in her long meditations and her ecstasies, she often had before her eyes the stone images of these virgin martyrs.

Now, the existence of these two figures is more than doubtful. What we know of them consists of

---

62 HENRI MARTIN says the opposite (*Histoire de France*, vol. VI, p. 142); but in the sources he cites— Trial of Condemnation , 2nd public interrogation—Saint Michael is not named.
Joan expresses herself in these words: *"la voix d'un ange"* (see also the 7th secret interrogation).

63 J. FABRE, *Procès de condamnation*, pp. 173–174.

legends that are highly contested. Around the year 1600, a censor of the University, Edmond Richer, who believed in angels but not in *saint Catherine* nor in *saint Marguerite*, suggested that the apparitions perceived by the young girl had presented themselves to her as the saints she had venerated since childhood. "The Spirit of God, who governs the Church, accommodates itself to our weakness.", he said[64].

Later, another doctor of the Sorbonne, Jean de Launoy, wrote: "The life of Saint Catherine, virgin and martyr, is entirely fabulous, from beginning to end. No faith should be given to it." [65]. Bossuet, in his *Histoire de France pour l'instruction du Dauphin*, does not mention the two saints.

In our own day, M. Marius Sepet, a graduate of the *École des Chartes* and member of the *Institut*, in his preface to the *Vie de sainte Catherine* by Jean Miélot[66], makes explicit reservations concerning the documents that served to establish this work: "The life of Madame Saint Catherine, in the form it has taken in manuscript 6449 of the French collection at the National Library, can in no way claim canonical value. [67]."

64 EDMOND RICHER, *Histoire de la Pucelle d'Orléans*, manuscript, Bibl. nat.

65 See A. FRANCE, *Vie de Jeanne d'Arc*, vol. I, p. LIX.

66 Hurtel edition, 1881, p. 35. See also F. X. FELLER, *Dictionnaire historique*.

67 Eminent critics, several of whom are Catholics and even prelates, have established, in more recent works, that the hagiographers have committed numerous errors. Mgr Duchesne, director of the École de Rome and member of the Académie française, who enjoyed great authority in the religious world, proved that several saints, among them Saint Maurice of the Theban Legion, patron of the cathe-

Let us note once again that the more recent case of the Curé of Ars presents many analogies with that of Joan of Arc. Like her, the famous thaumaturge was a seer and conversed with Spirits, especially with Saint Philomena, his habitual protectress. He also endured the harassment of an inferior Spirit named *Grappin*. Yet, just as Catherine and Margaret, Philomena is only a symbolic name; it signifies "one who loves humanity.[68]"

If the names attributed to the Invisible Powers who influenced the life of Joan of Arc have only relative importance and are, in themselves, very questionable, it is quite otherwise—as we have already seen—with the objective reality of these Powers and the constant action they exercised upon the heroine.

The Catholic explanation seems to us insufficient. We are inclined to see in them higher Entities who gather, concentrate, and put into action the divine forces at those hours when evil spreads across the earth, when



dral of Angers, never existed. He demonstrated that the *Saintes-Maries* never came to France, and that the legends concerning them in Provence are purely works of imagination.

More serious still: eight names of popes have been erased as inaccurate. By order from Rome, the list was revised; Pius X is no longer the 264th, but only the 256th. For example, Saint Clet and Saint Anaclet are in fact one and the same person. And if one could be mistaken to such a degree concerning figures who occupied the papal throne, how can we be certain of the existence of personalities even more hypothetical?

See the works of Mgr Duchesne entitled : *Catalogues épiscopaux des diocèses ; Origines chrétiennes* (lectures given at the Sorbonne).

68 See P. Saintyves: *Les Saints, successeurs des dieux*, pp. 109–112, and 365–370.

men, by their deeds, hinder or threaten the unfolding of the eternal plan.

These Powers are encountered, under the most diverse denominations, in widely different epochs. But whatever name one gives them, their intervention in history is not in doubt. In the fifteenth century, we may see in them the guardian spirits of France, the great souls watching more particularly over our nation.

Some will perhaps say: this is the supernatural. No! What is designated by that word are the higher regions, the sublime heights, and, so to speak, the crowning of nature. For by the inspiration of seers and prophets, by the mediating Powers, by the messenger Spirits, humanity has always been in communion with the superior planes of the universe.

Experimental studies, pursued for half a century[69], have cast a certain light upon the life of the Beyond. We now know that the spirit-world is peopled with innumerable beings, occupying every degree of the evolutionary scale. Death does not change us morally. We find ourselves again in space with all the qualities we have acquired, but also with our errors and our faults. From this it follows that the earthly atmosphere swarms with lower souls, eager to manifest themselves to human beings—making communication sometimes dangerous, requiring laborious preparation and much discernment from experimenters.

These studies also demonstrate that above us are legions of benevolent and protective souls: the souls of men who have suffered for goodness, for truth, and

69 See, *After Death* and *Into the Unseen*, *passim*.

for justice. They hover above poor humanity, to guide it along the paths of its destiny. Beyond the narrow horizons of earth, a whole hierarchy of invisible beings is ranged in light. It is Jacob's ladder of legend: the ladder of higher Intelligences and Consciences, ascending and rising toward radiant Spirits, toward mighty Entities who are the depositaries of divine forces.

These invisible Entities, as we have said, sometimes intervene in the life of nations, though not always in a manner as striking as in the time of Joan of Arc. Most often, their action remains hidden, obscure—first to safeguard human freedom, and above all because, if these Powers wish to be known, they also wish man to make the effort to become capable of knowing them.

These great events of history are comparable to sudden clearings between clouds when the sky is overcast: openings through which the deep, luminous, infinite heavens are revealed to us. Then the gaps close again, for mankind is not yet mature enough to grasp and comprehend the mysteries of higher life.



As to the choice of forms and means by which these great Beings intervene in the earthly sphere, we must recognize how weak our knowledge is to evaluate or judge them. Our faculties are powerless to measure the vast plans of the invisible. But we know the facts are there—uncontestable, undeniable. From time to time, through the darkness that envelops us, in the midst of the ebb and flow of events, in decisive hours, when a nation is in peril, when humanity has strayed from its path, then an emanation, a personification of the Supreme Power descends among us to remind men that above them exist infinite resources, that they may draw—through their thoughts, through their appeals—societies of souls which, one day, they will join through merit and effort.

The intervention in human affairs of these higher Entities—what we may call the *anonymes de l'espace*, the anonymous ones of space—constitutes a profound law upon which we must insist, striving to render it more comprehensible.

In general, as we have said, the superior Spirits who manifest themselves to people do not give their names. Or if they do, they borrow symbolic names which characterize their nature or the kind of mission entrusted to them. Why then, when here below men are so jealous of their slightest merits, so eager to attach their names to the most ephemeral of works—why do the great missionaries of the Beyond, the glorious messengers of the invisible, persist in preserving anonymity or in assuming allegorical names? Because the rules of the earthly world and those of the higher worlds, where the Spirits of redemption dwell, are very different.



Here below, personality dominates and absorbs all. The tyrannical "I" asserts itself: this is the sign of our inferiority, the unconscious formula of our selfishness. Our present condition being imperfect and temporary, it is logical that all our acts should gravitate around our personality, that is, around this "I" which maintains and assures the identity of the being in its lower stage of evolution, amid the fluctuations of space and the vicissitudes of time.

In the higher spiritual spheres, it is quite otherwise. Evolution continues under more ethereal forms—forms which, at a certain height, combine, unite, and realize what might be called the interpenetration of beings. The higher the Spirit ascends in the infinite hierarchy, the more the angles of its personality are effaced, the more its "I" expands and blossoms into universal life, under the law of harmony and love. Undoubtedly the identity of the being remains, but its action becomes ever more fused with universal activity—that is, with God, who, in reality, is pure act.

In this lies infinite progress and eternal life: to draw ever closer to the Absolute Being without ever fully reaching Him, and to merge ever more completely our own work with the eternal work.

Having reached such heights, the Spirit no longer bears this or that name; it is no longer an individual, a personality, but rather one of the forms of infinite activity. It is called *Legion*. It belongs to a hierarchy of forces and lights, as a spark belongs to the fire that engenders and nourishes it. It is an immense association of Spirits, harmonized among themselves by laws of luminous affinity, of intellectual and moral symphony, by love which makes them one. A sublime fraternity, of which that of the earth is only a pale and fleeting reflection!

At times, from these harmonious groups, from these dazzling constellations, a living ray detaches itself; a radiant form separates and comes, like a projection of celestial light, to explore, to illuminate the dark corners of our world. To aid the ascent of souls, to fortify a creature at the hour of a great sacrifice, to support the head of a Christ in agony, to save a people, to redeem a nation on the brink of ruin—such are the sublime missions which these messengers from the Beyond come to fulfill.

The law of solidarity requires that the superior beings attract to themselves the younger or lagging spirits. Thus an immense magnetic chain stretches across the immeasurable universe, linking souls and worlds together.

And since the highest form of moral greatness is to do good for good's sake alone, without selfish return, the beneficent Spirits act under the double veil of silence and anonymity, so that the glory and merit of their acts may revert to God alone and return to Him.

Thus are explained Joan's visions, her voices, the apparitions of the archangel and of the saints—who never existed as individual personalities baptized with those names, but who were nevertheless living realities, luminous beings detached from divine centers, who made of Joan the liberator of her country.

Michael (*Micaël*), the strength of God; Margaret (*Margarita*), the precious pearl; Catherine (*Katarina*), the pure virgin: all symbolic names that characterize moral beauty, a higher strength, and reflect a ray of God.

Joan of Arc was therefore a mediator between two worlds, a powerful medium. For this, she was martyred, burned. Such, in general, is the fate of messengers from on high: they are exposed to the persecutions of men, who will not, or cannot, understand them. The examples they give, the truths they spread, are a hindrance to earthly interests, a condemnation of human passions and errors.

It is the same in our own day. Although less barbaric than the Middle Ages, which sent them in masses to the stake, our age still persecutes the agents of the Beyond. They are often misunderstood, scorned, ridiculed. I speak of sincere mediums, not of impostors—who are numerous and intrude everywhere. These latter degrade one of the most respectable things in this world, and thereby assume heavy responsibilities for the future. For all is paid, sooner or later; all our acts, good or bad, return upon us with their consequences. Such is the law of destiny[70].

The manifestations of the invisible world are constant, as we have said, though not always of the same purity. Fraud and charlatanism sometimes mingle with sacred inspiration: beside Joan of Arc, we find Catherine of La Rochelle and Guillaume the shepherd, who were impostors. There are also genuine mediums who deceive themselves, acting at times under the sway of auto-suggestion. The source is not always pure; the vision is sometimes confused. Yet there are phenomena so radiant that doubt cannot prevail before them. Such were the mediumistic facts that illumined the life of Joan of Arc.



In mediumship, as in all things, there is infinite variety, gradation, a sort of hierarchy. Almost all the great predestined ones—the prophets, the founders of religions, the messengers of truth, all who have proclaimed the higher principles that nourish human thought—have been mediums, for their lives were in constant relation with the higher spiritual spheres.

Elsewhere I have shown[71], supported by numerous and precise testimonies, that genius itself, in many respects, can be considered as one of the aspects of

---

70 See *Life and Destiny*, chap. 18 et 19.

71 See *Into the Unseen*, chap. 26, Glorious Mediumship.

mediumship. Men of genius are, for the most part, inspired in the highest sense of the word. Their works are like beacons lit by God in the night of the centuries, to guide the march of humanity.

The whole philosophy of history is summed up in two words: the communion of the visible and the invisible. It is expressed through higher inspiration: men of genius, great poets, scientists, artists, celebrated inventors—all are executors of the divine plan in the world, of that majestic design of evolution that carries the soul toward the heights.

At times, the noble Intelligences who preside over this evolution incarnate themselves, to render their action more effective and direct. Then you have Zoroaster, Buddha, and, above all, Christ. At other times, they inspire and sustain missionaries charged with giving new impulse to the flights of human thought: Moses, Saint Paul, Mohammed, Luther belong to these. But in all cases, human freedom is respected. Hence the countless obstacles these great Spirits encounter on their path.



The most striking fact that marks the coming of these heavenly messengers is the religious idea upon which they lean. That idea alone suffices to exalt their courage and to gather around them, nearly always humble, powerless of material means, vast multitudes, ready to embrace the teaching whose grandeur they have perceived.

All have spoken of their communications with the invisible; all have had visions, heard voices, and acknowledged themselves as mere instruments of Providence in the accomplishment of a mission. Left to themselves, they would not have succeeded; the influence from above was necessary, indispensable, for the triumph of their idea, against which so many enemies raged.

Philosophy too has had its glorious inspired ones. Socrates, like Joan of Arc, perceived voices—or rather a voice—that of a familiar Spirit he called his *daimon*[72]. It made itself heard in every circumstance.

One may read in Plato's *Theages* how Timarchus would have avoided death if he had heeded this Spirit's warning: "Do not go," Socrates told him, when Timarchus rose from a banquet with his accomplice Philemon, intending to assassinate Nicias. "Do not go; the voice tells me to hold you back." Though warned twice more, Timarchus departed, failed in his enterprise, and was condemned to death. At the hour of execution, he confessed too late that he should have obeyed the voice: "O Clitomachus," he said to his brother, "I die because I would not follow the counsel Socrates gave me."

Another time, the voice warned the sage not to continue along a road he was traveling with friends. They refused to listen, went on, and were trampled by a herd.

Having so often recognized the accuracy of the counsels dictated by this voice, Socrates had every reason to believe in it. He reminded his companions that of all the predictions he had transmitted from it, none had ever proved false.

72 In Greek, *daïmon* means familiar spirit, genius.

Let us recall also the philosopher's solemn declaration before the tribunal of the Ephors, when life or death was at stake for him:

*"That poetic voice of the daimon, which never ceased to make itself heard throughout my existence, which never ceased, even in the most trivial circumstances, to turn me aside from anything that could have harmed me—behold, it is now silent, though things befall me which might be regarded as the worst of evils. Why is this? Doubtless because what is happening is, in truth, a good for me. We are deceived, it seems, in supposing that death is a misfortune."*

In France too, our philosophers were visited by the Spirit: Pascal had his hours of ecstasy; Malebranche composed his *Search for Truth* in complete darkness; and Descartes relates how a sudden intuition, swift as lightning, inspired in him the idea of his Methodic Doubt—the philosophical system to which we owe the liberation of modern thought. In his *Annales médico-psychologiques*[73], Brierre de Boismont reports: "Descartes, after a long retreat, was followed by an invisible presence that urged him to pursue his search for truth."

Schopenhauer, in Germany, likewise acknowledged the influence of the Beyond: *"My philosophical postulata,"* he said, *"came to me without my intervention, in moments when my will was as if asleep... My person seemed a stranger to the work."*

Almost all renowned poets have enjoyed invisible assistance. Among them we may cite[74]: Dante and Tasso, Schiller and Goethe, Pope[75], Shakespeare, Shelley,

---

73 1851, p. 543.

74 See *Into the Unseen*, chap. 26, Glorious Mediumship.

75 Pope wrote, as he himself stated, under the inspiration of

Camoëns, Victor Hugo, Lamartine, Alfred de Musset[76], and many more.

Among painters and musicians, Raphael, Mozart, Beethoven, and others deserve mention, for inspiration poured forth ceaselessly upon them in powerful streams.

It is often said: "These ideas are in the air." And indeed they are, for the souls of the Beyond suggest them to men. There lies the source of the great movements of opinion in every field, and there too the cause of revolutions that upheave nations, only to regenerate them.

We must then acknowledge it: the phenomenon of mediumship pervades the ages. All of history is illumined by its light. Sometimes it concentrates upon one eminent personality and shines with dazzling brilliance—that is the case of Joan of Arc. At other times it is diffused, distributed across a multitude of interpreters, as in our own day.

Mediumship has often been the inspirer of genius, the educator of humanity, the means by which God uplifts and transforms societies. In the fifteenth century, it served to draw France out of the abyss into which she had fallen.

Today, it is as if a new breath sweeps across the world, reviving countless souls sunk in materialism, and truths long buried in shadow and forgetfulness. Phenomena of vision, of audition, of apparitions of the departed, of manifestations of the invisible through incorporation,

---

Spirits. His works contain prophecies concerning the future of England, some of which have already been fulfilled.

76 Speaking of his own way of writing, Musset said:
*"One does not work, one listens, one waits.*
*It is like a stranger speaking in your ear."*

writing, raps, and more, have become innumerable; they multiply daily around us.

The investigations of several study societies, the experiments and testimonies of eminent scientists and leading thinkers—whose names we have cited—leave no doubt as to the reality of these facts. They have been observed under conditions that defy any suspicion of fraud. We shall cite but a few, among those that bear striking resemblance to the phenomena of Joan of Arc's life.

First, the voices:

In *Human Personality*, F. Myers recounts the mysterious voice heard by Lady Caidsly, at a moment when her life was in danger.

François Coppée likewise speaks of a mysterious voice that called his name at grave moments in his life, when, once in bed, he lay awake with worry:

*"Assuredly I am not asleep at such times,"* he affirms. *"And the proof is that, despite the intense emotion and the pounding of my heart, I always answered immediately: 'Who is there? Who speaks to me?' But the voice never added anything beyond its simple call*[77]*."*

In the *Revue scientifique et morale du Spiritisme* (July 1909), Dr. Breton, naval physician and president of the Psychical Study Society of Nice, reports the following fact: "Ms. Lolla had married M. de R., a Russian officer. Her father-in-law died. Some time later, the young woman accompanied her mother-in-law to the family chapel to pray at the tomb. Kneeling and praying, she distinctly heard a voice say to her: 'You too shall be a

77 See the newspaper *le Matin*, 7 October 1901.

widow, but you will not have the consolation of praying at my son's tomb.' Mrs. de R., upon hearing this voice, fainted. Her mother-in-law came to her aid, and soon, upon recovering, she explained the cause of her emotion.

The Russo-Japanese war broke out. Colonel de R. perished in Manchuria. His body, with others, was placed in a coffin and transported to Mukden to be sent to Russia. But during the general retreat of the Russian army, the detachment transporting them was forced to abandon the coffins. Despite many searches, the fate of those remains was never discovered.

Thus the prophecy of the Spirit—the colonel's father—was fulfilled: the young widow never had the consolation of praying at her husband's grave."

Let us now speak of apparitions. Examples of them are not rare in our own day, and in certain cases their authenticity has even been established by means of photography.



The *Revue* of January 15, 1909, contains an account by W. T. Stead of such an occurrence. The great English publicist is as well known for his loyalty as for his courage and selflessness. Whenever truth demanded it, he knew how to stand firm against all of England. One recalls how, disregarding his personal interests and forgetting the millions he was to inherit from Cecil Rhodes, he dared to cite Rhodes publicly as one of the principal architects of the South African War. He even went so far as to demand that he himself be sentenced to hard labor.

During that same war, Stead visited a photographer, an uneducated man but one endowed with second sight, to see what might be obtained, for the study of the occult world had always been a source of attraction for him. With Stead entered an apparition that had already shown itself in the photographer's studio a few days earlier. It was agreed to attempt photographing it together with the writer. During the operation, in response to a question, the being—unseen by human eyes—gave the name of *Piet Botha*. Among all the Bothas known to Stead, none bore that Christian name. Yet in the photograph there clearly appeared beside him the distinct, characteristic face of a Boer.

After peace was concluded, when General Botha came to London, Stead sent him the photograph. The very next day, one of the South African delegates, Mr. Wessels, arrived at his home. Deeply intrigued, he said: "That man never knew you! He never set foot in England! He is one of my relatives; I have his portrait at home." —"Is he dead?" asked Stead. —"He was the first Boer commander killed at the siege of Kimberley," replied Wessels, "his name was *Petrus Botha*, but we shortened it to *Piet*."



At the sight of the photograph, the other delegates from the Free States also recognized the Boer warrior.

Sometimes, and this is one of the strongest reasons in favor of their authenticity, apparitions present themselves to very young children—beings incapable of calculation or deceit.

The *Annales des Sciences psychiques* of February 1–16, 1909, cite several such cases. In one, a little girl of two and a half repeatedly saw her younger sister, who had recently died, in different places, and would stretch out her hand to her. In another case, a three-year-old child, at the very moment of her little brother's death, perceived one of her deceased aunts and ran toward her, following her movements.

We also read in Brierre de Boismont (*Annales médico-psychologiques*, 1851, pp. 245–246):

"A young man of eighteen, without any tendency toward enthusiasm, romanticism, or superstition, was living in Ramsgate for his health. During a walk to a neighboring village, he entered a church at dusk and was struck with terror on beholding the specter of his mother, who had died a few months before after a long and painful illness. The figure stood between him and the wall, remaining motionless for a considerable time. He returned home, but the same apparition appeared in his room on several successive evenings. Becoming unwell, he hastened to Paris where his father lived. He resolved not to speak of the vision, fearing to add to his father's grief over the loss of a beloved wife.



"Obliged to sleep in his father's room, he was surprised to find a light burning all night, contrary to their habits and quite against their taste. After several hours of insomnia caused by the brightness, the son rose to extinguish it. His father awoke immediately in great agitation and ordered him to relight it. Astonished at his father's anger and the signs of terror on his face, he asked the reason but received only vague replies.

"Within a week, unable to sleep under the light, the son once again dared to extinguish it; but his father leapt from bed trembling, scolded him, and relit the lamp. He then confessed that every time he was in the dark, the ghost of his wife appeared, remaining immobile, and would not vanish until the light was relit.

"This confession deeply impressed the young man. Fearing to increase his father's sorrow by relating what had happened in Ramsgate, he soon left Paris for an inland town sixty miles away, where his brother was at school, to whom he had not spoken of the events.

"He had scarcely arrived when the schoolmaster's son asked him: 'Has your brother ever shown signs of madness? Last night he came down in his shirt, out of his senses, declaring that he had seen his mother's spirit. He dared not return to his room and fainted from fright.'"

We could add many more facts of the same order[78]. The inhabitants of the unseen neglect no means of manifesting themselves to us, to prove the realities of survival.

On this subject, Sir Conan Doyle, the great English writer, sent us a photograph taken on November 11, 1923, in London, at the Cenotaph of the Unknown Soldier, during the minute of silence and recollection. In it, one sees a multitude of young men's faces, among which the eminent author claims to recognize that of his son, fallen at the front.

Great Spirits have a marked preference for the phenomenon of incorporation, for it allows them to manifest with greater consciousness and fuller intellectual resources. The medium, plunged into slumber by an invisible magnetic influence, abandons for a few moments their organism to Entities who take hold of it and come into contact with us through voice, gesture, and attitude. Their language is at times so commanding, so solemn, that no doubt remains as

78 See especially *Into the Unseen*, chapter 20 (*Apparitions and Materialization of Spirits*).

to their character, nature, or identity. While it is easy to counterfeit physical manifestations—such as rapping tables, automatic writing, or spectral apparitions—the same is not true of phenomena belonging to the higher order of intelligence. Talent cannot be forged, still less genius. We have often been present at such scenes, and each time they left within us a profound impression. To live, even for a brief instant, in the intimacy of great Beings is among the rarest joys granted on earth. It is through this mediumship of incorporation that we were able to converse with guiding Spirits, with Jeanne herself, and to receive from them the teachings and revelations we have recorded in our works.

Yet, if this faculty is a source of exaltation for the observers, it offers little satisfaction to the medium, who upon awakening retains no memory of what occurred during their absence from the body.



Mediumship lies dormant in countless individuals. Everywhere, around us, among young women, young girls, young men, subtle faculties are germinating; potent fluids are being elaborated, capable of serving as links between the human brain and the intelligences of space. What is lacking are the schools and methods needed to develop these elements with science and perseverance, and to bring them to their full worth. In the absence of methodical preparation and sustained study, these seeds cannot yield all the fruits of truth and wisdom they might contain. Too often, for lack of knowledge and regular training, they wither or bear only poisonous flowers.

Gradually, however, a new science and a new faith are arising and spreading, bringing to all the knowledge of the laws that govern the invisible universe. Soon, people will learn to cultivate these precious faculties, to make of them instruments of the great Souls, custodians of the secrets of the Beyond. Experimenters will renounce narrow views, the routine procedures of an outdated science; they will strive to employ the powers of the spirit through elevated thought—the supreme motor, the link uniting the divine worlds to the lower spheres—and a ray from on high will descend to fertilize their research. They will understand that the study of the great philosophical problems, the practice of duty, the dignity and integrity of life are essential conditions of success. If science and method are indispensable in the domain of psychic experimentation, no less important are the generous impulses of the soul through prayer, for they constitute the magnet, the fluidic current that attracts beneficent powers and repels harmful influences. Jeanne's entire life demonstrates this truth abundantly.

The day when all these conditions are united, the new spiritualism will fully enter upon the path of its destiny. At the very hour when so many beliefs waver beneath the breath of passion, when the human soul sinks into matter, and in the midst of the general collapse of character and conscience, it will become a means of salvation, a force, a living and active faith, uniting heaven and earth and embracing souls and worlds in an eternal and infinite communion.

# V
# VAUCOULEURS

*Je pars. Adieu, vous que j'aimais!*

*P. Allard*

Let us return to the course of Joan's story. We have seen her leave Domremy. From that day forward, trials would arise at every step. And those trials were to be all the crueler because they came from those of whom she might have expected sympathy, affection, and help. Of her, one might apply the words: *"She came among her own, and her own received her not.*[79] *"*



The painful struggles that were to besiege her repeatedly in later years Joan experienced already at the very beginning of her mission. She—so submissive to her parents' authority, so faithful to her duties, so deeply attached to her father and her mother—was compelled to disobey their command and, in secret, slip away from the home that had given her birth.

Her father had, in a dream, received a revelation of her designs. One night, he dreamed that his daughter would leave her country, her family, and go forth with armed men. He was profoundly troubled by this and spoke of it to his sons, commanding them that, rather

79 Gospel. St John, I, 11.

than allow her to depart in such a manner, *"they should drown her in the Meuse. And if you do not do it yourselves,"* he added, *"then I shall do it myself!"*

Joan was obliged to conceal her purpose, for she was resolved "to obey God rather than men."

At Rouen, her judges would reproach her with this: *"Did you believe you were doing right,"* they asked her, *"in leaving without the permission of your father and mother?"* To which she replied: *"I obeyed well my father and my mother in all other things—save in this departure. But afterward, I wrote to them, and they forgave me."*

Thus she showed her deference and filial submission to those who had raised her. Yet the judges pressed further: *"When you left your father and your mother, did you not think you were sinning?"* Then Joan gave utterance to the fullness of her thought in this noble reply: *"Since God commanded it, it had to be done. Even if I had had a hundred fathers and a hundred mothers, and had been the daughter of a king, still I would have gone!*[80]*"*



Accompanied by one of her uncles, Durand Laxart—whom she had picked up in passing through Burey, the only member of her family who believed in her vocation and encouraged her in her mission—she presented herself to Robert de Baudricourt, commander of Vaucouleurs on behalf of the Dauphin. The first reception was harsh. Yet Joan did not lose heart. She had been forewarned by her voices. Her resolution was unshakable; nothing could divert her from her goal. She declared it with firm conviction to the good people of

80 J. FABRE, *Procès de condamnation*, p. 139.

Vaucouleurs: "Before mid-Lent, I must be with the king, even if I wear my legs down to the knees!"

Little by little, through her persistence, the rough captain began to listen more closely to her words. Like all who came near her, Robert de Baudricourt fell under the sway of this young girl. After having her exorcised by Jean Tournier, parish priest of Vaucouleurs, and convincing himself that there was nothing evil in her, he no longer dared to deny her mission or to pile obstacles in her way. He provided her with a horse and an escort. Already the knight Jean de Metz, captivated by Joan's burning conviction, had promised to lead her to the king. "But when?" he had asked her. She answered quickly: "Sooner today than tomorrow, sooner tomorrow than later!"

At last she departed, and the final words of the captain of Vaucouleurs were these: "Go, and let happen what may!" A tepid, hardly encouraging phrase. What did it matter to Joan? She did not listen to voices from the earth, but to those from on high, and these voices stirred and sustained her. In her soul, strength and confidence grew with the uncertainties and dangers of the coming days. She often repeated a saying from her homeland: "Help yourself, and God will help you!"



The future was menacing. Everything around her inspired fear. But she carried within her divine strength! And thus she offered an example for all pilgrims of life. Humanity's road is strewn with pitfalls: everywhere ruts, sharp stones, brambles, thorns. To overcome them, God has placed within us the resources of a hidden energy we can bring forth, drawing upon invisible powers—those mysterious aids from above—which multiply our personal strength a hundredfold and ensure victory in the struggle. *Help yourself, and God will help you!*

She set out, accompanied only by a handful of brave men. They traveled day and night. One hundred and fifty leagues had to be crossed through hostile provinces to reach Chinon, where Dauphin Charles resided—mockingly called "the King of Bourges," for he ruled only a fragment of his kingdom. Charles drowned his misfortunes in pleasures, surrounded by courtiers who betrayed him and secretly conspired with the enemy. Joan had to pass through Burgundian lands, allies of England, trek under the rain along hidden paths, ford overflowing rivers, and sleep upon soaked ground. Never did she hesitate. Her voices told her constantly: "Go, daughter of God, go; we will come to your aid!" And she went, she went, in spite of obstacles, in the midst of dangers.

She hurried to the rescue of a prince without hope and without courage. And see what admirable mystery! It was a child who came to lift France from the abyss. What did she bring with her? Was it military aid, an army? No, nothing of the sort. What she brought was faith—faith in herself, faith in the future of France, that faith which uplifts souls and moves mountains.

What did Joan say to all who gathered along her path? "I come on behalf of the King of Heaven, and I bring you the aid of Heaven!"

# VI
# CHINON, POITIERS, TOURS

*Walk boldly, victory will follow.*

*Paul Allard*

Most historians believe that Joan entered Touraine through Amboise, following the Roman road that runs along the left bank of the Loire. From Gien she would have first come to Blois, by way of the Sologne. From Amboise she is said to have crossed the Cher at Saint-Martin-le-Beau, the Indre at Cormery, and then made a halt at Sainte-Catherine-de-Fierbois, where there stood a sanctuary dedicated to one of her patron saints. According to an old tradition, after Charles Martel defeated the Saracens—exterminating them in the wild woods in the midst of which this chapel rose (*ferus boscus*, Fierbois)—he laid his sword in that oratory. Rebuilt in 1375, it was often visited by knights and men-at-arms, who, to obtain the healing of their wounds, vowed to make a pilgrimage there and to leave their swords at the shrine.

Along the way, a troop—likely bribed by the treacherous La Trémoille and charged with abducting

Joan—lay in ambush. Yet, at the sight of the maiden envoy, these bandits stood as if nailed to the ground[81].

According to the identical testimonies of Poulengy and Novelonpont, the journey from Vaucouleurs to Chinon lasted eleven days. From this, Abbé Bosseboeuf concludes that Joan arrived there on Wednesday, February 23[82]. Wallon, Quicherat, and others place the date at March 6.

And now, the town comes into view, with its three castles blending together into one long gray mass of crenellated walls, towers, and keeps.

As her small caravan entered Chinon, it wound its way through steep streets lined with Gothic houses, their slate-covered façades adorned at the corners with wooden statuettes. At once, marvelous tales began to spread—on doorsteps, or at evening gatherings before blazing hearths—about the young girl arriving from the marches of Lorraine, come to fulfill prophecies and to bring an end to the insolent fortune of the English.



Joan and her escort lodged "with a good woman, near the château[83]," doubtless in the house of the gentleman Reignier de la Barre, whose widow or daughter welcomed the Maid with joy. She remained there two days without obtaining an audience[84]. Later, she was accommodated within the castle itself, in the tower of Coudray.

At last, the long-desired audience was granted. It was evening. The glow of torches, the blare of fanfares, the pageantry of the reception—would not all this dazzle

81 J. FABRE, *Procès de réhabilitation*, t. I, pp. 150-151.
82 Bulletin of the Archaeological Society of Touraine, vol. XII.
83 J. FABRE, *Procès de condamnation*, p. 150.
84 *Procès*. Deposition of Dunois.

and intimidate her? No, for she came from a world more radiant than ours. From long before, she had known magnificences beside which all this staging appeared pale indeed. Beyond Domrémy, beyond the earth itself, in times preceding her birth, she had frequented dwellings more glorious than the court of France, and she had retained their intuition.

More vibrant than the clash of arms and the sounding of trumpets, she heard within herself a voice that spoke and repeated: *Go, daughter of God, I am with you!*

Among my readers, some will find such words strange. Yet this is the moment to say—to recall—that the spirit exists before the body; that before its most recent earthly birth it has traversed vast periods of time, inhabited many realms, and that with each new incarnation in this world, it descends bearing a whole store of qualities, faculties, aptitudes, drawn from that obscure past through which it has passed.



Within each of us there lies, in the depths of our consciousness, an accumulation of impressions and memories resulting from our former lives, whether upon the earth or in space. These memories slumber within us: the heavy cloak of flesh muffles and stifles them. But sometimes, under the impulsion of some outward agent, they awaken suddenly; intuitions surge forth; hidden faculties reappear; and for an instant we become once again a being different from the one perceived in us[85].

You have surely noticed those plants that float upon the still waters of ponds. There is an image of the human soul. It floats upon the dark depths of its past; its roots

85 See my book, *Life and Destiny.*

plunge into unknown and distant regions, whence it draws the vital sap—the brilliant flower that will bud, unfold, and bloom in the field of earthly life.

In the vast hall of the château where Joan was brought, three hundred lords, knights, and noble ladies in dazzling attire were assembled. What impression must that sight have produced upon the humble shepherdess! What courage she must have summoned to confront all those licentious or inquisitive gazes, that throng of courtiers whom she sensed as hostile!

There were present Regnault de Chartres, Chancellor of France, Archbishop of Reims, a priest with a dried-up soul, perfidious and envious; La Trémoille, the grand chamberlain, a jealous and suspicious man, who dominated the king while secretly intriguing with the English; the harsh and arrogant Raoul de Gaucourt, grand master of the king's household; the marshal Gilles de Retz, the infamous magician better known under the name of Bluebeard; and then titled courtesans, cunning priests, greedy and avaricious. Around Joan there hovered an atmosphere of disbelief and malevolence. Such was the circle in which Charles VII lived, enervated by the abuse of pleasures, far from war, surrounded by his favorites and his mistresses.

Suspicious and mistrustful, the king, wishing to put Joan to the test, had placed a courtier upon his throne and concealed himself among the crowd. But she went straight to him, knelt, and spoke with him at length in a low voice; she revealed to him his secret thoughts, his doubts concerning his own birth, his hidden hesitations. And the face of that melancholy monarch, says the Chronicle, was suddenly lit with a ray of confidence and faith[86]. The bystanders, astonished, understood that an extraordinary phenomenon had just taken place.

And yet, *"no one could be found who might believe that the fate of the proudest kingdom of Christendom was entrusted to such hands, nor that the feeble arm of a poor village girl was reserved to accomplish a task in which the counsels of the wisest and the courage of the strongest had failed.*[87]*"* It was still necessary to endure many

86 J. Fabre, *Procès de réhabilitation.* Testimony of the chamberlain Guillaume Gouffier, vol. II, p. 286. Pierre Sala, author of *The Bold Deeds of the Great Kings and Emperors*, a work published in 1516, received from the chamberlain Guillaume Gouffier, Lord of Boisy, "the secret that had passed between the King and the Maid. Being greatly beloved by this King," says Pierre Sala, "he had been entrusted with his confidences. The King had fallen so low that he no longer knew what to do and thought only of finding some remedy for his life, for he was hemmed in on all sides by his enemies. One morning he entered his oratory, alone; and there he made a humble supplication and prayer to Our Lord in the depths of his heart, without uttering a word, devoutly entreating that, if he were truly the rightful heir to the kingdom of France, it might please Him to preserve it for him, or, failing that, at least grant him the grace of escape and refuge in Spain or in Scotland."
The Maid, Pierre Sala further relates in substance, having had a revelation of these things while still in the fields, repeated them to the King as soon as she was presented to him, comforting him and affirming on God's behalf that he was indeed the true son of the King and the rightful heir to the crown of France.
See manuscript of the Bibliothèque nationale, no. 191. J. Quicherat cites, along with Sala, who preserved the confidences of the Lord of Boisy, two other entirely concordant versions; *ap. Procès*, vol. IV, pp. 257, 272, 279. See also the very important letter of Alain Chartier, *ap. Procès*, vol. V, p. 133.

87 DUPANLOUP, *Panégyrique de Jeanne d'Arc*, 1855.

humiliations, to undergo the examination of matrons attesting to her purity. Sent to Poitiers, Joan was to appear there before a commission of inquiry composed of some twenty theologians, including two bishops, those of Poitiers and of Maguelonne.

*"It was a fine spectacle,"* says Alain Chartier, who wrote under the immediate impression of the scene, *"to see her dispute, a woman against men, an ignorant girl against doctors, alone against so many adversaries."* All her replies revealed great quickness of mind and a surprising presence of wit. At every moment she burst forth with unexpected and original sallies that reduced to nothing the pitiful objections of her examiners.

The official record of the interrogations at Poitiers has been destroyed. Some historians place responsibility for this on the agents of the French crown, who showed such ingratitude and culpable indifference toward the Maid during her long captivity. What remains is only a summary of the conclusions reached by the doctors called to give their opinion on Joan[88]: *"In her,"* they declared, *"we find no evil, but only good, humility, virginity, devotion, honesty, simplicity[89]."*

We also possess the testimonies from the trial of rehabilitation. Father Seguin, of the Order of Preaching Friars, spoke with simple good humor: *"I, who speak, asked Joan what language her voice spoke. — 'A better one than yours,' she replied. And indeed, I speak Limousin. Questioning her again, I said: 'Do you believe in God?' — 'Yes, better than you,' she replied."*

88 Manuscrit 7301 de la Bibliothèque nationale.

89 J. FABRE, *Procès de réhabilitation*, t. I, p. 170.

Another of her judges at Poitiers, Guillaume Aimery, objected: *"You say that God has promised you victory, and yet you ask for soldiers. What use are soldiers, if victory is assured?" — 'In God's name,' Joan replied, 'the soldiers will fight, and God will grant the victory*[90]*.'*

And when asked for signs, that is to say miracles, she replied: *"I have not come to Poitiers to give signs. But lead me to Orléans, and I will show you the signs for which I am sent."*

Once again, she was examined by a council of matrons, presided over by the Queen of Sicily, to confirm her virginity.

Emerging triumphant from all these trials, she still had to wait more than a month before marching against the English. Only when the situation at Orléans became desperate did Dunois obtain permission to send her, as a last resort, at the head of a convoy of provisions.

Joan first came to Tours to have her armor and standard prepared. The city was in the grip of great agitation. The inhabitants worked feverishly at defensive works. As early as 14 October 1428, Marshal de Gaucourt, bailiff of Orléans and grand master of the royal household, had informed them that the English had laid siege to Orléans and intended thereafter to march upon Tours[91]. The city thus made ready to resist. Everywhere, says the text, *"masons, carpenters, men of arms"* labored with feverish activity. They worked with zeal to restore the ramparts, to dig and widen the ditches, to repair and set in place the bridges. On the towers and walls, wooden sentry boxes were erected. *"Cannon embrasures"*



90 J. FABRE, *Procès de réhabilitation*, t. I, pp. 152, 153.

91 See *Registres des Comptes de la ville de Tours*, t. XXIV.

were cut into the walls. Bombards and culverins, stone balls, gunpowder—all that made up the artillery of the time—were stored within the city. The enemy might come: he would be answered.

The ancient city of the Turones then held great importance. It was called the *second Rome* because of its many churches, monasteries, and above all the pilgrimage of Saint Martin, which drew visitors from all Christendom.

To picture its situation in Joan's time, let us ascend in thought one of the towers of the collegiate church of Saint Martin—the Charlemagne Tower, for example, preserved to this day and containing the tomb of Luitgarde, wife of Charlemagne, whence it takes its name.

The view of the city, from above, would have been much the same as that of any great French city of the Middle Ages, and it is worth pausing a moment to recall it.



The walls formed four continuous lines of fortifications and towers. Within, the city was a labyrinth of narrow streets and constricted squares, lined with rows of houses with pointed gables and serrated roofs, with stories projecting one over another, statuettes by the doorways, carved beams, tall dormer windows, and panes of colored glass. To complete this picturesque ensemble, large wrought-iron signs, cut into fantastic shapes, swayed in the wind in place of house numbers. Some bore historical or heraldic meaning, others were emblematic, commemorative, or religious. Thus, in the Grand'Rue, one could see the signs *"at the Unicorn," "at the Magpie," "at the Golden Paternosters," "at the Watchful*

*Ass"*; on Saint Martin's square: *"at the Preaching Monkey," "at the Screech-Owl"*; in Rôtisserie street: *"at the Three Tortoises,"* and many more.[92]

From this high point, behold the forest of sharp gables, steeples, and walls, from which emerged the three masses of the cathedral, of which only the main nave was nearly complete, the towers rising scarcely ten or twenty meters above the ground; the abbey of Saint-Julien; and the far more imposing mass of the collegiate church of Saint Martin, of which only two towers remain today.

At our feet lay the whole city, with its fifty churches or chapels, its eight great cloisters enclosed by walls, its many inns and noble residences: a veritable forest of spires, pinnacles, turrets, and tall Gothic chimneys. Then the maze of intersecting streets and narrow crossings, thronged with people and horses. Listen to the hum, the murmur of the city rising to you. Hear the chiming of the hours from every bell tower.



Let a ray of sunlight fall upon the scene; contemplate the river with its shifting reflections, and in the distance, the vine-covered slopes and the vast forests covering the two plateaus, especially to the south, forming a deep green frame for the city spread across the valley floor. See all this, and you will have an idea of what Tours looked like the day Joan d'Arc made her entry, followed by her military household[93].

According to the testimony of her chaplain, Jean Pasquerel, she lodged with Jehan du Puy, royal counselor

92 Docteur GIRAUDET, *Histoire de la ville de Tours.*

93 This company was composed of Jean d'Aulon, her squire; the two knights who had accompanied her from Vaucouleurs; two pages; and her two brothers, Jean and Pierre d'Arc, who had come to join her.

and alderman, in his house near the church of Saint-Pierre-le-Puellier, which many archaeologists identify with the so-called "House of Tristan."

It was at Tours that Brother Pasquerel, then lecturer at the Augustinian convent of the city, was attached to Jeanne's service as chaplain. He followed her faithfully until her capture at Compiègne, a year later.

It was also at Tours that the brave girl received her military equipment, her sword, and her banner. At her direction, an armorer of the city fetched the sword deposited by Charles Martel at Sainte-Catherine-de-Fierbois. It lay buried behind the altar, and no one in the world knew of its presence there. But for the heroine, this sword was to emerge from the dust of centuries and once more drive out the foreigner.

Another armorer of Tours made for Joan a suit of armor, gleaming white[94].

Obeying the instructions of her voices, Joan had a white banner made by a craftsman of Tours, to serve as her standard and rallying sign. It was fringed with silk and bore, along with the image of God blessing the fleurs-de-lis, the motto *"Jhésus Maria."*[95] The heroine never separated the cause of France from the higher cause of divine inspiration, from which her mission flowed.

---

94 According to the accounts of Master Hémon Regnier, treasurer of the wars, published by Quicherat (*Procès de Jeanne d'Arc*, vol. V, p. 158), payment was made "to the master armorer, for a complete suit of armor for the said Maid, one hundred *livres tournois*."

95 In the same registers of the treasurer of the wars appears the following entry: "Paid to Hannes Poulvoir, painter residing in Tours, for having painted and provided materials for a large standard and a smaller one for the Maid, twenty-five *livres tournois*."

Joan left Tours around 25 April 1429, to go to Blois, where the war leaders and the bulk of the army awaited her. Twelve days later, on a date of imperishable memory, she won the battle of the Tourelles and lifted the siege of Orléans.

When she departed from Tours, the entire population crowded into the streets and squares to see and acclaim her. She rode gracefully on her fine warhorse, in her white armor gleaming in the morning light. Banner in hand, the sword of Fierbois at her side, she shone with hope and faith; one might have thought they beheld the angel of battle, a messenger from heaven.

# VII
# ORLÉANS

*Entering Orléans, how great and beautiful she was!*
*The trembling soldiers pressed around her.*
*The mothers held out their children for her blessing.*
*And all prostrated themselves at the sight of her coming.*

*Paul Allard*

The journey from Tours to Orléans was a triumphal procession. Everywhere, Joan scattered joy along her path. If the courtiers still suspected and disdained her, at least the people believed in her, in her liberating mission. Even the English were struck with stupefaction. They remained immobile in their entrenchments as the Maid rode at the head of the relief army. The inhabitants of Orléans, intoxicated with enthusiasm, forgot their peril, streamed out of the city walls, and rushed in crowds to meet her. According to an eyewitness, *"they already felt comforted, and as though no longer besieged, by the divine virtue said to dwell in this simple Maid, whom they gazed upon most affectionately, men, women, and even little children alike.*[96]"

The campaigns of Joan on the Loire offer us a spectacle unique in history: the captains of Charles VII—Dunois, La Hire, Gaucourt, Xaintrailles—marched to the enemy under the orders of an eighteen-year-old girl!

Difficulties beyond number rose before her. A formidable circle of bastilles had been raised by the English around Orléans. Within a short time, there would be famine, then the surrender of one of the greatest and strongest cities of the kingdom. Facing them were the best soldiers of England, commanded by its most skillful generals—the very men who had inflicted upon France a long series of defeats. Against such an obstacle this young girl was to contend. She had with her brave men, it is true, but they were demoralized by successive disasters, and too poorly organized to avoid further routs.



A first assault, attempted in Joan's absence on the bastille of Saint-Loup, had been repulsed. Warned, the heroine leapt onto her horse and raised her banner high; she electrified the soldiers and, with irresistible impulse, led them to the attack.

*"It was the first time,"* writes Anatole France, in one of the rare passages where he renders her justice, *"it was the first time Joan had seen men fight, and no sooner had she entered the battle than she became its leader, because she was the best. She did better than the others, not that she knew more; she knew less. But she had greater heart. When each thought of himself, she alone thought of all; when*

96 E. LAVISSE, *Histoire de France*, t. IV, p. 53.

*each sought to guard himself, she guarded nothing, having already offered herself entirely in advance. And this child, who, like every human creature, feared suffering and death, to whom her voices, her presentiments had foretold that she would be wounded, went straight ahead and remained, under crossbow bolts and leaden hail, standing on the edge of the fosse, her standard in hand, to rally the fighters*[97]*."*

By this vigorous attack, she broke through the English lines. One by one, the bastilles were carried. In three days, Orléans was delivered. Then came the battles in succession, like flashes of lightning in a burning sky. Each assault brought a victory—Jargeau, Meung, Beaugency! At last, at Patay, the English were routed in open field, and their general Talbot was taken prisoner. Then followed the march to Reims, and Charles VII was anointed King of France.

In two months, Joan had repaired every disaster: she had reconstituted, moralized, disciplined, and transfigured the army; she had lifted every spirit. *"Before her,"* said Dunois, *"two hundred English would put a thousand French to flight; with her, a few hundred French made an entire army retreat.*[98]*"*

Some authors, such as M. Thalamas[99], have thought themselves able to say that the situation of Orléans in 1429 was not as grave as is commonly asserted. The English, they argued, were not numerous. The Burgundians had withdrawn. The city, well-provisioned,

97 A. FRANCE, *Vie de Jeanne d'Arc*, t. I, pp. 335-336.

98 J. FABRE, *Procès de réhabilitation*, t. I. Déposition de Dunois.

99 Conference given in Tours, on April 30, 1905.

could have held out for a long time, and the Orléanais might have freed themselves by their own efforts.

But not only are all historians—Michelet, Henri Martin, Wallon, Lavisse, and others—unanimous in testifying to the desperate plight of the besieged, here too is the judgment of another writer, little suspect of partiality toward Joan. Anatole France wrote: *"Tossed between doubt and fear, consumed with anxiety, sleepless, restless, making no progress, the Orléanais began to despair.*[100] *"*

Meanwhile, the English awaited reinforcements promised by the Regent. Five thousand men were gathering at Paris under Sir John Fastolf, well supplied with provisions, to march to the aid of the besieging forces[101].



Let us recall also the deposition of the Duke of Alençon at the trial of rehabilitation. He spoke of the formidable bastilles raised by the English. *"Had I been,"* he said, *"in one or another of them with only a small number of men-at-arms, I would have dared to defy the strength of an army. And indeed, it seems that the assailants could never have taken them. Moreover,"* he added, *"the captains who took part in the operations declared to me that what was done at Orléans savored of the miraculous.*[102] *"*

To these testimonies we must add the statement of one of the besieged, Jean Luillier, a notable merchant of the city. He declared: *"All my fellow citizens and I believe that had the Maid not come to our aid, we should soon have*

100 A. FRANCE, *Vie de Jeanne d'Arc*, t. I, p. 164.

101 Ibid., p. 430. (They only arrived in time for the Battle of Patay.)

102 J. FABRE, *Procès de réhabilitation*, t. I, p. 176.

*fallen into the hands of the besiegers. It was impossible that the Orléanais could long resist forces so greatly superior.*[103] "

The enthusiasm of the townspeople measures the peril they had endured. After the deliverance of their city, the Orléanais *"offered themselves to Joan, to do with them and their goods as she willed,"* says the *Journal du Siège*[104].

This part of Joan's life is rich in phenomena of premonition, which must be added to those already noted.

Her voices had told her that, upon her entry into Orléans, the English would not stir. And so it happened.

The barges that were to cross the river to bring in provisions could not proceed, as the wind was unfavorable. Joan said: *"Wait a little. Everything will enter the city."* And indeed, the wind shifted and filled the sails[105].

She felt no concern for Marshal de Boussac, who had gone to meet the second convoy of provisions, saying: *"I know well that no harm will befall him."* And so it was.

Little by little, the joy of Orléans spread through all of France. As Joan's victories multiplied, the king announced them to his loyal cities, inviting the people to praise God and honor the Maid, who *"had always been present herself in the execution of all these things*[106]. *"* Everywhere the news was received with delirious joy,



103 J. FABRE, *Procès de réhabilitation*, t. I, pp. 260-261.

104 Pp. 91-92.

105 *Procès*. Déposition de Dunois. - *Journal du Siège*.

106 Letter from Charles VII to the inhabitants of Narbonne, *Trial*, vol. V, pp. 101, 104. – ARCERE, *History of La Rochelle*.

and the people devoted themselves to an ever-growing cult of the heroine.

For nearly five hundred years, Orléans has celebrated the anniversary of these events. At the gracious invitation of the mayor, I have had the chance to attend several of these solemnities. These are the notes I wrote then, under the immediate impression of the moment:

The belfry, the old witness of the siege—the very one that signaled the movements of the English—chimes every quarter hour. Its resonant vibrations spread over the city; they slip through the narrow, winding streets of old Orléans, penetrate deep into the houses, and awaken in every heart the memory of the deliverance. Soon, at its call, the bells of all the parishes begin to sway. Their bronze voices rise into the air; they form a mighty concert, dominated by the deep notes of the belfry, and they stir the dreaming soul.

The whole city is decorated, festooned with flags. Banners float over the public buildings; at every balcony, at every window, the national colors mingle with the colors and arms of the Maid.

Crowds pack the squares and streets. Many have come from the surrounding countryside; others from distant parts of France, and even from abroad. A telling detail: every year the English, in great numbers, come to take part in the festivals of the Maid of Lorraine. Cardinal Vaughan, Archbishop of Westminster, was seen there among the French prelates. A people that acts thus is not a people without greatness.

Nowhere has the memory of Joan remained so alive. In Orléans, everything speaks of her. Every street corner, every monument recalls some detail of the siege.

For four centuries, France neglected Joan. Silence and shadow enveloped her memory; Orléans alone did not forget.

As early as 1430, one year after the raising of the siege, the commemorative ceremony and procession were instituted; and each time, the municipal authorities and the clergy, in noble emulation, seek the means to lend the festival new charm. A rare and touching spectacle: all powers unite to render this manifestation more resplendent. The memory of Joan alone today can restore unity to minds and hearts, as she restored the unity of France at the hour of supreme disasters and collapse.

On the evening of May 7, at eight o'clock, Joan, victorious at the Tourelles, re-entered the besieged city. An affecting, unforgettable ceremony consecrates this memory every year. The mayor, preceded by the heroine's banner—white, strewn with golden fleurs-de-lis—and followed by the municipal councilors, leaves the Hôtel de Ville and comes to the cathedral parvis to place the sacred standard in the hands of the bishop, surrounded by his clergy and foreign prelates.

Under a black, rain-laden sky, the basilica of Sainte-Croix lifts its massive towers. The troops form a square; the cannon thunders; the belfry, the cathedral bourdon, the bells of the churches peal at full voice. The doors of the vast edifice open; the procession of bishops and priests, with measured steps, crosses the threshold and arranges itself beneath the wide portals. Before them, the banners of Saint Aignan and Saint Euverte, patrons of the city, are unfurled. Miters and croziers gleam in the torchlight borne by horsemen. Fires suddenly kindled within the towers bathe them in fantastic color. A crimson light spreads over the rose windows, the ogives—over all the lacework of stone on the façade, over the floating banners, the stoles, and the surplices. Five hundred voices intone the *Hymn to the Standard*:

*Standard of Deliverance,*
*To victory you led our forebears.*
*Sons of those valiant men, let us say as they did:*
*Long live Joan! Long live France!*

A shiver, a mighty breath passes over the attentive, reverent crowd. Heads bow before the white, *fleurdelisée* banner, which slowly ascends the steps and vanishes beneath the vaults, like the phantom of the Maid of Lorraine returning on the night of her anniversary. The gates swing shut, the fires go out, the harmonies fall silent; the crowd disperses, and the basilica remains dark and still in the night.



May 8, ten o'clock. Under the sun's rays, the cathedral displays a festoon of oriflammes and flags. The interior decoration is restrained and of great effect. Tall banners in red and gold, the colors of Orléans, adorn the choir. From the pillars of the naves hang the armorial bearings of the Bastard of Orléans and the other companions of the Maid. At the height of the organ loft, dominating all, appear Joan's arms[107], set within a virginal frame of white draperies. Not a seat remains empty in the vast nave. All France—army, magistracy, clergy, municipal authorities, burghers, artisans—is represented in this throng. The graceful dresses and flowered hats of the

107 These arms are: azure, a silver sword palewise with a golden hilt, surmounted at the point by a royal crown Or; on the flanks, fleurs-de-lis.

young women mingle with the gold-braided uniforms, the red robes of the judges, and the black coats of the civil officials.

The office begins with Gounod's *Mass in Memory of Joan of Arc.* Martial fanfares unite with the harmony of the organ; then a choir of young girls sings Gounod's *The Voices of Joan.* Their pure voices descend from the high gallery like celestial accents. One would say an echo of the angelic spheres, an evocation of the martyred Maid who seems to hover, a radiant spirit, beneath these vaults. For an instant, one forgets the earth, its sorrows, its pains. The impression is grand and profound; many eyes fill with tears.

I lift my thought, my prayer toward Joan, and a ray of sunlight, filtering through the armorial stained-glass window, envelops me with its light, while, all around, the shadow covers the packed multitude of listeners.

Then comes the panegyric, preached by the Bishop of Orléans. He brings us back to earth. His words are ardent. He sets forth the city's situation during the siege:

*"Assuredly,"* he says, *"it defends itself well, the noble city! Paris is English, so be it: Orléans will remain French. Paris is only the head of the country: Orléans is its heart. So long as the heart beats, there is hope. Aldermen, people, burghers, clergy, men-at-arms decide to die rather than surrender. The suburbs will be burned; the churches dismantled; the watch will be kept by day and by night; the merchants will fight as if it were their habitual trade; the king shall be given time to send reinforcements; and, by the living God! we shall see to whom the fortune of battles will smile!

"Alas! the king sent neither money nor soldiers; the besieger tightened his lines; the bastilles rose week by week; provisions were exhausted; hunger—the horrible hunger—held sway[108]. Another fortnight, and Orléans would fall; and the little king of Bourges would cease to be even the little king of Bourges; and France would descend into that tomb where dead nations lie..."

A little later, he depicts the rapture of the inhabitants after Joan's victories:

*"Ah! those eight days that followed Patay—how good it must have been to live them! How sweet the renewal must have seemed, and how luminous the broad sheet of our Loire, and how fragrant our golden valley! Can you picture those visits of thanksgiving to all your churches; those hymns that never ceased; those outpourings of enthusiasm around the heroes of the marvelous epic; that people drawing breath for the first time after the oppressions of the Hundred Years' War; that city, in a word, acclaiming itself in the triumph of the Maid and the resurrection of the Fatherland?"*



The orator descends from the pulpit. The crowd surges onto the parvis, mingles with the army, among bishops, banners, and relics, and the traditional procession unwinds—two kilometers long—beneath a cloudless sky, through streets decked with flags. It will pass the stations of victory that Joan made in besieged Orléans.

On the site of the fort of the Tourelles, a modest cross recalls the memory of her who, as the inscription says, *"by her valor, saved the city, France, and her king."* There the procession makes its final halt, while the cannon

108 See, in the *Journal du Siège*, the joy with which the slightest arrival of provisions is noted.

booms again and the military bands salute the standard. The cortege returns to its starting point, then disperses. The joyful crowd will give itself over to its pleasures, while Joan's truest friends go apart to pray and reflect.

# VIII
# REIMS

*I come to deliver to the Dauphin the kingdom of France.*

*Saint-Yves d'Alveydre*

The prophecy of Joan concerning Orléans had been fulfilled. One task remained: the march to Reims and the coronation of Charles VII. Without losing an instant, the Maid applied herself to its realization. She departed from the Orléanais and pursued the Dauphin into the depths of Touraine. She first rejoined him at Tours, then followed him to Loches, urging him relentlessly to put everything into action for the success of this daring enterprise.



But this indolent prince, weak of will, hesitated between the exhortations of the heroine and the warnings of his counselors, who deemed it rash to risk a journey of sixty leagues across a land bristling with fortresses and strongholds held by the enemy. To their objections, Joan invariably replied: *"I know it well; yet I take no account of it. We shall succeed!"*

The enthusiasm of the people and the army spread from place to place. Voices cried out that they must take advantage of the disarray of the English, who had abandoned the Loire, retreating upon Paris and leaving behind their baggage and artillery. Never had they been dealt so crushing a blow. Stricken with terror, they imagined that ghostly armies were advancing against them in the sky.

The echo of these events resounded throughout France. With hope, energy revived. The current of opinion grew so strong that Charles VII could no longer persist in his apathy. He showered honors upon the liberator and her family, yet he himself remained without vigor, without courage. He did not even go to see the people of Orléans. His influential counselors—La Trémoille and Regnault de Chartres—were uneasy, secretly exasperated by Joan's triumphs, which cast them into the shadows, jealous of a prestige that now drew to her all eyes and all hopes. They asked themselves whether their power and fortune were not about to be engulfed in this mighty and irresistible popular tide which had driven back the English invasion.

At last, the cry of the people rose into a clamor, and it was necessary to yield. An army of twelve thousand combatants was gathered at Gien. Gentlemen hastened from all quarters, and those too poor to equip themselves asked to serve as foot soldiers. The departure took place on June 29, with little money, few provisions, and inadequate artillery.

On July 5, they arrived before Troyes. The city, strong, well-provisioned, and defended by an Anglo-Burgundian garrison, refused to open its gates. The French army, lacking resources, could not undertake a long siege. After only a few days, the soldiers were reduced to eating beans and unripe grain plucked from the fields.

The king assembled a council to deliberate on what course to take. The Maid was not even summoned. The chancellor laid out the dire situation and posed the question: Should the army retreat, or continue its march toward Reims? Each of those present was to give his opinion in turn. Robert le Masson, lord of Trèves-sur-Loire, observed that since the king had undertaken this expedition not because it seemed easy, nor because he had a powerful army or the money to pay it, but because Joan had declared it was the will of God and that no resistance would be found, it was fitting above all to consult the heroine. This proposal was accepted.

At that very moment, Joan, already warned by her Voices, struck sharply at the door. She entered, and addressing the king, said: *"Gentle Dauphin, if you will remain but two days before your city of Troyes, it will be yours, by force or by love—doubt it not!"* The chancellor replied: *"If we could be certain within six days, we would well wait!"* — *"Doubt it not!"* Joan repeated.

Immediately she went through the encampments, organizing the attack, communicating to all the ardor that animated her. The night passed in feverish preparations. From atop the walls and towers, the besieged saw the French camp astir with frantic activity. By torchlight, knights, squires, and soldiers vied with one another to fill the ditches, prepare fascines and ladders, and construct shelters for the artillery. The spectacle was fantastic and awe-inspiring.

When dawn whitened the horizon, the inhabitants of Troyes, to their terror, saw that all was ready for a furious assault: columns of attack arrayed at the most favorable points, with reserves behind them; the few pieces of artillery, well sheltered, ready to open fire; archers and crossbowmen at their posts. The whole army, ranged in silence, awaited the signal. Standing at the edge of the moat, her standard in hand, Joan prepared to have the trumpets sound the charge. Seized with dread, the besieged sued for terms.

The conditions were easily arranged. The king had every interest in showing clemency to cities willing to submit. On the following day, July 10, the English garrison departed, leading away some French prisoners of war whose fate had been overlooked. Seeing Joan, these unfortunate men threw themselves at her feet, imploring her aid. She opposed their departure with firm resolve, and the king was obliged to pay their ransom.

Following the example of Troyes, Châlons and Reims likewise opened their gates to Charles VII.



At Châlons, Joan had the joy of meeting several inhabitants of Domremy who had come forth to greet her, among them Gérardin, a farmer whose son Nicolas was her godchild. To them she opened her thoughts and her heart, confiding her hopes and fears, recounting her struggles, her victories, the splendor of the coming coronation, and the rising again of France, humbled and wounded. Near these simple, rustic men, who brought her so vivid a remembrance of childhood, she felt at ease, pouring herself out entirely. She told them how little these glories touched her, and what joy it would bring her to return to her village, resume her peaceful life and rustic labors in the midst of her family. But her mission bound her to the king, and she must submit to the will of Heaven. The struggle against the English troubled her less than the intrigues of court and the perfidy of the great. *"I fear only treason,"* she told them[109]. And indeed, it was by treason that she was to perish. For every great envoy, there is ever a traitor lurking in the shadows, plotting his ruin.

Against the deep azure of the sky stood out the lofty towers of the Cathedral of Reims, already centuries old in Joan of Arc's time. The three gaping portals revealed the vast naves, resplendent with the light of thousands of candles, thronged with a motley crowd of priests, lords, men-at-arms, and burghers in festive attire. The vibrations of sacred chants filled the vaults, while at intervals the blare of martial fanfares broke forth in strident notes.

The confraternities, the guilds with their emblems borne aloft, all who could find no place within the basilica, crowded the forecourt. A throng of common folk—townspeople and peasants from the surrounding countryside—pressed upon the approaches of the edifice, held back with difficulty by iron-clad horsemen and archers clad in the liveries of France. Pages and squires held by the bridle the splendid mounts of the king, the peers, and the captains of war. All eyes turned to the black steed of the Maid, held fast by a soldier of her suite.

Let us pass beneath the lofty Gothic nave and advance to the choir. The king, surrounded by the twelve peers of the realm—both lay and ecclesiastical—or their deputies, and by the constable, Charles d'Albret, who

109 J. FABRE, *Procès de réhabilitation*, t. I.

bore the sword of France, had just been made a knight. Near him, standing with her back against the right-hand pillar, in the very spot still pointed out to this day, was Joan, clad in full armor, holding in her hand her white standard, that banner which, *"having borne the toil, must also share the honor.*[110]*"*

The king received the holy anointing from the hands of the Archbishop of Reims, Regnault de Chartres. The latter took from the altar the crown, which the twelve peers held aloft with their hands above the head of the monarch. Once crowned, Charles of Valois was robed in the royal mantle of blue, strewn with golden fleurs-de-lis. It was then that the Maid, overcome with emotion, flung herself at his feet, embraced his knees, and said:

*"Gentle Sire, thus is accomplished the will of God, whose pleasure it was that I should raise the siege of Orléans and bring you to this city of Reims to receive your rightful consecration, that thereby it might be shown that you are the true king and heir of the crown of France."*



The trumpets resounded anew, and the procession was formed. When, in the great doorway, the king appeared, the crowd surged forward, and cries of *Noël! Noël!* burst forth.

The fanfares made the lofty vaults tremble. Songs and joyful shouts rose to the skies—and to these calls there came the answering echoes of a thousand unseen voices. They were there, all the great Spirits of Gaul, to celebrate the awakening of their native land. They were there, all those who had loved and served, even unto death, the noble realm of France. They hovered above

110 J. FABRE, *Procès de condamnation*, p. 189.

the frenzied multitude. Behold Vercingetorix, followed by the heroes of Gergovia and Alesia! Behold Clovis and his Franks! Then Charles Martel with his companions, and Charlemagne, the mighty emperor, who with his sword *Joyeuse* salutes Joan and King Charles. Then Roland and the valiant knights! And the countless throng of warriors, priests, monks, and common men whose bodies lie beneath heavy tombstones or crumbled into the dust of centuries—all those who had given their lives for France. They too cried *Noël!* to hail the resurrection of the fatherland, the rebirth of Gaul!

The procession wound its way through the narrow streets and constricted squares. Beside the king rode Joan, bearing her banner; then followed princes, marshals, and captains, richly arrayed, mounted on splendid coursers. Pennons, pennants, and banners floated in the wind. Yet amid the lords in sumptuous attire and the warriors in glittering armor, all eyes sought with eagerness the maiden who had led them into the city of consecration—she who had foretold it herself in her village, when she was still but a humble peasant girl, an unknown shepherdess.



The whole city was in jubilation. People had come from afar for the coronation. Jacques d'Arc, Joan's father, had arrived two days before from Domremy, accompanied by Durand Laxart. They lodged at the inn of the l'Ane rayé in the Rue du Parvis. It was a moving scene when the heroine, accompanied by her brother Pierre, beheld her aged father once more. She fell at his knees, begging forgiveness for having left him without his consent, adding that it had been the will of God.

At Joan's entreaty, the king received them and granted to the inhabitants of the villages of Greux and Domremy exemption from all tailles and imposts. The expenses of Jacques d'Arc were borne by the public treasury, and a horse was given him at the city's expense for his return home.

Joan showed herself in the streets, receiving with modesty and kindness the humble and the supplicant. The people thronged about her; all wished to touch her hands, her ring. Not one doubted that she had been sent by God to bring an end to the calamities of the kingdom. This was Sunday, July 17, 1429, and that date marks the highest summit of the epic of Joan of Arc.

Yet Michelet erred in saying that her mission was to end at Reims, and that she disobeyed her Voices in continuing the struggle. This assertion is refuted by the heroine's own words, by her declarations to the examiners at Poitiers and to the judges at Rouen. She affirmed it most clearly in her letter of summons to the English captains before Orléans, dated March 22:

*"Wherever I find your men in France, I will make them depart, whether they will or no... I am come on God's behalf to drive you forth from all France*[111]*."*

There can be no doubt. The notion that Joan's mission ceased at Reims was advanced only at the time of the trial of rehabilitation, in order to conceal from posterity the disloyalty—one might say the crime—of Charles VII and his counselors, to divert the heavy responsibilities that weighed upon them. To this end, history was falsified, mutilated, testimonies altered,

111 J. FABRE, *Procès de condamnation*, p. 97.

the register of the interrogations at Poitiers destroyed, and thus was consummated an odious act, a work of falsehood and iniquity[112].

Yet it was not without apprehension, not without regrets, as we have seen, that Joan pursued her arduous path. A few days later, riding between Dunois and Chancellor Regnault de Chartres, she said: *"How I wish it might please God that I could return now, laying down my arms, and go back to serve my father and mother, and keep their flocks with my sister and my brothers, who would be so glad to see me again*[113]*."*

These words show plainly that neither the splendor of her triumph nor the brilliance of the court had dazzled her. She had reached the very summit of her glory. The adoration of an entire people was hers. In truth, she stood then as the foremost figure in the realm, her prestige eclipsing that of Charles VII himself. And yet she longed only for the peace of the fields and the sweetness of her father's hearth. Neither her victories nor the power she had gained had changed her. She remained simple and modest amid all grandeur. What a lesson for those whom the least success intoxicates, whom pride inflates, and upon whom fortune's favor casts a fatal vertigo!



112 Jean Chartier, secretary of the royal archives, tells us quite naïvely in his history of Charles VII that "the chronicles make us aware of the events chosen by the king to be entrusted to history, in the sense and light under which he intended them to be appreciated." It was the king who had his scribes declare that Joan's mission ended at Reims.

113 *Procès de réhabilitation.* Déposition de Dunois.

# IX
# COMPIÈGNE.

*I fear only treason.*

*Joan.*

"To Paris!" cried the Maid the day after the coronation. "To Paris!" repeated the whole army[114]. Had they marched straight upon the capital, as Joan wished, there was every chance of entering it, aided by the disorder that reigned among the English. But Charles VII lost precious time, which the Duke of Bedford put to good use by reinforcing Paris: he summoned from England an army of relief, raised by Cardinal Winchester, uncle of King Henry, and originally destined to combat the Hussites.



Here, Joan's star begins to pale. After the triumphs, the resplendent victories, there come the dark hours, the hours of trial, before prison and torment. As the renown of the heroine spreads, as her glory surpasses all other glories, hatred rises around her; intrigues are woven among the great lords whose plans, whose shadowy machinations she has thwarted. All those perfidious courtiers whom she eclipses, those churchmen whose minds are steeped in gall, who cannot forgive her for

114 HENRI MARTIN, *Hist. de France*, t. VI, p. 200.

declaring herself, above their authority, sent from Heaven, and for preferring to their counsels the inspirations of her Voices; even many of those war-chiefs, vanquished in a hundred battles and who now find themselves surpassed in military science by a peasant girl—all these men, wounded in their pride, have sworn her downfall. They await the propitious hour; and that hour is near.

The English, for their part, are thunderstruck by their reverses. Their principal army is destroyed; their best captains are dead or captive; their soldiers desert in terror of the Maid. They scarcely doubt the superhuman power of her whom they call "the witch of France." And had Charles VII, immediately after his coronation, marched on Paris, the great city would have surrendered without combat. Six weeks are lost in hesitation; then, when at last they arrive before the capital, no precautions have been taken; Joan's orders are not carried out; the ditches are not filled in; the assault is not pressed. She has been given as lieutenants the two commanders most hostile to her—"the most ferocious men who ever existed," says Michelet: Raoul de Gaucourt and Marshal de Retz, the odious magician who would later mount the scaffold for the crime of sorcery[115].

The king refused to show himself. In vain was he sent message upon message. He did not come. The Duke of Alençon rode to fetch him at Senlis; he promised to come, and broke his word. At the assault on the Saint-Honoré gate, Joan, as always, showed herself heroic. All day long she stood upon the edge of the ditch, beneath

115 In the dungeons of his castles at Suze, Tiffauges, and elsewhere, were found the bones of several hundred children, whose blood had been used in his conjurations.

a rain of projectiles, urging the soldiers to the attack. Toward sunset she was struck deep in the thigh by a crossbow bolt and had to lie down upon the slope. She did not cease exhorting the French, sometimes crying out: "The king! the king! let the king show himself!" But the king did not come. Toward eleven o'clock at night, several captains came to seize her and carried her off against her will.

The army fell back to Saint-Denis, where the king had arrived and was making preparations to withdraw again to the castles of the Loire. Joan could not bring herself to turn her eyes from the spires of Paris: "she was as though enchained before the great city by a superhuman force[116]." On the very next day she wished to renew the assault. But what had happened? Passage was no longer possible. By order of the king, the bridges had been cut and retreat imposed.

Thus was accomplished one of the greatest infamies of history. Those very men to whom God had sent a messianic savior conspired against her. They succeeded in thwarting the mission of Joan of Arc and, in the strong phrase of Henri Martin, "in making God a liar." Their selfishness, their blindness were such that the providential action was suspended by their own unworthiness.

After the failure before Paris, there unfolds for Joan a long period of uncertainties, of turmoil, of inner torment. For eight months she will experience the alternation of successes and reverses: success at Saint-Pierre-le-Moutier, failure at La Charité. She feels that

116 H. MARTIN, *Hist. de France*, t. VI, p. 209

fortune is abandoning her. On the ramparts of Melun, her Voices tell her: "Joan, you will be taken before Saint John's Day!"

This reversal of fortune must be attributed solely to the ill will of men, to the ingratitude of the king and his counselors, who raised against her a thousand obstacles and brought her enterprises to ruin.

Was she thereby diminished? In no way. It is from this moment that she became truly great—greater than her victories had made her. Her trials, her captivity, her martyrdom, so nobly endured, would raise her above the most illustrious conquerors and render her sublime in the eyes of posterity. From the depths of her prisons, before the tribunal of Rouen, from the height of her funeral pyre, she will appear to us more imposing than amid the tumult of battles or in the intoxication of triumph. Her bearing, her sufferings, her inspired words, her tears, her painful agony, will make of her one of the purest glories of France, a subject of admiration for the centuries, an object of envy for all peoples! Adversity would place upon her brow a sacred aureole. By her heroic acceptance of suffering, by the greatness of her soul in the face of defeat and before death, she became a just cause of pride for the women of France, and an object of veneration for all in whom vibrates the sense of moral beauty and the love of their country.



The glory of arms is fair; but genius, sanctity, and suffering alone have right to the apotheoses of history!

The siege of La Charité having failed, Joan was recalled to court; but soon inaction weighed upon her, and once again her ardor carried her away. Leaving the king to his pleasures and his revels, at the head of a devoted band she threw herself into besieged Compiègne. And it was there that, during a raid, the governor of the city, Guillaume de Flavy, having lowered the portcullis, she could not re-enter the stronghold and was taken by the Count of Luxembourg, of the Burgundian party.

What share of responsibility belongs to the Sire de Flavy in this event? Some have seen in it a premeditated treason. The chancellor, Regnault de Chartres, had but recently passed through Compiègne and held conferences with the Duke of Burgundy. Yet most historians—Henri Martin, Quicherat, Wallon, Anatole France—believe in the loyalty of that captain[117]. Despite their affirmations, his role at the time of Joan's capture has remained equivocal and ill-defined. According to indications received from beyond, we are inclined to believe there was no prior premeditation, but rather that advantage was taken of the occasion to rid themselves of a personality grown troublesome to certain ambitions.



If no plot had been laid beforehand against Joan, there was nevertheless treason, in the sense that Guillaume de Flavy made no attempt to rescue her. Cornered by the Burgundians at the angle of the Margny road and the boulevard that defended the bridgehead, but a few paces from the gate, she might easily have been saved. At that critical instant, the captain of Compiègne held the boulevard with several hundred men. He saw all that was happening, made no effort, and abandoned Joan to her fate. In this, the treachery seems flagrant.

---

117 *See H. Martin, History of France, vol. VI, p. 231; Wallon, Joan of Arc, p. 211; Quicherat, New Insights, pp. 77–85. Neither Lavisse nor Michelet take a position.*

Joan was at first confined in the castle of Beaulieu, some distance from Compiègne, then transferred to the keep of Beaurevoir, belonging to the Count of Luxembourg. For six months she was moved from prison to prison—at Arras, at Drugy, at Le Crotoy—until, on the 21st of November, at the urgent and menacing summons of the University of Paris, she was sold to the English, her cruel enemies, for ten thousand livres tournois, plus a pension granted to the soldier who had effected her capture.

Jean de Luxembourg was of high lineage, but of narrow heart and meager fortune. On his escutcheon he had inscribed a dispirited device: *"To the impossible, no man is bound."* How much more vibrant the cry of his contemporary Jacques Cœur: *"To a valiant heart, nothing is impossible!"* Heavily in debt, almost ruined, Luxembourg would not resign himself to poverty, nor therefore refuse the ten thousand golden livres offered by the King of England. At this price, he sold Joan and delivered her up.

Ten thousand livres in gold! It was an enormous sum for the time. Yet the English were at the end of their resources, unable even to pay their officials. For lack of money, the course of justice was suspended in Paris for several weeks. The clerk who drew up the acts of parliament was forced to halt his work for want of parchment[118]. But when it was a matter of buying Joan, the English knew how to raise that great sum. And how did they do it? By a method familiar to them: they levied a heavy tax upon all Normandy. And here is a fact to be

118 *Registers of Parliament, vol. XV, February 1431, according to H. Martin, vol. VI, p. 245.*

marked: it was with French money that the blood of Joan of Arc was bought!

Deep in her prisons, Joan's greatest concern is not for her own fate, but rather this thought, sadly expressed: *"I shall no longer be able to serve the noble country of France!"* Upon hearing the news that the good people of Compiègne, if the town were taken, were threatened with being put to the sword, she threw herself from the top of the tower of Beaurevoir in order to join them: *"I had heard tell,"* she would explain to her judges, *"that those of Compiègne, all of them down to the age of seven years, were to be put to fire and sword; and I preferred to risk death rather than to live after such destruction of good people*[119]*."*

Step by step, from dungeon to dungeon, she at last arrived at Le Crotoy, on the borders of Normandy, occupied by the English. She was shut up in a defensive tower guarding the mouth of the Somme. From the barred window her gaze stretched across a panorama of sandflats and then, beyond, to the immensity of the sea. It was the first time she beheld the great expanse of water, and the spectacle made a deep impression on her.

The sea! With its foaming waves, its boundless horizons, its shifting reflections!

She, so sensitive to the harmonies of sky and earth, to sunlit days and starry nights, lost herself in the contemplation of the vast expanse—now of a silvery gray, now of an intense blue, studded in the evening with the shimmering of stars. She lent an astonished ear to the mysterious murmurings of wind and wave.



119 J. Fabre, *Trial of Condemnation*, 5th secret interrogation.

When, at the hour of high tide, the lament of the waves, the sobbing of the Ocean, rose up to her, an immense feeling of sadness overwhelmed her.

The English are coming—the English who bought her dearly! Since Compiègne, she had been the captive of the Burgundians, her adversaries, it is true, but men of the same tongue and the same race, who had shown her some consideration. Now, what could she expect from these fierce foreigners, whom she had so often defeated and who, having sworn her a savage hatred, had never missed a chance to insult her? A dreadful anguish tore at her soul, and she prayed.

But the voice said and repeated: *Take everything with grace!*

She had to wait thus, at Le Crotoy, for three weeks. One day, the ladies of Abbeville came to visit her, to console her, and their tears, for a moment, mingled with her own[120].



120 WALLON, *Jeanne d'Arc*, p. 222.

# X
# ROUEN; THE PRISON

*He whom God chooses for a holy task,*
*Liberating soldier, priest, apostle, or martyr,*
*Must strengthen his heart, silence every complaint;*
*It is beautiful to fight; it is great to suffer.*

*Paul Allard*

Joan is now in the hands of the English. They gagged her so that she could not communicate with the people, and led her, under heavy escort, to the castle of Rouen. There, she was thrown into a dungeon, shut inside an iron cage: *"They had a sort of cage forged for me,"* *she tells us,* *"in which they placed me. I was tightly confined; I had a heavy chain around my neck, another at my waist, and others on my feet and hands. I would have succumbed to such dreadful misery if God and my Voices had not granted me their consolations. Nothing can express their touching solicitude and the ineffable comfort they gave me. Dying of hunger, half clothed, surrounded by filth and bruised by my irons, I drew from my faith the courage to forgive my executioners."*

Atrocious treatment! Joan was a prisoner of war; she was a woman, and yet they locked her like a wild beast in an iron cage! Later, it is true, the English contented themselves with chaining her feet to a heavy beam.

Thus began a passion of six months—an ordeal without precedent in history, more harrowing even than that of Christ. For Christ was a man, and here we are dealing with a young girl of nineteen, abandoned to brutal, stupid, and lustful soldiers. Five of them—the scourings of the English army, as all historians affirm—kept watch night and day in her cell.

Imagine what a young woman, bound in chains, could expect from such vile men, intoxicated with rage against the one they held responsible for all their defeats. These wretches subjected her to constant abuse. More than once, they tried to violate her, and when they failed, they beat her savagely. She complained of this to her judges during the trial, and often, when they entered her prison to interrogate her, they found her in tears, her face swollen and bruised from blows she had received[121].



Think of the horrors of such a situation—the thoughts of the woman, the fears of the virgin—exposed to every insult, every outrage, deprived of rest and sleep, her body broken, her strength annihilated amid continual anguish and dread. Alone among these infamies, she refused to lay aside her male attire, and they reproached this act of modesty as though it were a crime!

Nor were her visitors less vile than her guards. The Count of Luxembourg, who had sold her, once came to mock her in her dungeon. He was accompanied by the Earls of Warwick and Stafford, and the Bishop of

---

121 H. MARTIN, *Hist. de France*, t. VI, pp. 258, 290.

Thérouanne, chancellor of the King of England: *"I have come to ransom you,"* he said, *"on the condition, however, that you promise never again to take up arms against us."* — *"You mock me,"* she cried. *"I know well that you have neither the will nor the power to do so."* And as he insisted, she added: *"I know well that these English will kill me, thinking by my death to win the kingdom of France. But even if they were a hundred thousand more than they are now, they will never have the kingdom."* These words made them furious. The Earl of Stafford drew his dagger to strike Joan. Warwick restrained him[122].

Later, her judges entrusted to an unworthy priest—Loyseleur, traitor and spy—the task of sneaking into her prison in secular dress. Pretending to be a fellow prisoner from Lorraine captured by the English, he gained Joan's confidence and persuaded her to confess to him. During their conversations, notaries, secretly hidden, listened through an opening made for that purpose and recorded all the confidences of the heroine.

The English believed that a "spell" was attached to her virginity and that, if she lost it, they would have nothing more to fear from her. An examination conducted by the Duchess of Bedford, assisted by Lady Anna Bavon and several matrons, confirmed that Joan's virginity was intact. A detail revealing the baseness of his character: the Duke of Bedford, Regent of England, was secretly present at this examination.

It was shortly afterward that the Lord Constable, Count of Stafford, driven as much by superstition as by

---

122 J. Fabre, *Trial of Rehabilitation.* Deposition of the knight Aimond de Macy, who was present at the scene, vol. II, p. 143.

a hideous passion, had Joan's dungeon opened and tried to do violence to her.[123]

Who could tell what she suffered in the darkness of her prison! Abandoned by all, betrayed and sold for the weight of gold, she endured all the pangs of suffering. She knew those hours of anguish, of moral torture, when everything grows dark around us, when the voices of Heaven seem to fall silent[124], when the invisible remains mute, just as all the furies, all the earthly hatreds are unleashed and rush upon us.

All missionaries have endured those sorrowful hours, and she endured them more than any, poor child, exposed defenseless to the vilest outrages. Why does God permit such things? It is to probe the soul and the heart of His faithful, to test their faith in Him; it is so that their merits may grow yet greater, and that the crown He reserves for them may shine with even more brilliance and beauty.



But, one will ask, how could Joan, exhausted, laden with irons, escape the infamous attempts of her visitors and her jailers? How could she preserve that flower of purity which was her safeguard, according to the opinion—widely held at that time—that a virgin could not be convicted of sorcery?

Well, here is how! In those terrible hours, more feared by her even than death itself, the invisible intervenes. In the cold and gloomy prison, a radiant legion enters. Beings whom she alone sees and whom she calls "her

123 J. Fabre, *Trial of Rehabilitation*. Depositions of Martin Ladvenu and Isambard de la Pierre, vol. II, pp. 88, 99.

124 The Spirits did not always come to her aid. Her voices did not forewarn her of the snares and artifices of Loyseleur; they did not intervene during the many visits.

brothers of paradise" come to assist her, to sustain her, to give her the strength needed to escape what would have been an abominable sacrilege.

These Spirits comfort her and tell her: "To suffer is to grow, to rise higher!" Amidst the darkness that surrounds her, a light shines forth; sweet songs reach her, like an echo of the harmonies of space.

Her voices console her and repeat: "Take courage! You will be delivered by a great victory!" In her simple faith, she believes that this deliverance means freedom. Alas! As our ancestors, the Druids, once taught, it was "deliverance through death"—death by martyrdom. So it had to be, to give to this saintly figure all her sublime radiance.

Is it not the privilege of superior souls to be destined to suffer for a noble cause? Must they not pass through the crucible of trial to reveal all the virtues, all the treasures, all the splendors that lie within them? A great death is the necessary crown of a great life, of a life of devotion and sacrifice. It is initiation into a higher existence. But, in those painful hours, in that supreme purification, these souls are upheld by a superhuman strength, a strength that enables them to face everything, to overcome everything!

# XI
# ROUEN; THE TRIAL

*But I enter, trembling, into this darkness!*
*Thy holy will be done, O my God!*
*P. Allard*

We now come to the trial.

Indeed, at the same time as this captivity — so harsh, so horrible — Joan had to endure the long and tortuous phases of a trial such as the world had never before seen.

On one side, all that the spirit of evil can distill of hypocritical blackness, cunning, perfidy, and servile ambition: seventy-one clerics, priests, and doctors, Pharisees with hardened hearts, all men of the Church, but for whom religion was nothing more than a mask concealing burning passions — cupidity, intrigue, and narrow fanaticism.

On the other side — alone, without support, without counsel, without defender — a child of nineteen years, innocence and purity incarnate, a heroic soul in a virgin's body, a heart sublime and tender, ready for every sacrifice to save her country, to fulfill her mission with fidelity, and to set the example of virtue in duty.

Never has human nature risen so high on one side, and on the other fallen so low.

History has established the responsibilities. I wish to say nothing that might rekindle political or religious hatreds. Is not the name of Joan of Arc, among all glorious names, the one that ought to rally every sentiment of admiration, no matter from what quarter it comes?

The Church has sought to clear itself of the accusation that weighed upon it for centuries. To do so, it strove to lay the whole odium of Joan's condemnation upon Pierre Cauchon, Bishop of Beauvais. It repudiated him, loaded him with its curses. But was Cauchon the only great culprit?

Let us recall one fact. On May 26, 1430—three days after Joan's capture before Compiègne—the vicar general of the Grand Inquisitor of France, sitting in Paris, wrote to the Duke of Burgundy to beg him, and "to enjoin him, under penalty of law, to send to him as prisoner a certain woman named Joan the Maid, vehemently suspected of crimes savoring of heresy, to appear before the promoter of the Holy Inquisition[125]." Thus that redoubtable tribunal of the Holy Office, by then little more than a shadow, reappeared, emerging from the gloom to demand the greatest victim that ever stood before it. And the University of Paris—the foremost ecclesiastical body in France—supported its claim.



Anatole France, well informed on this point, tells us[126]:

125 Trial, vol. I, pp. 8 and following.

126 A. FRANCE, *Vie de Jeanne d'Arc*, t. II, p. 179.

"In the case of the Maid, it was not only a bishop who set the Most Holy Inquisition in motion, it was the daughter of kings, the mother of learning, the fair bright sun of France and Christendom—the University of Paris. It claimed the privilege of judging causes of heresy, and its opinions, sought from every quarter, carried authority over the whole world where the cross is planted."

For a year, it had demanded that the Maid be handed over to the inquisitor, as one suspected of sorcery.

The same author further tells us[127]:

"After consultation with the doctors and masters of the University of Paris, the Bishop of Beauvais presented himself, on July 14, at the camp of Compiègne and claimed the Maid as belonging to his jurisdiction. He supported his demand with letters addressed by the *alma mater* to the Duke of Burgundy and to the Lord of Luxembourg."



It was the second time the University had demanded Joan of the duke; it feared she might be delivered "by indirect means" and removed from its grasp. At the same time, the envoy bore offers of money.

Pierre Cauchon, Bishop of Beauvais, who had been driven from his see by the people for having allied himself with the English, did indeed instruct and direct the trial himself. He played the most important role therein—this is beyond dispute. Yet the vice-inquisitor, Jean Lemaître, approved all his choices regarding the composition of the tribunal and often sat at his side. And when the Bishop of Beauvais was prevented from

127 Id., *Ibid.*, t. II, p. 195.

presiding, Jean Lemaître presided alone. This is attested by all the documents[128].

The vice-inquisitor signed and certified the minutes of the hearings as authentic. These were drawn up in triplicate by the tribunal's clerks. One copy still exists in the library of the Chamber of Deputies, bearing the seal of the Inquisition.

In trials of heresy, it was the law that all decisions and judgments be made jointly by two judges: the bishop and the inquisitor. So it was at Rouen, as everywhere else. It is thus impossible not to recognize that Cauchon acted under the cover of inquisitorial jurisprudence.

Nor was that all. The bishops of Coutances and Lisieux were consulted during the trial, and both approved the prosecution. One particular detail deserves mention: the Bishop of Lisieux, Zanon de Castiglione, declared for condemnation on the sole ground that Joan was of too humble a condition to have been inspired by God. Truly, one may ask what the apostles of Christ—those humble craftsmen and fishermen of Galilee—and what Christ Himself, the carpenter's son, would have thought of such an answer.



The bishops of Thérouanne, Noyon, and Norwich were also present at the trial; all three took part in admonishing the Maid.

Cauchon surrounded himself with eminent personages and renowned theologians. He placed upon the tribunal men such as Thomas de Courcelles, later called "the light of the Council of Basel and the second Gerson"; Pierre Maurice and Jean Beaupère, both

128 J. Fabre, *Trial of Condemnation*, 4th secret interrogation. Declaration of P. Cauchon to Joan.

former rectors of the University of Paris; doctors and masters in theology, such as Guillaume Erard, Nicole Midi, Jacques de Touraine; and numerous abbots with crozier and miter from the great abbeys of Normandy.

Yet of all these eminent clerics, not one showed impartiality. All were partisans of the English and enemies of Joan. The promoter, Jean d'Estivet, Cauchon's damned soul, a man without faith or scruple, distinguished himself in particular by his hatred and his violence against the accused. No heed was given to Joan's legitimate request that an equal number of clerics from the French party be admitted to the tribunal. She also appealed to the pope and to a council; it was in vain.

All the judges, assessors, canons, and doctors of theology received from the English, for each session, an indemnity equivalent to about a hundred francs in modern currency. The receipts are annexed to the trial. Nearly one hundred assessors were called, though they did not all sit at the same time. The most hostile to Joan also received gifts.



There were several consultations of the Sorbonne, notably that of April 19, confirmed by the four faculties on May 14: all concluded against the Maid.

It must also be noted that the inquisitor general, Jean Graverend, preached a sermon at Saint-Martin-des-Champs in Paris after Joan's execution, in which he repeated all the terms of the accusation and approved the sentence. Shortly afterward, the pope appointed Pierre Cauchon to the episcopal see of Lisieux.

If, later, he was struck with excommunication, it was not in punishment of his crime, but merely for having refused to pay a fee demanded by the Vatican. For a matter of money, this prelate was threatened with papal thunderbolts, from which he had been spared as long as he was guilty only of condemning the liberator of his country[129].

In truth, not a single voice in Christendom rose to protest against the iniquitous judgment of which Joan was the victim—not among the clergy who had remained French, nor among those who had gone over to the English. On the contrary, a circular from Regnault de Chartres, Archbishop of Reims, to his diocesans, reveals the shameful state of mind of Charles VII and his counselors.

In a relation written from the charters of the city hall and magistracy of Reims, there survives the analysis of a message from the chancellor to the inhabitants of his archiepiscopal city, expressed in the following terms:

He gave notice of Joan's capture before Compiègne, and declared that, "inasmuch as she would not heed counsel, but did all according to her own pleasure... God had permitted Joan the Maid to be taken, because she had given herself over to pride, and because of the rich garments she had assumed, and because she had not done what God commanded her, but had done her own will[130]."

Yet, however ill-advised Charles VII may have been, immediately after Joan's capture he was the object of urgent and solemn solicitations in favor of the heroine.

Jacques Gélu, lord archbishop of Embrun, his former preceptor, wrote to his royal pupil, reminding him of what the Maid had done for the crown of France.

---

129 J. FABRE, *Procès de réhabilitation*, t. II, pp. 222-223.

130 H. MARTIN, *Histoire de France*, t. VI, p. 234.

He urged him to examine his conscience, and to assure himself whether "it was not his offenses against God which had brought about this misfortune."

"I recommend to you," he added, "that for the recovery of this maiden and for the ransom of her life, you spare neither means nor money, nor any price whatsoever, lest you incur the indelible reproach of a most blameworthy ingratitude."

He counseled him to order prayers everywhere for Joan's deliverance, that forgiveness might be obtained for some possible failing. "Thus spoke that old bishop, who remembered having been counselor to the Dauphin in evil times, and who dearly loved the king and the kingdom[131]."

Joan might have been ransomed from the Count of Luxembourg. Nothing was done. She might have been rescued by force: the French held Louviers, at but a short distance from Rouen. They remained inert. Those who, before the journey to Reims, had spoken of attacking Normandy, were now silent.



At the very least, something might have been attempted by way of procedure, to obstruct the tribunal's sentence by the same forms to which her judges pretended to show respect. The Bishop of Beauvais, director of the trial, was suffragan of the Archbishop of Reims. The latter could have required him at least to communicate the debates. He refrained from all intervention.

The family of Joan might have protested, appealing to the pope or to a council; the English might have been threatened with reprisals upon Talbot and the other

131 V. A. FRANCE, *Vie de Jeanne d'Arc*, t. II, pp. 185-186.

prisoners of war, to save the life of the Maid. Nothing was attempted!

"It was with deliberate intent," says Wallon[132], "that Joan was abandoned to her fate; her death itself entered into the calculations of those detestable politicians... Regnault de Chartres, La Trémoille, and all those wretched personages, in order to preserve their ascendancy in the king's councils, sacrificed, with Joan, the prince, the country, and God Himself."

All things considered, the responsibility for Joan's torment and death appears to us to fall equally upon the Church and upon the two crowns of England and France.

Yet, as regards the Church, one fact must be recalled. If so many priests and prelates, if the Inquisition itself, took part in the trial of condemnation of Joan of Arc, it was also under the direction of the grand inquisitor, Jean Bréhal, that the trial of rehabilitation was conducted. If there were priests who condemned the Maid, there were also priests—among them not the least illustrious—who glorified her: the learned Gerson, for instance, and the Archbishop of Embrun.

Assuredly, Joan having been burned as a sorceress, the crown of France neither wished nor could allow itself to remain under the charge of having bargained with hell. Yet to obtain that revision of the trial which would clear it, three years of negotiation with the Roman court were required; all the influence of the king and his counselors had to be exerted—an influence which the Roman pontiff had strong interest in preserving in those



---

132 WALLON, *Jeanne d'Arc*, p. 358.

days of schism, when three popes had lately disputed authority over Christendom. Powerful pressure had to be applied before the revision was granted.

"The tribunal of rehabilitation," says Joseph Fabre, "which made France wait twenty-five years, sanctioned the impunity of the executioners even while it proclaimed the innocence of the victim. Moreover, though it declared Joan free of the crime of heresy, it admitted that had she been guilty she would have deserved the flames, and thus consecrated, after the example of her first judges, that baleful principle of intolerance of which she had been the victim[133]."

Late and insufficient though it was, let us accept that reparation as it came. Let us recall that expiatory processions were held in the principal cities of France, with the clergy taking a prominent part. Let us recall also that in later times the English themselves glorified the memory of Joan: one of their poets, Southey, proclaimed her the greatest heroine of humankind. Numerous voices in England were raised to demand that honorable amends be made, in the public squares of Rouen, by representatives of the crown and Parliament.

On its side, the Roman Church, after long and minute inquiry, proceeded to the canonization of Joan, whose statue today rises in most of the churches of France.

Let us remember all this, and let us say that before the great figure of Joan, all resentment must vanish, all hatred must fall. On that august name no conflict of parties or of nations must take place. For if that name



133 J. FABRE, *Procès de réhabilitation*, t. II, p. 223.

is, above all, a symbol of patriotism, it is also—above all—a symbol of peace and reconciliation.

Joan belongs to all, assuredly, but above all to France. And yet, if any exception were to be made within the nation in favor of some group or body, if Joan might belong to some rather than to others, inflexible logic would require that it be to those who have understood her life, who have penetrated her mystery, to those who still today seek, in the study of the invisible world, those forces, those supports, those succors which secured her triumph, and which they would employ for the moral good and salvation of their country.

Returning to the judges of Rouen: when one studies the phases of the trial, it becomes evident that in the minds of those sophists with frozen hearts, in the thoughts of those priests sold to the English, Joan was condemned in advance. Had they not all seen, with spite and rage, a woman raise up in the name of God—of whom they called themselves representatives—the cause they had betrayed, believing it lost, the cause of France?



These men had now but one aim, one desire: to avenge upon this woman their authority threatened, their position compromised. To them, as to the English, Joan was destined for death. But that death alone was not enough, either for their politics or for their hatred. She must die dishonored—renouncing her mission herself—and her dishonor must reflect upon the king and upon all France.

For this, only one resource remained: to wrest from her a retraction, a denial of her own mission. She must avow herself inspired by hell; a trial for sorcery would bring her to it. To reach that end, they would shrink from no means: ruse, espionage, ill-treatment, all the torments and horrors of a hideous prison, where Joan's chastity was exposed to the vilest outrages. Threats, even torture itself—everything was deemed lawful.

But Joan resisted all.

Picture, in thought, that vaulted hall, where a dim and mournful light filters through narrow openings. One might take it for a sepulchral crypt. The tribunal is assembled. Some sixty judges sit beneath the presidency of the Bishop of Beauvais, to whom the English have promised the archbishopric of Rouen, if only he serves their interests well. And above them—bitter irony—the image of the crucified Christ stretches across the wall. At the back of the hall, at every exit, gleam the weapons of English soldiers, their faces hard and filled with hatred.

Why this display of force? To judge a child of nineteen years! Joan stands there, pale, trembling, weighed down by chains; she is weakened by the sufferings of a long captivity. She stands there, alone in the midst of enemies who have sworn her destruction.



Alone? Oh no! For if men abandon her, if her king forgets her, if the nobles of France do nothing to snatch her from the English—neither by force nor by ransom—there are at least invisible beings who watch over her, who sustain her, who inspire replies so striking that at times they strike terror into her judges.

And what tumult! what uproar! In their fury, in their rage, the judges sometimes go so far as to cry out against one another, to quarrel among themselves. The questions rain upon her. They strive by hypocritical artifices to entangle the accused, they harry her with interrogations so subtle, so difficult, that—according to the words of one assessor, Isambard de la Pierre—"the greatest clerks present could scarcely have answered them without much pain[134]."

And yet she answered them—sometimes with admirable subtlety, sometimes with such depth of sense, with words so sublime, that none doubted she was inspired by Spirits. A hush of awe would fall upon the assembly when she declared, speaking of them: *"They are here, though unseen!"* But these men were too far sunk in their crime to draw back.

Thus they sought to crush Joan, body and soul. They subjected her to interrogation after interrogation—up to two in a single day, each lasting three hours. And all that time she was forced to remain standing, laden with heavy chains.

But Joan would not be intimidated. That sinister hall was to her as a new battlefield. There her great soul, her manly courage, shone forth. The invisible Power that inspired her burst out in vehement words that terrified her accusers.



She addressed the Bishop of Beauvais: *"You say you are my judge. I know not if you are. But take good heed not to judge me wrongly; for in so doing you would place yourself in great peril. I warn you, that if Our Lord chastise you, I shall have done my duty in telling you so."* And again: *"I am come from God's hand. I have nothing to do here. Leave me to the judgment of God, from whom I came.*[135]*"*

They posed to her this insidious question: *"Do you believe yourself to be in the grace of God?"*

134 J. FABRE, *Procès de réhabilitation*, t. I, pp. 93-94.

135 J. FABRE, Trial of Condemnation, pp. 66, 71, 158.

—"If I am not, may God set me there; and if I am, may He keep me there."

—*"You think then it needless to confess, though you be in mortal sin?"*

—"I have never committed mortal sin."

—*"How can you know that?"*

—"My voices would have reproached me; my Spirits would have abandoned me!"

—*"And what do your voices say?"*

—"They say to me: 'Fear not; answer boldly; God will help you[136]!'"

They sought to convict her of magic, of sorcery, claiming she had used objects of mysterious power. *"Did you help your standard more, or the standard help you?"* She replied: *"The victory, whether of the standard or of Joan, was all God's."*

—*"But was your hope of victory founded in your standard or in yourself?"*

—"In God, and nowhere else[137]."



How many others, in her place, would have faltered before the temptation to claim the glory of their victories! Pride steals even into the purest and noblest hearts. We are nearly all prone to magnify our deeds, to exaggerate their scope, to glory in them without cause. And yet, all comes to us from God; without Him we are nothing, we can do nothing. Joan knew this. Amid the aura of glory that surrounded her, she made herself humble, small, attributing solely to God the merit of the work accomplished. Far from boasting of her mission,

---

136 *Procès, passim.*

137 J. FABRE, Trial of Condemnation, p. 184.

she reduced it to its true measure: she had been but an instrument in the service of the Supreme Power:

*"It pleased God to act thus through the deeds of a simple maiden, in order to repel the king's adversaries*[138]*."*

But what an instrument of wisdom, of intelligence, of virtue! What profound submission to the will from above! *"All my deeds and words are in God's hands, and I await all from Him."*

One day, the Bishop of Beauvais entered the dungeon. He was clad in his sacerdotal vestments; seven priests accompanied him. Joan had been forewarned by her voices: she knew that this interrogation would be decisive. Her voices had told her to resist bravely, to defend the truth, to defy death. And so, at the sight of the priests, her exhausted body straightened, her features grew radiant, her gaze shone with a deep and piercing brilliance.



*"Joan,"* said the bishop, *"will you submit to the Church?"*

A terrible question in the Middle Ages, on which the fate of the heroine depended!

*"In all things I refer myself to God," she replied, "to God who has always guided me."*

*—"That is a grave word. Between you and God there is the Church. Will you, yes or no, submit to the Church?"*

*—"I came to the king for the salvation of France, by God's command and His holy Spirits. To that Church above, I submit in all I have said and done."*

*—"Thus you refuse to submit to the Church? You refuse to renounce your diabolical visions?"*

138 J. FABRE, Trial of Condemnation, p. 152.

—*"I refer myself to God alone. As for my visions, I accept the judgment of no man!"*

This was the central point of the trial. It was above all a question of whether Joan would subordinate the authority of her revelations to the will of the Church. At the trial of rehabilitation, judges and witnesses alike sought only to prove that Joan had hesitated, then accepted the authority of the pope and of the Church — an argument still used today by those who would introduce the heroine into the Catholic paradise.

At the trial of condemnation, however, Joan's replies show her resolved; her thought was clear, her speech assured. She had a profound sense of the cause she defended. In truth, a solemn debate was being played out between two inflexible principles. On the one side: rule, tradition, the supposed infallibility of a power immobilized for centuries. On the other: inspiration, the sacred rights of individual conscience. And that inspiration here manifested itself under one of the most moving, most suggestive forms that history has ever shown.

It must be recognized: far better than the testimonies of the rehabilitation, the interrogations at Rouen show Joan in her full greatness, in the radiant brilliance of her impassioned replies — replies in which her voice vibrated, and in which, as one witness said, *"her glance shot forth lightning."* She fascinated even her judges. Nowhere, in no company, did she appear more beautiful, more imposing.

*"I refer myself to God alone!"* she had declared. And then, before such resolution, such will as nothing could bend, there could be no more doubt.

On May 9th, Joan was brought into the torture chamber. The torturers stood ready with their sinister apparatus. The instruments were prepared; they were heated red in the fire. Still Joan persisted. She defended France and the ungrateful king who had abandoned her: *"If you were to tear my limbs from my body,"* she said, *"and draw my soul out of it, yet would I not tell you otherwise*[139]*!"*

She was not delivered to the torture—not from pity, not from compassion, but simply because, in her weakened state, it was clear she would expire in the midst of the torments. And they desired a public death, a brilliant spectacle, to strike the imagination of the crowd.

Her judges left nothing undone to make her suffer. With refined cruelty, they took pleasure in describing to her the horrors of death by fire. That punishment she dreaded most of all: *"I would rather be beheaded,"* she said, *"than be thus burned."* But far from being moved by her cry, they pressed the matter all the more. Crushed beneath the weight of her chains, closely guarded by brutal enemies, in the depths of that abyss of misery where not one ray of pity, not one word of comfort descended, sometimes a cry of revolt rose to her lips, and she appealed to God, *"the great Judge,"* against the wrongs inflicted upon her. And she added: *"Those who would take me from this world may well depart from it themselves before me."* Another time she said to her examiner: *"You will not do to me what you say, without it turning to your harm in body and soul*[140]*!"*

---

139 J. FABRE, Trial of Condemnation, p. 324.

140 J. FABRE, Trial of Condemnation, p. 321.

And indeed, several of her judges met a miserable end. All endured the scorn of the public and the reproaches of their own conscience. Cauchon died overwhelmed with remorse; the people exhumed his corpse and flung it upon the refuse heap. The promoter, Jean d'Estivet, perished in a sewer. Others appeared at the trial of rehabilitation, twenty-five years later, far more as accused than as witnesses. Their demeanor was pitiful; their words revealed the torment of their conscience and the sense of their infamy.

The truth was not always respected in the transcription of the accused's words. One day, when she was being questioned about her visions, a prior response was read to her. Jean Lefèvre recognized a mistake in the record and pointed it out to Joan, who then asked the clerk Manchon to reread. He reread, and Joan declared she had said the very opposite.[141]

Another time she reproached them: *"You write down what is against me, and not what is for me!"*



Despite everything, Joan's superhuman energy, her inspired language, her greatness in suffering, ended by making an impression on her judges. Cauchon himself perceived that here was a being apart, sustained by Heaven. Already the hideous consequences of his crime rose before him; at moments, the voice of conscience thundered within, threatened him. Terror invaded the prelate's soul. But how could he draw back? The English were there; they followed the trial with feverish attention; they awaited, with dark fury, the hour of Joan's immolation—after she had been tortured and

141 H. WALLON, *Jeanne d'Arc*, p. 230. - J. FABRE, Trial of Rehabilitation, t. I, p. 358.

dishonored. The Bishop of Beauvais saw but one way: to make the victim disappear by assassination, to avoid a public crime by a secret one. He thought to poison her, and had a fish sent to her of which she ate. At once she was seized with violent sickness and fell ill. Her weakness was extreme. They feared for her life. They surrounded her with perfidious care, for she must not die obscurely: the English had paid dearly for her, and they had destined her for the stake. But her robust constitution prevailed. And no sooner had she recovered than her moral sufferings began again. They took advantage of her weakness; they pressed her unceasingly; they demanded her abjuration. Nothing had been spared to bring her to this: espionage, lies, attempted violation, even poison. The virgin whom a whole people admired had been drenched with ignominy by her judges, by her jailers.

A scene — one might say a comedy — was arranged in the cemetery of Saint-Ouen. There, before the people and the English, before her assembled judges, at the head of whom stood a cardinal and four bishops, Joan was summoned to declare her submission to the Church. She was urged, she was besought to spare herself, not to condemn herself to the fire. The executioner stood there, indeed, with his sinister cart at the foot of the platform on which she was placed—the executioner who, if she refused, would lead her to the Old Market, where the stake awaited her!

And then, beneath that somber light falling from the sky as though with reluctance, amidst the sadness that emanates from the graves and sepulchers around her, she felt seized by a profound despondency.

Her thoughts turned away from that field of the dead; she saw again her old land of Lorraine, her dense woods where birds sang, those beloved haunts of her youth. She thought she heard once more the songs of spinners and shepherds, those sweet and plaintive accents borne upon the wings of the wind. She beheld again her thatched cottage, her mother, and her aged father with white hair, whom she had seen at Reims, and who would grieve so deeply at the news of her death. In her awoke the regret for life. To die at twenty—is it not cruel indeed?

And, for the first time, the angel faltered. Christ Himself too had His hour of weakness. On the Mount of Olives, did He not long to turn aside the cup of gall? Did He not say: *"Let this chalice pass from me!"*

Joan, at the end of her strength, signed the paper that was presented to her. Remember that she neither read nor wrote. And, besides, the paper she signed was not the one that would be recorded. A vile substitution had taken place. They had not even recoiled from this odious act. Today it is proven that the formula of abjuration preserved in the trial record, signed with a cross, is a forgery. That formula, in both its content and its length, was not the one Joan signed. Not one of the witnesses at the trial of rehabilitation affirmed its authenticity; five denied it outright. The document we possess is extremely long. Three witnesses — Delachambre, Taquel, Monnet — declared: *"We stood close by; we saw the paper; it contained only six or seven lines.*[142]*"* Migiet added[143]: *"Its reading lasted no longer than the time of a Pater."* Another witness declared: *"I know positively that the paper I read*

142 J. FABRE, Trial of Rehabilitation, t. II, pp. 19, 63, 134.

143 *Ibid.*, t. I, p. 365.

*to Joan and which she signed was not the one mentioned in the trial*[144]*."* This witness was none other than the clerk Massieu, who had himself pronounced for Joan the formula of abjuration.

Joan, troubled, neither heard nor understood the formula. She signed without swearing an oath, without full consciousness of her act. She herself affirmed this to her judges a few days later, saying: *"What was in the schedule of abjuration, I did not understand. I revoked nothing except insofar as it would please God.*[145]*"*

Thus, what threats, violence, and the whole apparatus of torture had not been able to wrest from her, was obtained by entreaties, by hypocritical solicitations. That tender soul allowed herself to be deceived by false shows of sympathy, by counterfeit gestures of kindness. But that very night, the voices spoke again, imperious, in her prison. And on May 28th, Joan declared to her judges: *"The voice told me it was treason to abjure. The truth is that God has sent me. What I did was well done."* And she resumed the man's clothing they had forced her to lay aside.



What had happened after the abjuration, when — contrary to the promise of placing her in a "Church prison" under the guard of a woman — she had been taken back to her foul dungeon? The following testimonies will tell:

*"Joan revealed to me that, after her abjuration, she was violently tormented in prison, molested and beaten, and that an English lord attempted to violate her. She said*

144 *Ibid.*, t. II, p. 76.

145 J. FABRE, Trial of Condemnation, p. 367.

*publicly, and said to me, that this was the cause for which she resumed male attire.*[146] ”

*“In my presence, Joan was asked why she had put on man's dress again; she replied that she had done it to defend her modesty, because she was not safe, in a woman's dress, among her guards, who had sought to attack her honor.*[147] ”

*“Several others and I were present when she excused herself for having put on that attire, saying and affirming publicly that the English had done her great wrong and violence in prison when she wore a woman's dress. In fact, I saw her weeping, her face full of tears, disfigured and outraged in such a way that I had pity and compassion for her.*[148] ”

In that English prison, Joan drained the cup of bitterness to the very dregs; she descended to the deepest abyss of human misery. All her suffering is summed up in these words to her judges: *“I would rather die than endure longer imprisonment!*[149] ”

And, in those dreadful hours, far away in the castles of the Loire, Charles VII, to the languid sound of viols and rebecs, gave himself up to the pleasures of the dance, to every joy of indulgence. Amidst feasts, he forgot the one who had given him his crown!

In the face of such facts, thought is saddened and hearts are troubled. One is tempted to doubt eternal justice. Like Joan's own cry of anguish, our lament rises into the boundless heavens, and only a mournful silence answers our appeal.

146 J. Fabre, *Procès de réhabilitation*, vol. II, pp. 88–89. Deposition of Brother Martin Ladvenu.

147 Ibid., vol. II, p. 41. Deposition of the notary Manchon.

148 Ibid., vol. II, p. 98. Deposition of Brother Isambard de la Pierre.

149 J . FABRE, *Procès de condamnation*, p. 366.

And yet, let us look within and sound the great mystery of suffering. Is it not necessary for the beauty of souls and the harmony of the universe? What would good be without evil, which serves as its contrast and makes its brilliance stand forth? Would we value the blessing of light, if we had not suffered the night? Yes, earth is the Calvary of the just, but it is also the school of heroism, of virtue, of genius; it is the vestibule of blessed worlds where every sorrow borne, every sacrifice accomplished, prepares us joys of compensation. Souls are purified and made beautiful through suffering. All felicity is purchased by pain. Those who are sacrificed have the fairest share. All pure hearts suffer upon the earth: love goes not without tears. Emptiness and bitterness dwell at the core of earthly indulgence, and specters creep even into our sweetest dreams.

But all is fleeting in this world. Evil endures but for a time; higher up, in the superior spheres, the reign of justice unfolds in eternal duration. No, the trust of believers, the devotion of heroes, the hopes of martyrs — these are not vain illusions! Earth is but a footstool for mounting to Heaven.

Let these sublime souls be our examples, and let their faith shine upon us across the centuries! Let us banish from our hearts sorrow and vain discouragement. Let us learn to draw from our trials and sufferings all the fruit they offer for our elevation. Let us strive to make ourselves worthy to be reborn in fairer worlds, where there is no more hatred, nor injustice, nor coldness of heart, and where lives unfold in ever deeper harmony and ever brighter light.

After her retraction, Joan was declared a relapsed heretic, a schismatic, and condemned without appeal. There remained nothing for her but to die — to die by fire! Such was the sentence of her judges!

These judges, these believers of the fifteenth century, did not wish to recognize the mission of Joan of Arc. They were willing to believe in those distant manifestations spoken of in the Bible; they delighted in turning their thoughts to times when missionaries, when messengers from on high, descended to earth and mingled among men. They were willing to believe in a God whom they immobilized in the depths of heaven, to whom they sent sterile praises every day. But for the God who lives, who acts and manifests in the world with all the spontaneity, youth, and freshness of life, for the great Spirits who stand before them, breathing upon their missionaries the breath of powerful inspiration, they had nothing but hatred, insult, and dishonor!



The judges of Rouen and the doctors of the University of Paris declared Joan inspired by hell. And why? Because the defenders, the representatives of the letter, of the formula, of routine, possessed only a superficial knowledge—a knowledge that withers the heart, deprives thought of nourishment, and in certain cases can lead even to injustice, even to crime. Thus it is that, in every age, the men of the letter have been, without realizing it, the executioners of the ideal and of the divine. Thus it is that, beneath the iron wheel of despotism, the most beautiful, the greatest, the most generous things in this world have been crushed.

The consequences were not long in coming. They were terrible for the Church. As Henri Martin tells us[150]:

"In condemning Joan, the doctrine of the Middle Ages, the doctrine of Innocent III and of the Inquisition, pronounced its own condemnation. It had first burned sectarians, then dissenters who taught a pure Christian morality; now it has burned a prophet, a messiah! The Spirit has withdrawn from it. Henceforth it will be outside of it and against it that the progress of humanity and the manifestations of Providence's government on earth will be accomplished."

Yes, humanity has advanced; progress has been realized in the world. No longer can the messengers of God be put to death on the cross or at the stake. The dungeons and the torture chambers have been closed, the gallows have disappeared. Yet other weapons are still raised against innovators, against the heralds of new ideas: mockery, sarcasm, slander — the silent and unrelenting struggle.



But if the dreadful institutions of the Middle Ages, if the entire apparatus of torture, scaffolds, and pyres could not halt the march of truth, how could it be impeded today? The hour has come when human beings will no longer acknowledge, in the realm of thought, any authority but their conscience and their reason. That is why we must remain faithful to our eternal right to judge and to understand.

The time approaches — the time has come— when all the errors of the past will be brought forth into the light of day, before the tribunal of history. Already the

150 H. MARTIN, *Histoire de France*, t. VI, p. 302.

words and actions of the great missionaries, martyrs, and prophets are being revisited and explained. They shine before the eyes of all with a new brilliance. Soon it will be the same with societies and institutions of the past. They too will be judged, and they will retain their moral power and authority only if they can offer humankind greater means and resources to think, greater freedom to love, to rise, and to progress.

# XII. – ROUEN; THE EXECUTION

*With ardor, Joan kissed the image of Christ.*

*Casimir Delavigne*

It is May 30, 1431. The drama nears its end. It is eight o'clock in the morning. All the bells of the great Norman city toll mournfully. It is the death knell, the toll of the dead. Joan is told that her last hour has come.

"Alas!" she cries, weeping, "do they treat me so horribly and cruelly that my pure and intact body, which was never corrupted, must today be consumed and reduced to ashes! Ah! I would rather be decapitated seven times than thus be burned... Oh! I appeal to God against the great wrongs and injustices done to me[151]!"

This thought of death by fire weighs on her painfully. She pictures in advance those rising flames, that death approaching slowly, that prolonged agony of a living being feeling the searing bites that devour her flesh. This was the death reserved for the worst criminals—and Joan, the innocent virgin, Joan the liberator of a people, is to suffer it!

Here is revealed all the baseness of her enemies, those whom she had defeated so many times. Instead of rendering to her courage and genius the homage that civilized soldiers accord to an adversary fallen into their

151 J. FABRE, *Trial of Rehabilitation*, vol. II, p. 104. Deposition of Brother Jean Toutmouillé.

hands by ill fortune, the English reserved for Joan—after the worst of abuses—an ignominious end. Her body would be consumed, her ashes cast into the Seine. She would have no tomb where those who loved her might come to weep, to lay flowers, to keep alive the tender cult of remembrance.

She climbs into the sinister cart, and they make their way to the place of execution. Eight hundred English soldiers escort her. A dismayed crowd presses along her path. The procession emerges by the rue Ecuyère into the square of the Old Marketplace. There, three platforms stand. The prelates and officers have taken their places upon two of them. There, enthroned, is the Cardinal of Winchester in his Roman purple, and beside him the bishops of Beauvais and Boulogne, along with all the judges and English captains. Between the estrades rises the pyre, terrifying in height—an enormous heap of wood towering above the whole square. They want the ordeal to be long, that the maiden, vanquished by suffering, might beg for mercy, renounce her mission and her voices.



The act of accusation is read—seventy articles in which is amassed all that the most venomous hatred could devise to distort facts, deceive opinion, and make the victim an object of horror. Joan kneels. At this solemn moment, on the threshold of death, her soul rises above earthly shadows; she glimpses eternal splendors. She prays aloud, long and fervently. She forgives all—her enemies, her executioners. In the sublime outpouring of her thought and heart, she unites two peoples, embraces two kingdoms. At her words, emotion sweeps through the crowd; ten thousand present burst into sobs. Even the judges, those human-faced tigers—Cauchon, Winchester—all weep. But their emotion is short. The cardinal gives a sign. Joan is bound to the fatal stake with iron chains; a heavy iron collar is fastened around her neck.

At that moment, she turns to Isambard de la Pierre and says: "I beg you, go fetch me the cross from the nearby church, to hold it upright before my eyes, until the step of death.[152]" And when the cross is brought to her, she covers it with kisses and tears. At the instant she is to die a horrible death, abandoned by all, she wants before her eyes the image of that other victim who, on a rugged hill of the East, gave his life as witness to the truth.

At this solemn hour she sees again her short but dazzling life. She recalls all those she loved, the peaceful days of childhood at Domrémy, the gentle face of her mother, the grave features of her aged father, her companions of early youth: Hauviette and Mengette, her uncle Durand Laxart who led her to Vaucouleurs; then the devoted men who accompanied her to Chinon. In swift vision the Loire campaigns pass before her, the glorious battles of Orléans, Jargeau, Patay, the martial fanfares, the joyous cries of the delirious crowd.

She relives, she re-hears all this at the final hour. As in a last embrace, she would bid farewell to all these things, all these beloved souls. Having none of them before her eyes, it is in the image of the dying Christ that she sums up all her memories, all her affections. To him



152 J. FABRE, *Trial of Rehabilitation*, vol. II, p. 100. Deposition of Brother Isambard de la Pierre.

she directs her farewell to life, in the last outpourings of her broken heart.

The executioners set fire to the pyre; whirlwinds of smoke rise into the air. Flames leap, run, and twist among the piled wood. The Bishop of Beauvais approaches and cries from the foot of the pyre: "Abjure!" But Joan, already encircled by fire, replies: "Bishop, it is by you that I die; I appeal from your judgment to God!"

The flame, red and fierce, mounts higher, licking her virginal body; her garments smolder. She writhes in her iron bonds; then, in a piercing voice, she hurls to the silent, terrified crowd these blazing words:

"Yes, my voices came from on high. My voices did not deceive me! My revelations were from God. All that I have done, I did by the order of God[153]!"

And her robe catches fire, becoming one with the sparks of the inferno. A gasping cry bursts forth, the supreme appeal of the martyr of Rouen to the victim of Golgotha:

"Jesus!"

And nothing more was heard but the crackling of the flames…

Did Joan suffer greatly? She herself assures us not. "Powerful fluids," she tells us, "were poured upon me. And besides, my will was so strong that it commanded the pain."

**Joan is dead!** All of space is suddenly illumined. Above the earth she rises, she soars, leaving behind her a shining trail. She is no longer a material being, but a pure spirit, an ideal creature of light and purity. For

---

153 J. FABRE, *Trial of Rehabilitation*, vol. II, p. 91. Deposition of Brother Martin Ladvenu.

her, the heavens have opened to their infinite depths. Legions of radiant Spirits advance to meet her or form a procession at her side. And the hymn of triumph, the chorus of celestial welcome resounds:

*"Hail! Hail to she whom martyrdom has crowned! Hail to you who, through sacrifice, have won eternal glory!"*

Joan has entered into the bosom of God, into that inexhaustible center of energy, intelligence, and love that animates the entire universe with its vibrations. Long she remained immersed there. Then, one day, she went forth again, more radiant, more beautiful, prepared for missions of another order, of which we shall speak later. And God, in reward, granted her authority among her sisters of heaven.

Let us collect ourselves; let us salute this noble figure of the virgin, this maiden with an immense heart, who, after saving France, died for her before she was twenty years old.



Her life shines like a celestial ray through the dreadful night of the Middle Ages. She came to bring men, with her powerful faith and confidence in God, the courage and energy needed to overcome a thousand obstacles; she came to bring to betrayed, dying France, salvation and renewal. For the price of her heroic abnegation, alas! she gathered only bitterness, humiliation, and treachery—and, as the crown of her short but marvelous career, a passion and a death so cruel that they can only be compared to those of Christ.

The father of Joan, struck to the heart by the news of his daughter's martyrdom, died suddenly; he was soon followed to the grave by his eldest son. The mother had only one goal left in this world: to pursue with perseverance the revision of the trial. She made petition after petition; she addressed entreaty upon entreaty to the king and to the pope—long in vain.

In 1449, when Charles VII entered Rouen, she had some hope, but Pope Nicholas V responded with evasions, and the king remained frozen in his ingratitude. In 1455, with Calixtus III, she had more success, for the people of France themselves supported her claim. The court was forced to listen to the voice of the nation. It had been made clear to the king that his honor was stained by the heresy that had been used as a pretext for the heroine's death. The rehabilitation was done in the interest of the French crown far more than in respect for the memory of Joan.

At all times, Joan has been sacrificed to the interests of caste and party. Yet there are thousands of humble and modest souls who know how to love her for herself, with selfless devotion. Their thoughts of love rise toward her across the expanse of space. To these, she is far more sensitive than to the pompous demonstrations organized in her honor. They are her true joy and her sweetest reward, as she has affirmed more than once in the intimacy of our study gatherings.



Long was Joan misunderstood, misrepresented. She is still, even today, by many who admire her. But it must be acknowledged that the error was possible. Those who sacrificed her—among them a king—strove to hide their crime from the eyes of posterity. They labored to distort her role, to diminish her mission, to veil her memory. For this reason, the register of the interrogations at Poitiers was destroyed; certain documents of the Rouen trial, according to Quicherat, were falsified; and the testimonies of the rehabilitation were rendered with constant concern to protect exalted reputations.

It is said, in the Rouen records, that on the very morning of her execution, at her final interrogation, conducted in prison without notaries or clerks and annotated only later by Cauchon, Joan renounced her voices. This is false. She never renounced her voices. At one moment, exhausted, she submitted to the Church: in that alone consists the abjuration of Saint-Ouen.

It is through such treacheries that Joan's memory remained shrouded so long. At the beginning of the nineteenth century, only a weakened image, an incomplete, distorted legend of her remained. But the immanent justice of history willed that truth should emerge. From among the people arose patient workers: Michelet, Henri Martin, Senator Fabre, Quicherat above all, director of the École des Chartes—priests as well. These conscientious workers searched yellowed parchments, scoured dusty libraries. Many forgotten manuscripts were discovered. In the royal ordinances of the time, in the Chronicles of Saint-Denis, in archives preserved in the Bibliothèque des Chartes, in the expense accounts of the "good towns," were found revelations that heightened still more the stature of the heroine. Justice was tardy for her, but it has been dazzling, absolute, universal.

Thus, modern France has a great duty: to repair, at least morally, the faults of ancient France. All eyes must turn toward that noble and pure image, toward that radiant figure who is the angel of the fatherland. All the children of France must engrave in thought and in heart the memory of the one whom Heaven sent us in the hour of disasters and collapse. Across the ages, an eternal homage must rise toward that valiant spirit who loved France even unto death, who forgave upon the pyre all betrayals, all treacheries—toward she who offered herself as holocaust for the salvation of a people.

The sacrifice of Joan of Arc had immense scope. Politically—as will be shown in the second part of this work—it forged the unity of France. Before her, ours was but a fractured land, torn by factions. After her, there was a France. Joan stepped resolutely into the furnace, and with her expiring soul, national unity emerged.

Every work of salvation is accomplished through sacrifice. The greater the sacrifice, the more superb and imposing the work. Every redemptive mission concludes and is crowned by martyrdom. This is the great law of history. So it was with Joan as with Christ. It is thus that her life bears the divine seal. God, the supreme artist, reveals Himself therein by incontestable and sublime traits.



The sacrifice of Joan has an even greater reach: it will remain a lesson and an example for generations, for centuries to come. God has His purpose in reserving such lessons for humanity. Toward these great figures of martyrs will turn the thoughts of all who suffer, all who bend under the weight of trial. They are so many hearths of energy, of moral beauty, where souls frozen by the cold of adversity may come to be warmed. Through the centuries, they cast a luminous trail, like a wake drawing us toward radiant realms. These souls passed through the earth to give us a glimpse of the other world. Their deaths gave birth to life, and their memory has consoled countless fainting and sorrowful souls.

# SECOND PART
# THE MISSIONS OF JOAN OF ARC

# XIII
# JOAN OF ARC AND THE IDEA OF THE FATHERLAND

*Glory to our immortal France!*
*Glory to those who died for her,*
*To the valiant, to the martyrs, to the strong!*

*Victor Hugo*

In the first part of this work, we recalled the principal events in the life of Joan of Arc, and we sought to explain them with the help of insights drawn from the psychical sciences. We have spoken of the heroine's triumphs and sufferings; we have recalled her martyrdom, which stands as the crowning point of that sublime career.



It now remains for us to examine and bring to light the consequences of Joan of Arc's mission in the fifteenth century. From this perspective, we must first pose the following question: What does France owe to Joan?

Above all, as we know, it owes her its very existence; it owes her the fact of being a nation, a fatherland. Until then, the idea of a fatherland was something vague, confused, almost unknown. City contended against city; province warred against province. No union, no true sense of solidarity bound together the different parts of the land. Great fiefs divided France among themselves, and every powerful lord strove to cast off all authority.

When Joan appeared, the states of Burgundy, Picardy, and Flanders were allied with the English; Brittany and Savoy remained neutral; Guyenne lay in the hands of the enemy. It was Joan, the first, who summoned forth in souls the sacred image of the common fatherland—of a fatherland torn, mutilated, and dying.

It will be objected, perhaps, that the word *fatherland* was scarcely in use at that time. But, if the word was lacking, Joan gave us the thing itself[154]. And that is what

---

154 It results from recent research that Jean Chartier was the first to use the word *patrie*, in the following passage from his *History of Charles VII*, p. 147:
"According to the proverb which says that it is lawful and praiseworthy for each person to fight for his fatherland."
Master Jean Chartier—who was not, as has been believed, the brother of the poet Alain Chartier (the one made famous by the supposed kiss of Dauphine Margaret of Scotland, and immortalized by an admirable page in honor of Joan of Arc)—held, in 1449, the position of *chronicler of France*. In other words, he was the official historiographer of the court. He wrote under the direct inspiration of the sovereign, and he discharged his literary functions in such a manner as to please the king, that the latter ordered him to accompany him on the war against the English.
M. Michaud, of the Académie française, together with MM. Poujoulat, Bazin, Champollion-Figeac, and others, have given, in their *New Collection of Memoirs Relating to the History of France*, several extracts from Jean Chartier, notably this one, which is highly significant:
"In the year 1429, at the beginning of the month of June, the king raised a great army at the persuasion of the Maid, who said that it was the will of God that the king should go to Reims to there be anointed and crowned; and whatever difficulties and doubts the king and his council may have raised, it was concluded, by the urging of that

must be remembered. The very notion of a fatherland was born from the heart of a woman—from her love, from her sacrifice.

Amid the tempest that broke upon her, through the dark cloud of grief and misery that enveloped her, France beheld this radiant figure pass by, and she was left as though dazzled. She did not even understand, nor feel in its fullness, the extent of the aid that Heaven had sent her. And yet, despite all, the sacrifice of Joan imparted to France powers hitherto unknown. The first among nations, France became, in truth, a nation. And from that time forth, her national unity—sealed by the blood of the heroine—neither vicissitudes, nor social upheavals, nor disasters without parallel, have ever been able to destroy!

We are not unaware that, in our own time, the idea of the fatherland undergoes a kind of eclipse, even a decline. For some years now, it has been fiercely criticized, even combated in our country. A whole class of writers and thinkers has labored to expose its abuses and excesses, to undermine the principle itself, and to extinguish its cult within souls.



---

same Joan, that the king would summon as many men as he could gather to undertake the journey of his coronation at Reims."

The *Chronicle of Charles VII, King of France*, first composed in Latin and translated into French by Jean Chartier, was published in three volumes in the *Bibliothèque elzévirienne* by MM. Plon, Nourrit & Co., under the editorship of M. Vallet de Viriville, the learned professor of the École des Chartes, who also produced an edition of the *Trial of Condemnation of Joan of Arc*, translated from the Latin and published in its entirety for the first time in French by Firmin-Didot & Co.

Before anything else, in this debate now engaged, it would be fitting to define clearly and precisely what is meant by *fatherland*. The idea presents itself to the mind under two aspects. At times, abstract for certain minds, it becomes a moral person and represents the accumulated acquisitions of centuries—the genius of a people in all its facets and in every manifestation: its literature, its art, its traditions, the sum of its efforts through time and space, its glories and its reverses, its great memories. In a word, it is the whole work of patience, of suffering, of beauty, which we inherit at birth, a work in which still vibrates and palpitates the soul of generations gone by.

For others, the fatherland is something concrete. It is the geographical expression, the territory itself, with its established boundaries.

For the idea of fatherland to be truly beautiful and complete, it must unite these two forms within a higher synthesis. Considered under only one aspect, it would be but a parade gesture, or else a vague, indistinct abstraction.



Here again the idea appears under its two forms: the spirit and the letter. According to the point of view, some will seek the moral and intellectual greatness of their fatherland; others will aim chiefly at its material power, and for them the flag will be the symbol of that power. In every case, it must be acknowledged that, in order to survive and cause the radiance of its genius to shine ever more widely across the world, a fatherland must safeguard its independence and its liberty.

In the immense work of the development and evolution of human races, each nation contributes its own note to the universal symphony; each people represents one of the facets of universal genius. It is destined to manifest that genius, to embellish it through its labor across the ages. Every form of human endeavor, every element of action, is necessary for the evolution of the planet. The idea of fatherland, by incarnating them, by making them concrete, awakens among these elements a principle of emulation and of rivalry that stimulates them, makes them fruitful, and raises them to their highest power. The gathering together of all these modes of activity will one day create the ideal synthesis that will constitute the planetary genius, the apogee of the great races of the earth.

But for now, in the phase of human evolution through which we pass, the competitions and struggles that the idea of fatherland provokes among men still have their reason to be. Without them, the genius proper to each race would risk growing dull, weakened in the easy possession and well-being of a life exempt from shocks and perils. In the time of Joan of Arc, this necessity was still more pressing. Today, with the human spirit more evolved, we must strive to clothe these struggles, these rivalries, in forms ever more noble and pure, to strip them of all savagery, to draw from them all the benefits that can enrich the common heritage of humanity. They will take on the aspect of tasks ever more lofty and fruitful, through which the future shall be built; thought and form will therein find their expression ever more magnificent and sublime.

Thus, one day, after a slow, confused, and painful incubation, will emerge the soul of the great fatherlands. From their union shall arise a civilization of which that of our present time is but the rough draft. To the bloody struggles of the past will succeed the nobler struggles of intelligence, applied to the conquest of the forces of nature and to the realization of Beauty in art and in thought, to the creation of works where splendor of expression will be wedded to profundity of idea. And this will intensify the culture of souls, awaken sentiment more fully, and hasten the progress of all toward the summits where eternal and perfect Beauty reigns.

Then the earth will vibrate with one thought, will live with one life. Already humanity is seeking itself, in confusion. Thought gropes for thought in the night; and over the iron roads and vast sheets of water, peoples call to one another, stretch out their arms. The embrace is near: through united efforts shall begin the giant work of preparing the human dwelling for a life broader, more beautiful, more joyous.

The new spiritualism will contribute powerfully to this coming together of minds, by putting an end to the antagonism of religions, and by giving as the foundation of belief, no longer dogmatic teaching or revelation, but experimental science and communion with the departed. Already, its hearths are kindled across every point of the globe; their radiance will spread ever outward, until men of every race are united in a common conception of their destiny upon the earth and beyond.

The delegates of twenty-four nations, gathered in a Congress in Paris in September 1925, founded the International Spiritist Federation, which now extends to the very confines of the globe and constitutes a regenerating force whose influence is already making itself felt in the world of thought and of science.

Let us return to Joan of Arc. Certain writers have judged that her intervention in history was, in fact, rather unfortunate for France[155], and that the union of the two countries under the crown of England would have created a powerful nation, preeminent in Europe, destined for the highest greatness[156].

To speak thus is to misunderstand both the character and the aptitudes of the two peoples—utterly dissimilar, and such that no event, no conquest, could have succeeded in fusing them entirely at that time. The English character displays eminent qualities, which we have been glad to acknowledge[157], but it is marked by a self-interest that has at times gone as far as ferocity. England recoiled before no means in the pursuit of her designs. The French, on the other hand, for all their many faults, mingle with them a spirit of generosity, almost chivalric.

Nor are their aptitudes less diverse. The genius of England is above all maritime, commercial, colonizing. The genius of France inclines rather toward the vast domains of thought. The destinies of the two nations are different, and their roles distinct within the harmony of the whole. In order to follow their natural paths and to preserve the fullness of their own genius, each of them had, above all, to maintain freedom of action,



155 See the *Mercure de France*. « La malencontreuse Jeanne d'Arc », 1907.

156 The terrible civil war of the Two Roses, York and Lancaster, which broke out shortly after the Hundred Years' War and nearly led England to ruin, shows that even within that country unity had not yet been achieved. How, then, could it have been established with elements as disparate as those that would have been added by the conquest of France?

157 See *Life and Destiny*, chapter on the Will.

to safeguard independence. United under a single domination, these two aspects of human genius would have clashed, hampered in their respective development.

It is for this reason that, in the fifteenth century, when the genius of France was threatened, Joan of Arc became, upon the great chessboard of history, the champion of God against England.

Joan of Arc played a great military role; yet today, militarism has fallen into disrepute. Under the name of pacifism, many thinkers—most of them inspired by the most honorable intentions—carry on in our country a vigorous campaign against anything that recalls the warlike spirit of the past and the conflicts between nations.

It is true that the idea of the fatherland has given rise to undeniable abuses. That is the condition of all human things. Yet it remains both a right and a duty for all peoples to remember their glories and to take pride in their heroes.



Militarism, it is said, is an evil. But is it not a necessary evil? Universal peace is a beautiful dream, and the settlement of all international disputes by arbitration is something eminently desirable. But one must ask whether an assured and prolonged peace might not bring with it evils of another order.

To see clearly into this question, one must rise above the narrow horizons of present life and embrace the vast perspective of the ages allotted to the evolution of human souls. Our current existence, we know, is but a single point in the immensity of our destinies; everything that relates to it can neither be fully understood nor rightly judged if we ignore what precedes and what follows it.

What are the true ends we pursue through our multiple lives, across the succession of our existences on earth and on other worlds? The goal of the soul in its course, as we have shown[158], is the conquest of the future—the building of its destiny by persistent effort. Now, indefinite peace, on inferior worlds and within societies still but little evolved as ours, encourages the growth of weakness and sensuality, which are poisons of the soul. The exclusive pursuit of comfort, the thirst for wealth and ease, which characterize our time, are causes of enfeeblement of will and conscience. They destroy all virility within us, rob us of every spring of action, every power of resistance in the hour of adversity.

Struggle, by contrast, awakens within us hidden treasures of energy that accumulate in the depths of the soul and become one with consciousness. Long turned toward evil in the lower stages of evolution, these forces, through progress and ascent, gradually transform into energies for good. For it is the very law of evolution to transmute the darker powers of the soul into beneficent strengths. This is the divine and supreme alchemy.

The threat of the foreigner may be as salutary to peoples still in the course of evolution as trials are to individuals. They bring union within. In the struggles that follow, defeats themselves prove more useful than triumphs: misfortune draws souls together and prepares their fusion. Defeats are blows struck upon a nation; but, like the sculptor's hammer, these blows render it more beautiful, for each one awakens emotions deep within hearts and calls forth hidden virtues. It is also in



158 See our book, *Life and Destiny*, passim.

resistance to adverse fortune that characters are tempered and ennobled.

In the grand evolution of being, the most essential quality is courage. Without it, how could one overcome the innumerable obstacles that strew the path? That is why, on inferior worlds—the dwelling places and schools of new souls—struggle is the universal law of nature and of societies; for in struggle the being acquires the primal energies necessary to trace its immense trajectory through time and space.

Do we not see it already in this life? The child who, from the beginning, receives a strong education, who is tempered by great examples or by trials, who learns sacrifice and austerity while still young—is he not better prepared for an important role, for profound action? While the child who is too coddled, accustomed to abundance, to the satisfaction of whims and caprices, loses all virile quality, the springs of his soul slacken. Too much comfort weakens. To avoid delay upon the path, one needs necessities that spur, dangers that provoke effort.

Thus, whatever is done, peace and harmony among men can never be completely assured except through an elevation of character and of conscience. Our happiness, our perfect security—let us not forget—stand in direct proportion to our capacity for good. We can only be happy in the measure of our merits. War, like all the scourges that strike humanity, will disappear only with the causes born of our errors and our vices.

Since I wrote these lines in my first edition, the great war has swept over us like a crushing wave and nearly destroyed us. When one reflects upon the ravages this war has caused—the millions of human lives sacrificed, the countless sufferings it has brought about and will continue to bring for a long time yet—the idealism of armed struggle, the prestige of heroic virtues, fades and grows dim. A veil of sadness and mourning has spread over France, and Joan herself laments the woes we have had to endure. Here is what she recently dictated to us on this subject:

"It is necessary to soften everything that provokes the brutal clash between peoples. Let the love of God, of country, and of neighbor unite beings, and let spirituality make their union easier. War was born of passions. Let the passions of evil disappear, and let the cult of love draw hearts together. I want my beloved France, my gentle France, to be respected and honored. Brutal war must be replaced by a fraternal work of conciliation among the different human beliefs. The rapprochement of peoples will not be achieved without shocks, certainly, for passions must be broken; but by establishing justice, one prepares the blossoming of higher love."



With the formation, after the war, of the League of Nations, the peoples have affirmed their will to understand one another, to unite in order to put an end to bloody conflicts, to homicidal struggles that, from time to time, tear humanity apart. Already, this institution has resolved many problems, settled grave and complicated disputes. Its authority grows little by little.

Will it succeed in realizing Joan's vision, by becoming the arbiter of universal peace? The future alone will tell us. Whatever the outcome, if offensive war can henceforth be considered a crime, the defense of one's country, in times of invasion, remains a sacred duty!

# XIV
# JOAN OF ARC AND THE IDEA OF HUMANITY

*I have never killed anyone.*
*Joan*

We will not claim that Joan of Arc was the first to bring us the notion of humanity. Long before her, and in every age, the cry of those who suffer had awakened in sensitive souls a sentiment of pity, of compassion, of solidarity. Yet, during the course of the Hundred Years' War, such qualities had become exceedingly rare—particularly in the rough soldiery that surrounded Joan, men who had turned war into a work of plunder and brigandage. Amid that age of iron and blood, the maiden of Lorraine makes us hear the language of pity, of kindness.

No doubt, she took up arms for the salvation of France; but when the hour of battle was past, she returned to being the woman of tender heart, the angel of gentleness and charity. Everywhere she opposed massacres; she always offered peace before launching an attack[159]. Three times before Orléans she renewed such offers. She tended to the wounded—even to the wounded

159 See his letter to the English: Trial of condemnation.

English[160]. She brought relief to the unfortunate; she suffered with all human suffering.

In that dark feudal night, the fifteenth century appears darker, more sinister still than those that preceded it. It was the century in which a king of Aragon killed his own son, and a count of Guelders his own father; in which a duke of Brittany had his brother assassinated, and a countess of Foix her sister. Through that blood-drenched cloud which rose before men's eyes, Joan appears to us as a vision from on high; her presence rests and consoles from the horror of slaughter. Did she not herself utter those gentle words: *"Never have I seen French blood flow without my hair standing on end*[161]*!"*

At the court of Charles VII, not only plunder and brigandage of every kind were common, but murders as well. The first chamberlain, who later became the king's favorite, the Sire de Giac, had murdered his wife, Jeanne de Naillac, in order to marry the wealthy Countess of Tonnerre, Catherine de l'Isle-Bouchard. He himself was later drowned at the instigation of the Constable of Richemont, whose policies he hindered, and of La Trémoille, who coveted his wife—after having so cruelly mistreated his own that she died of it. Another favorite of Charles VII, Le Camus de Beaulieu, was assassinated before the very eyes of the prince. The Count of

160 See the testimony of Louis de Contes: 'Joan,' he said, 'who was very compassionate, felt pity for such slaughter. She saw a Frenchman, who was leading prisoners, strike one of them on the head so violently that the man fell as if dead. She dismounted from her horse and had the Englishman confessed. She held his head and comforted him as best she could.' J. Fabre, *Trial of Rehabilitation*, vol. I, p. 213.

161 Deposition of her steward Jean d'Aulon.

Armagnac forced a will in his favor from Marshal de Séverac, whom he had imprisoned, and afterward had him killed[162].

It was into this monstrous environment that the good maid of Lorraine was called to intervene. Her task was thereby made all the more difficult, and her sensitivity multiplied for her the causes of suffering. Some writers have tried to portray Joan of Arc as a kind of virago, a warlike maiden exalted by the love of combat. Nothing could be more false; this opinion is contradicted by both her words and her actions. Indeed, she knew how to brave peril and expose herself to the blows of the enemy. But even in the midst of the camp or in the shock of battle, she never departed from the gentleness and modesty inherent in her womanly nature. She was good and peaceable by disposition. Never did she engage the English in battle without first inviting them to withdraw. When they retreated without fighting, as on May 8 before Orléans, or when they yielded under the French assault, she commanded that they be spared: *"Let them go,"* she would say, *"do not kill them. Their retreat is enough for me."*



During the interrogations at Rouen, she was asked: *"What did you love more, your banner or your sword?"* She replied: *"I loved my banner far more, even forty times more than my sword. I never killed anyone[163]!"*

To guard herself against the impulses of combat, she always carried her banner in her hand, for, as she explained: *"I did not wish to use my sword."* At times she would hurl herself into the thick of the fray, at the

162 According to Lavisse, *History of France*, vol. IV, pp. 24, 27.
163 Fourth public interrogation.

risk of being killed or taken. In those moments, her companions-in-arms said, she seemed no longer herself. Yet as soon as the danger had passed, her gentleness and simplicity reasserted themselves[164]. *"When she felt herself wounded,"* says the record, *"she was afraid and wept; but after a while, she said: 'I am consoled.'"* Her fears and her tears render her all the more touching in our eyes. They lend to her character that charm, that mysterious strength, which is one of the most powerful attractions of her sex.

Joan, as we have said, had a tender heart. The insults of her enemies cut her deeply: *"When the English called her harlot,"* said one witness, *"she would burst into tears."* Then, in the prayers she addressed to God, she purified her soul of all resentment, and she forgave.

At the siege of Orléans, one of the English commanders, Glasdale, heaped abuse upon her whenever he caught sight of her. On the day of the attack, he was in command at the fortress of the Tourelles and shouted insults at her from the top of the bulwark. Shortly after, when the bastille was taken by storm, this captain, fully armed, fell into the Loire and drowned. *"Joan,"* added the same witness, *"moved with pity, wept bitterly for the soul of Glasdale and the others, drowned there in such great number*[165]*."*

Joan of Arc is therefore not only the maiden of battles. As soon as the fighting ceased, the angel of mercy reappeared within her. As a child, we saw her

---

164 Trial of Rehabilitation. Testimonies of Dunois, the Duke of Alençon, Thibauld d'Armagnac, and President Simon.

165 J. Fabre, *Trial of Rehabilitation*. Deposition of Jean Pasquerel, vol. I, p. 227.

aid the poor and tend to the sick. Once she became a commander of armies, she knew how to ignite courage in the hour of danger; yet, as soon as the battle was over, she was moved by the misfortune of the vanquished and strove to lessen for them the sufferings of war.

Contrary to the customs of her time, and insofar as the higher interest of France allowed it—and even at the risk of her own life—she defended prisoners and the wounded whom others sought to kill. Even for the dying, she tried to make death less cruel.

In the Middle Ages, it was customary to "strike down the defeated." "People of low and middle rank," says Colonel Biottot[166], "were massacred, and sometimes even the great themselves. But Joan intervened; social rank was no crime—neither for the lowly nor for the mighty—and she wanted all spared, provided they had laid down their arms. At Jargeau, it was only with great difficulty that she rescued from death the Earl of Suffolk, who commanded the fortress after having led the siege of Orléans."

The English, when they held her in their power and conducted her trial, should have taken such generous acts of the Maid into account. Yet not a single voice was raised before her judges at Rouen to recall them. Her enemies thought only of satisfying their base resentment.

And yet it must be acknowledged: long before the expression had even been coined, Joan had already put the law of nations into practice. In this way she was ahead of the innovators who, in future times, would invite the world to embrace equality and fraternity

166 Colonel Biottot, *The Great Inspired Ones before Science.*

among individuals and among nations—who would evoke the principles of order, equity, and social harmony destined to govern a truly civilized humanity. From this point of view as well, the good Maid of Lorraine laid the foundations for a better future and for a new world.

We can see it clearly: Joan knew how to establish just measure in all things. In that well-balanced soul, love of country came before all else, but that feeling was never exclusive; her pity, her compassion were stirred at the sight of any human suffering.

In our own time, the word *humanity* has been much abused, and through a vain and puerile sentimentality we have often seen thinkers and writers sweep aside the interests and rights of France in favor of vague personages or hypothetical collectives. No one will ever persuade us that one can love "Blacks, Yellows, or Reds" one has never seen more than one's own kin—more than one's family, one's mother, or one's brothers. And France, too, is our mother.



Yes, no doubt, we must be kind and humane toward all. Yet in many cases, such reasoning is but a sophism. If we probed to the bottom of things, we would simply realize that certain great "humanitarians," by forging for themselves theoretical duties they well know they will never have to fulfill, seek thereby to evade other duties—urgent and immediate—toward those around them, toward France, their country.

Others, by an opposite excess, hate everything foreign; they harbor blind resentment toward peoples who once turned against us. Let us not allow misfortune to make us unjust, nor prevent us from recognizing the virtues and bravery of other nations! When asked,

"Does God hate the English?" Joan replied: *"As to God's hatred for the English, I know nothing. But He wills that they leave France and return to their own land.*[167] "

Like Joan, let us be fair and not hate our enemies. Let us know how to honor merit, even in an adversary. Let us defend our rights and our heritage when necessary, but let us provoke no one. From this perspective, the Maid of Lorraine gives us more than a lesson in patriotism—she gives us a living lesson in humanity.

When she takes up arms, it is far less in the name of the law of struggle than in the name of the law of love—less to attack than to defend and to save. Even beneath the armor, the finest qualities of womanhood shine through in her: the spirit of renunciation, the spontaneous and absolute gift of self, deep compassion for all who suffer, attachment carried to the point of sacrifice for the beloved being—husband, child, family, country—the resourcefulness of her practical sense and her intuitions in defending their interests—in a word, her devotion unto death to all that is dear to her.

In this sense, Joan of Arc synthesizes and personifies what is most noble, most delicate, and most beautiful in the soul of the women of France.

167 Eighth secret interrogation.

# XV
# JOAN OF ARC AND THE IDEA OF RELIGION

*I love God with all my heart.*

*Joan*

Joan held the beliefs of her time: *"I am a good Christian and I will die a good Christian,*[168]*"* she would answer her judges and examiners whenever they questioned her about her faith. It could not have been otherwise. It was within the convictions and hopes of her age that she had to draw the strength and impulses necessary for the salvation of France. The invisible world assisted her; it revealed itself to her under the forms and appearances familiar to the religion of the Middle Ages. After all, what do forms matter? They shift and change with the centuries. The essence of religious truth, however, is eternal, for it flows from divine sources.

The religious idea, in all its diverse aspects, penetrates deeply into the history and intellectual and moral life of humanity. It goes astray, it errs often. Its teachings and manifestations are debatable. But it rests upon invisible realities of a permanent and immutable order. Humanity

168 J. Fabre, *Trial of Condemnation*, pp. 166, 256, 302, etc.

perceives them only by successive degrees, in the course of its slow and painful evolution.

Human societies cannot exist without a religious ideal. Whenever they attempt to suppress or destroy it, moral disorder immediately increases, and anarchy raises its threatening head. Do we not see this in our own time? Human laws are powerless to restrain evil. To check the passions, one must possess inner strength and the sense of responsibility that springs from the awareness of the Beyond.

The religious idea cannot perish. It veils itself for a time only to reappear in other forms, better adapted to the needs of the age and the environment.

As we have said, Joan was inspired by the highest religious feelings. Her faith in God who had sent her was absolute; her trust in her invisible guides was boundless; she observed faithfully the rites and practices of her time. But when she professed her faith, she rose above all the established authorities of this world. The ardent belief of the heroine came directly from higher things; it depended on her conscience alone. And whom did she obey above all? Not the Church, but the voices she heard. Between her and Heaven there was no intermediary. A breath passed across her brow that brought her a mighty inspiration, and that inspiration governed her entire life, directing all her acts.



Let us recall the scene at Rouen, when the Bishop of Beauvais, followed by seven priests, entered her cell to question her:

**The Bishop:** "Joan, will you submit to the Church?"

**Joan:** "I refer myself to God in all things, to God who has always inspired me!"

**The Bishop:** "That is a grave reply. Between you and God there is the Church. Will you, yes or no, submit to the Church?"

**Joan:** "I came to the King for the salvation of France, by God and His holy spirits. To that Church above, I submit in everything that I have said and done!"

**The Bishop:** "So you refuse to submit to the Church; you refuse to renounce your diabolical visions?"

**Joan:** "I appeal to God alone. As for my visions, I accept the judgment of no man!"

In the rectitude of her reason, Joan clearly understood that this Church was not the Church of God. Eternal Power has no part in human iniquities. She could not demonstrate this with subtle or learned arguments; she expressed it instead in brief, clear words, sharp and brilliant like the flash of steel. She would obey the Church, but only insofar as its commands conformed to the will of Heaven: *"God must be served first!"*



Above all, what stands out in Joan of Arc's religious vision is communion—in thought and in action—with the invisible world, the divine world. From this communion come great works, from it flow the deepest intuitions. But such communion is possible only under certain conditions of moral elevation, and Joan possessed these to the highest degree. To instill them in those around her, she appealed to their religious sentiments, requiring them to confess and to receive communion; she expelled camp-followers from the army; she would not march against the enemy except to the sound of prayers and hymns. This may astonish our skeptical age; in reality, it was the only way to rouse in those coarse men of blind faith the exaltation that was necessary. As soon as that moral fervor ceased—when the intrigues of courtiers and the envy of rivals had done their work, when vice and bad passions regained the upper hand—then came the hours of failure and defeat.

To the higher powers, the forms of worship and religious ceremonies matter little; what they ask of humanity is the elevation of the heart and the purity of sentiment. That can be found in all religions, and even outside and above religions. We, as Spiritists, know this well—going about the world amid mockery and countless obstacles, proclaiming the truth, with no support other than the help of the Invisible Beings who have never failed us.

Above all, what characterizes Joan is her confidence—confidence in success, confidence in her voices, confidence in God. In the heat of battle, in the uncertain hours of combat, she made all who surrounded her share in that confidence. Her faith in victory was so great that it became one of the essential elements of ultimate triumph.



And this confidence filled her entire life. In her chains, before her judges, she still believed in final deliverance; she affirmed it again and again with steadfastness. Her voices had told her she would be delivered *"by a great victory."* This, however, was but a figure; in truth, it meant martyrdom. At first she did not understand it in that sense. She long expected help from men. Yet that misunderstanding was necessary. The promise of her voices was her supreme resource during the painful days of the trial. It was in them that she drew her unshakable assurance before the tribunal. And even at the hour of sacrifice, she went to her death with confidence. Her last cry, rising from the midst of the flames that consumed her, was once again the affirmation of her faith: *"No, my voices did not deceive me!"*

Scarcely a few doubts ever brushed Joan's mind—at Melun, at Beaurevoir, at Saint-Ouen in Rouen. Poor young girl! Who would dare reproach her for this, at her age and in so difficult a situation? The outcome remained hidden from her until the very end. How could she have advanced along her arduous path if she had known beforehand all that awaited her? It is a blessing from above that a veil conceals from us the hour of anguish, the painful ordeal that will crown our lives. Is it not better that our illusions fall away little by little, while hope persists in the depths of our hearts? The tearing away will then be less cruel.

Yet as Joan drew closer to the end of her career, the dreadful truth became clearer: *"I asked my voices if I would be burned. They answered: 'Trust in Our Lord and He will help you. Accept everything with grace; do not trouble yourself about your martyrdom. In the end, you will come to Paradise*[169]*.'"*



In those sinister hours, when all earthly hope collapses, the thought of God is the soul's supreme refuge. Indeed, that thought had never been absent from Joan's mind. On the contrary, it had ruled her entire existence. But in the hour of agony it filled her with a deeper intensity, preserving her from the weakness of despair. From infinite depths descended the consoling ray that illumined the dark dungeon where she had endured a thousand injuries and torments for nearly six months,

169 J. Fabre, *Trial of Condemnation*, pp. 325, 159.

and through her clear visionary gaze, a corner of Heaven opened. Earthly things grew veiled in sorrow. The hope of deliverance faded in her heart. The ingratitude and treachery of men, the savage malice of her judges, all showed themselves in their naked ugliness. The harsh reality stood before her. And yet, through the bars of her prison, there filtered the radiance of a more beautiful world. Beyond the dreadful gulf she must cross, beyond the torment, beyond death itself, she glimpsed the dawn of eternal things.

Suffering, we know, is the crown of a life well-lived. Nothing is complete, nothing truly great without it. It is the refining of souls, the halo that rests upon the brow of saints and the pure. There is no other gateway to the higher worlds. And this is what we must understand by the word *"Paradise"*—the only word capable, in that century, of expressing the idea of a spiritual life bathed in rays and harmonies that never fade.



Joan had no one on earth to whom she could confide her sorrow. But God does not abandon His messengers. Invisible yet present, He is the ever-faithful friend, the mighty support, the tender Father who watches over His afflicted children. It is because men forget Him, because they scorn the strength and help that come from above, that they now find no comfort in trials, no consolation in sorrow. If our society writhes feverishly, tossed about in the incoherence of ideas and systems—if evil grows within it, if nowhere can it find stability or inward peace—it is because it clings only to appearances and surfaces, while rejecting the true joys and profound resources of the invisible world. Believing happiness lay in material wealth, humanity has only increased the emptiness and bitterness of its soul. From all sides rise cries of anger, harsh demands. The very notion of duty grows faint, and the foundations of social order are shaken. Humanity no longer knows how to love, because it no longer knows how to believe. It turns to science. But science, crushed beneath the weight of its own discoveries, is powerless to give it trust in the future or inner peace.

On the very morning of her execution, Joan said to Master Pierre Morice: *"By the grace of God, this evening I shall be in Paradise*[170]*."*

She resigned herself to martyrdom, and faced it with a high heart and a noble soul. Was not death, even the cruelest death, preferable to what she had endured for six long months? The thought of death awakens in every young being a terrible anguish. Joan had suffered that anguish from the day she entered the iron cage of Rouen. What she endured there—was it not worse than death itself? Hopes, dreams of glory, grand designs—all had vanished like smoke. Who can ever tell what passed in that angelic soul during the long nights of her prison cell, as the fatal hour drew near?



*"I shall be in Paradise!"* she said. And we must understand in the same way those other words of hers that reflected the belief of her time: *"I asked of my voices for no other reward than the salvation of my soul*[171]. "To save one's soul—that was the axiom of Catholic conviction, the ultimate goal assigned by the religious ideas of the Middle Ages. Narrow though it may seem, this idea still held a kernel of truth. In reality, nothing is utterly saved,

---

170 J. Fabre, *Trial of Rehabilitation*, vol. II, p. 126.
171 Second public interrogation.

nothing is utterly lost, and divine justice provides for every fault a way of reparation, for every fall a means of rising again. This precept ought to be rephrased thus: *The soul must leave life better and greater than when it entered.* There are many ways to achieve this: through work, through study, through trial, through suffering. This is the true aim we must ever keep before us.

For Joan, these words bore an even more personal meaning. Her constant concern was to fulfill worthily the mission entrusted to her, and to secure for all her actions and her words the sanction of Him who never errs.

With Joan, religious feeling never degenerated into bigotry or childish superstition. She did not importune God with vain and endless requests. This is evident from her own words: *"I do not ask anything of Our Lord without necessity.*[172] *"* She did not hesitate to fight before Paris on the day of the Nativity, despite the reproaches some made on that account.

She loved to pray in church, especially at those hours when it was silent and deserted, when in the stillness of thought the soul rises most surely toward God. Yet in reality—whatever Anatole France may have said—the priests had little influence over her youth. As she affirmed during the interrogations at Rouen, it was her mother who taught her the things of religion: *"I learned my faith from no one but my mother.*[173] *"*

She said nothing of her voices and visions to the priest of her village, and took counsel only from herself regarding all that concerned her guiding Spirits: *"As for*

172 . Fabre, *Trial of Condemnation*, p. 255.

173 . Fabre, *Trial of Condemnation*, p. 49.

*believing in my revelations,"* she said at Rouen, *"I ask advice neither of bishop, priest, nor anyone else.*[174]"

Joan's faith in God was deep; it was the driving force of all her actions and allowed her to face the hardest trials. *"I have a good Master,"* she declared, *"namely Our Lord, from whom I expect everything, and from no other*[175]*."*

What do the vicissitudes of this world matter, if our thought is one with God—that is, with the eternal and divine law? Yet God is not only a master. He is a Father, whom we must love as children love the one who gave them life. Too few men feel or understand this; it is why they deny God in adversity. But Joan proclaimed in touching words: *"From all things I look to God, my Creator. I love Him with all my heart.*[176]"

In vain, the inquisitors—who neglected no means of tormenting her—sought to shake her faith and drive her to despair. With perfidious insistence, they pointed out her apparent abandonment, her disappointed hopes, the promises of Heaven unfulfilled. She invariably replied: *"That God has failed me, I deny!"* What an example for all those whom trial overwhelms, who accuse God of their misfortunes and often blaspheme Him!

For her, God was also Judge: *"I look to my Judge. He is the King of Heaven and of Earth*[177]*."* Simple words, yet they expressed the Power that stands above all the powers of this world. Throughout her life Joan had been the victim of human injustice. She had suffered the



174 . Fabre, *Trial of Condemnation*, p. 242, 311.

175 . Fabre, *Trial of Condemnation*, p. 242, 811.

176 . Fabre, *Trial of Condemnation*, p. 307.

177 Fabre, *Trial of Condemnation*, p. 307.

jealousy of courtiers and warlords, the hatred of nobles and priests. The judges of Rouen were guided not by equity but by prejudice and passion in condemning her. And so she turned to Heaven and appealed to the Sovereign Judge, who weighs all human actions in His eternal balance. *"I look to my Judge!"*—that is the refuge of the wronged, the dispossessed, of all those wounded by partiality. And no one ever calls upon Him in vain.

Nothing is more moving than her reply to this question: *"Do you know whether you are in the grace of God?"—"If I am not, may God put me there; if I am, may God keep me there. I would be the most sorrowful creature in the world if I knew I were not in God's grace!*[178] "

The candor of this angelic soul outwitted the cunning of her tormentors. Their insidious question could have destroyed her. Had she answered yes, she would have shown presumption; had she answered no, she would have admitted guilt and justified all suspicions. But her innocence triumphed over their treachery. She entrusted herself to the Supreme Judge, who alone searches hearts and consciences. Should we see in these words the mark of an exquisite faith, or one of those sudden inspirations with which she was often graced? Whatever the case, it remains one of the most admirable utterances ever given by this child of nineteen.



In all circumstances, Joan saw herself as an instrument of the divine will and did nothing without first consulting the invisible powers. She acted only on the command from above: *"It is the hour when it pleases*

178 Fabre, *Trial of Condemnation*, p. 71.

*God. We must work when God wills. Work, and God will work.*[179] ”

We see here that, according to her, divine intervention is not limited to her own life, but extends to all life. Every one of our actions must harmonize with the divine plan. Before acting, each of us should consult the depths of conscience, which is the divine voice within us. It will tell us in what direction our efforts should be guided. God works in us and with us only through our free cooperation. When our will and our deeds coincide with His law, our work becomes fruitful for good, and its effects flow into the whole of our destiny.

Yet few men listen to that voice which speaks within them at solemn hours. Swept away by passions, desires, hopes, and fears, they plunge headlong into the whirlpool of life, chasing what harms them most, intoxicated with possessions contrary to their true interests. Only later in life do their illusions fade, their errors dissolve, and the mirage of material goods vanish. Then comes the procession of bitter disappointments; and they realize that all their restless striving has been in vain, because they never paused to study and grasp God's purposes for them and for the world. Happy are those, then, who find in the prospect of future lives the chance to take up again the task they once failed, and to use their time better!

He who does not perceive the great harmony reigning over all things, nor the radiance of divine thought reflected in nature and within conscience, is unfit to bring his actions into accord with higher laws. When he



179 J. Fabre, *Trial of Rehabilitation*, vol. I, p. 178.

returns to the spiritual realm and the veil is lifted, he will feel the bitterness of discovering that everything must be begun anew—with a new spirit, a clearer and loftier conception of duty and destiny.

It may be objected that it is not always easy to know the hour of God; His will is obscure, sometimes impenetrable. Yes, no doubt—God hides from our eyes, and His ways often seem uncertain to us. But He conceals Himself only out of necessity, in order to leave us fuller freedom. If He were visible to every eye, if His will were affirmed with irresistible power, there would no longer be hesitation—and therefore no merit. The Intelligence that governs the physical and moral universe veils itself. Things are so ordered that no one is compelled to believe. If the order and harmony of the cosmos are not enough to convince, man is free. Nothing forces the skeptic toward God. God hides Himself in order that we may seek Him, for that search is the noblest exercise of our faculties, the principle of their highest development.



And yet, when a grave and decisive hour arrives, if we truly pay attention, there is always, around us or within us, a warning, a sign, dictating our duty. It is our inattention, our indifference to higher things, our neglect of their presence in our lives, that causes our irresolution and uncertainty. But for the soul that is awake, that calls, that seeks, that expects, these higher powers never remain silent. By a thousand voices they speak clearly to our spirit, to our heart. Events will occur, incidents will arise, pointing to the resolutions we must take. It is within the very fabric of events that God reveals Himself and instructs us. It is for us to seize and understand, at the right moment, the mysterious, half-veiled counsel He gives—never imposing, but always guiding.

In her straightforward wisdom, at once candid and profound, Joan knew how to define this providential action in life. When the judges of Rouen asked her: *"If you saw a way of escape at this moment, would you take it?"* she answered: *"If I saw the door open, I would go, and that would be the leave of my Lord*[180]*."*

At all times, the will from above was her guide. *"I must go,"* she said to Jean de Metz when he questioned her at Vaucouleurs, *"I must go and do it, because my Lord wills it."* — *"And who is your Lord?"* — *"It is God!"* she replied simply[181]. Neither peril nor danger could hold her back. Consider also these words in which she rises far above the glitter of human glory or sorrow, to the calm regions of serene purity: *"What does it matter, so long as God is pleased!"*

And this, which touches the sublime: Taken at Compiègne, dragged from prison to prison, to the dungeon, to the stake at Rouen, she blessed the very hand that struck her. When her judges sought to exploit her pain and shake her faith in the mission she had received from Heaven, she answered: *"Since it has pleased God, I believe it is for the best that I was taken*[182]*."*

This is greater and more beautiful than all her successes and all her victories.

In summary, it would be in vain to try to torture the texts and the facts in order to prove that Joan of Arc was, in every respect, perfectly orthodox. Her religious

180 Fabre, *Trial of Condemnation*, p. 168.

181 J. Fabre, *Trial of Rehabilitation*, t. I, p. 126.

182 Fabre, *Trial of Condemnation*, p. 137

independence shines through at every moment in her words: *"I submit to God alone."*

Does not the language of Joan, her fearlessness amid suffering and before death, recall our Gallic ancestors? Before that tribunal at Rouen, the maiden of Lorraine appears to us as the genius of Gaul rising up, magnificent, before the genius of Rome, to claim the sacred rights of conscience. She admitted no arbiter between herself and Heaven. All the dialectics brought against her, all the subtleties of argument, the force of eloquence itself—everything shattered against that firm will, that calm assurance, that unshakable trust in God and His messengers. The word of Joan triumphed over every sophism: at her accents they fell into dust. She was a dawn breaking through the darkness of the Middle Ages, illuminating them with a gentle light.

Consider that this was the very moment when the *Imitation of Christ* (1424) had just appeared, a work attributed to Gerson, though its true author remains unknown. It was one of the first cries of liberation from the Christian soul, seeking to free itself from dogma and to commune directly with God without any intermediary.



Yet Joan knew nothing of letters. She needed no prior studies: she had the intuition of truth. Her strength lay in her faith, in her profound piety—an independent piety, we have said, that rose above the narrow, petty conceptions of her time and soared straight to Heaven. That was her "crime," and the reason for her martyrdom.

And is it not one of the strangest spectacles of our troubled age, to see the Roman Church sanctify the very one it once condemned as a heretic? The memory of

Joan has always been fatal to the Church. Already in the fifteenth century, the trial of rehabilitation struck it a heavy blow. It led to the downfall of the Inquisition in France—and that, too, was one of the blessings Joan bestowed. That sinister tribunal received its deathblow in 1461, in the trial against the Waldensians.

It is no mere accident that all eyes are once again turning toward this ideal figure. There is in it an almost unanimous foreboding, an unconscious aspiration of civilized humanity, a sign of the future. In placing Joan of Arc upon its altars, the Roman Church has made a gesture heavy with consequences; it has, in truth, signed its own condemnation.

This young woman of the fifteenth century, who conversed directly with her voices and read so clearly into the invisible world, is the image of the humanity to come, which too will converse directly with the world of Spirits—without the mediation of official priesthoods, without the aid of rites whose meaning the Church has lost and whose virtue it has let fade away. The hour has come when, once more, the great soul of Joan hovers over the world, in communion with the invisible, inaugurating the reign of worship *in spirit and in truth.*



And since it is the law that all great and holy things must germinate in suffering and be consecrated by pain, it is fitting that the new times, the era of the pure Spirit, should be inaugurated under the patronage of the one who was the victim of theology and the martyr of mediumship.

Every religion is a reflection of eternal thought, mingled with the shadows and imperfections of human thought. At times it is difficult to separate the truths they contain from the errors accumulated by the work of centuries. Yet whatever is divine within them projects a light that illuminates every sincere soul. Religions are more or less true; they are above all stations along the path that the human spirit traverses in order to rise toward ever broader conceptions of the future of the soul and the nature of God. Their forms, their manifestations, are debatable; they are passing and changeable. But the deep sentiment that inspires them—their very reason for being—remains eternal.

Humanity, in its march toward its destiny, is called to shape for itself a religion ever purer—freed from the material forms and dogmas under which divine thought has too often been buried. It is a false and dangerous idea to wish to destroy the religious conceptions of the past, as some dream of doing. Wisdom consists in drawing from them the elements of life they contain, in order to build the edifice of future thought, whose summit will rise ever higher toward Heaven.



Each religion will contribute to the faith of the future with a ray of truth: Druidism and Buddhism will give their notion of successive lives; the Greek religion, the divine thought enclosed in nature; Christianity, the loftier revelation of love, the example of Jesus draining the cup of sorrow and sacrificing himself for the good of humankind. If the forms of Catholicism are worn out, the spirit of Christ is still alive. His teaching, his moral law, his love remain a consolation to hearts wounded by the harsh struggles of earthly life. His word can be renewed; the veiled aspects of his doctrine, once brought again to light, hold treasures of beauty for souls eager for spiritual life.

Our age will mark a decisive stage in the history of the religious idea. Religions, aged and weakened under the weight of centuries, need to be infused with other regenerating principles, to broaden their conceptions of the purpose of existence and of the laws of destiny.

Humanity seeks its path toward new centers of light. At times, a cry of anguish, a plaintive lament, rises from the depths of the soul toward Heaven. It is a call for more light. Thought stirs feverishly amid the uncertainties, contradictions, and threats of our age. It seeks a point of support to soar toward regions more beautiful and richer than all those it has traversed until now. A kind of deep intuition urges it forward; within the being lies an imperious need to know, to understand, to penetrate the august mystery of the universe and the secret of its own future.

And behold, little by little, the path grows brighter. The great law is revealed, thanks to the teachings of the Beyond. Through various means—typology, written messages, discourses spoken in trance—Spirit-guides and inspirers have, for half a century, provided us with the elements of a new religious synthesis. From the heart of space, a powerful current of moral force and inspiration flows down to the earth.

We have set forth elsewhere the essential principles of this teaching[183]. In our book *Christianity and Spiritism*, we have dealt more specifically with the religious question. On this vital problem, which stirs so many passionate contradictions, what is most important for

183 See *After Death* and *Life and Destiny*. Concerning the methods of communication with the invisible world, see especially *In the Invisible: Spiritism and Mediumship*.

the reader to know is the direct thought of our invisible guides: the views of the great Spirits of space, of the tutelary Beings who hover above us, far from human rivalries, and who—judging from on high—judge more justly.

This is why we reproduce below some recent messages, obtained through mediumship, among those that touch both upon the religious problem in its entirety and upon the canonization of Joan of Arc.

## MESSAGES

### June 1909. Improvisation in the state of trance:

"The Church is passing away. Its energy, its direction are artificial. That energy comes from the disorganization of the parties opposed to it. It alone still stands in the face of the materialist schools. It alone represents the soul in the face of materialism and science. From the moment when science consecrates the soul, the Church will collapse.



The Church is only a relative good. All those who are enamored of the life of the soul take refuge in the Church, because they have nothing else. Many souls cannot form for themselves a personal faith; they ask others for their belief, and find it easier to turn to the Church. Better to believe in Catholicism than to believe in nothing. But the day when a scientific, artistic, and literary philosophy arises that synthesizes the ideal, the present Church will disappear.

The Church has admitted into its domain the arts and letters, but not science. It rejects part of knowledge; therefore, it will have to yield its place to a philosophy that embraces the whole of human knowledge. We say philosophy, and not religion, because the latter word today has the sense of a sect."

"The Reformation attracted certain souls because it allowed morality to be joined to religion. At that time everything was permitted by the Church, provided one knew how to buy pardon with money. The sale of indulgences was public. Everyone saw morality on one side, religion on the other. The moral question shook the Church; today it will be science that finishes it. When men truly know, the Church will collapse."

"We do not weep for its disappearance. The Church is, in history, only one of the forms of the religious idea on its way. The Church has done good, and we prefer to see the good it has accomplished rather than the harm it has caused. Above all, we delight in seeing in it the great figure of Christ who founded it. We will always see the gospel in the mass; that is the true central point and not the elevation, as many believe. We love this gospel; it is what still draws us today into certain cathedrals. We love the Church; we revere it, as we revere all that has brought something great to humanity."



"Later, we will venerate even more the one who will bring a new word of life, that Spirit of Truth announced so long ago. He will be a man of science, a scholar, a philosopher, and above all, a man of exquisite sensibility. The Muslims await him as well. All religions have promised him. All souls must first feel disoriented, all must sense the necessity of his coming. The dissolution is deeper now than at the time when Christ appeared, and the desire for knowledge even stronger. All peoples are pressed and burdened by their governments. The hour is coming."

"It is upon the foundations of Christianity that the new religion will rise, just as Christianity rose upon Judaism. The old Church, like the Law of Moses, will be renewed, improved."

## JEROME OF PRAGUE
## July 1909; through trance mediumship:

"What are these dogmas and mysteries? Let us seek the true meaning of religions!"

"Religion surrounds itself with a dark and formidable apparatus. It believes that everything is known, discovered, fixed. A profound error!"

"Truth cannot be separated from God. It cannot merely be a symbol. It is a ray that descends from His divine brow. We have God within us—not through His body of flesh (the host)—but through His truth."



"It is through His messengers that the divine sacrifice is accomplished. God is in us by the radiations of His truth. But this truth is not yet known; it is only hoped for. One must know how to love it, for it to descend to us."

"Man is infinitely perfectible. It is a grave fault to destroy before him the perspectives of the future. Divine mercy gives him, along with hope, the perpetual possibility of repairing his faults."

"The Church says to man: Leave us to direct you. But it forgets that by doing so it makes itself responsible for the conduct of souls before God. And if the Church is God, then God would be responsible for the conduct of souls. That is false! Man might then fall asleep in the confidence that he was sufficiently guided."

"The Church has often been a stepmother to those who lived within it. It has crushed every intelligence that rose above a certain level. What ruined it was its love of matter, temporal power, the desire for domination. The intoxication of power overcame it. It drank from the cup of pride. That will be the cause of its decline, for matter cannot give life. Temporal power has already fallen; the others will follow. We must respect the Church as we respect old age, which accomplished great things in its youth. But today the crowds are leaving it. The naves are empty outside of great ceremonies."

"The Church no longer loves enough—that is why it is dying. To love more: that is the whole thought of Christ. He loved humankind more than Himself, as Joan loved France. This is what the Church no longer knows how to do. Souls should have been governed by love, not fear. John said: 'Love one another; that is the whole of religion!'"



"Christ loved Thomas, the doubter, even to the point of materializing and letting him touch His wounds. But the Church does not love those who doubt; it repels them. For faith to be real, it must have the love that makes it fruitful. Love is the lever of humanity. This is what the Church has forgotten, and this is why it is destined to weaken ever more."

"We must salute it, for it once received the thought of Christ. But now, it has given all it could give; its time is done. It has not understood this century. It thinks everything rests in the past. But instead of stirring the ashes of old memories, it should think of its duties toward the men of the present and prepare the times to come."

"No hatred! We must pity it and let it fade away gently. One does not cry out against those who are dying. Let peace be upon it! Let us pray for it!"

"As for its attitude toward Joan, it is explained thus: The Church wanted to make for itself a popular saint and thereby regain a little of its lost influence. And as patriotism weakens, it seeks to reclaim that idea for its profit. It picks up Joan's sword and turns it into a weapon to fight its enemies. But it cannot be its former victims who defend it now."

"A manifestation more material than spiritual! It should have acted differently, and held a new trial to establish the true responsibilities, to condemn Cauchon and clear Rome. The trial of rehabilitation was made from texts; it did not incriminate the judges, it upheld their validity. It is not enough to thunder against them from the pulpit; a more solemn act was needed. The Church lacked the courage of its actions and of its policy."



*Jerome of Prague*

## July 1909; through mediumistic writing:

"The Church is often in contradiction with its own teachings. It asks the soul to purify itself, to improve, to abandon its errors; yet it declares itself alone to be omniscient and omnipotent. It does not admit that its knowledge of the past can no longer suffice for today;

it believes the world has stopped beneath the nave of Gothic cathedrals. In reality, one cannot demand of the educated and skeptical man of your century what could once be demanded of those terrified by eternal punishments. Time has done its work; it has piled up ruins. Souls have been renewed, and only the Church has stubbornly tried to shore up its ancient edifice, continually rebuilding the formidable fortress. In doing so, it has slowly separated itself from the world; it has indulged in the satisfaction of power and pride, but it has forgotten the history of civilizations."

"The demands of evolution upon souls are so powerful that they renew both faith and science. Old beliefs fade away for others, and the Church, in turn, should ascend toward the light. It should be the natural path for souls going toward God, offering them all the resources demanded by intelligences enamored of beauty, of greatness, of a more perfect truth."



"The Church gives the same duties to the adult man as to the child. Its explanations, its commandments are the same for all. Everywhere it seeks unity and the fixation of souls upon the contemplation of its dogmas."

"Its continual concern for its survival and existence ought to have made the Church understand that it would be wise and strong to abandon, at the right time, the methods that had once sufficed to govern the world. One does not attract the man with the same words as the child; and what succeeded with the peoples of centuries past is insufficient today. Some perceptive minds have sensed this; they have attempted to give a mystical and spiritual sense to the dogmas, to show them as symbols of some great thought. But the Church, as an institution, is not open to sublime reflection. Mediocrities have seized power, and such attempts have been harshly repressed. For if this reform had been carried out for faith, it would have had to be carried out in conduct as well. One needed the courage to symbolize everything, to show that the Church had once guided peoples and kings only because they were still in childhood; one needed to condemn the errors, chastise the past, and openly repudiate all that was not in harmony with these new insights. That would have been political wisdom. For today the Church is no longer a religion in the proper sense of the word: it does not seek to unite souls, but to govern bodies by every means. To govern bodies, it must first master souls, and it thought to attract them by a few skillful gestures, by the glorification of some honored souls."



"In these troubled times, when the Church seems to be fighting its last great battle, it has wanted to give itself a powerful auxiliary in the person of Joan. It should have clearly branded her judges as impostors and shown them as agents of an authority not recognized. The Church, having so clumsily cast out so many great men from its bosom, could have easily sacrificed a few more, and here it had the perfect opportunity to place among its saints one of its victims, toward whom the pity of believing souls already extended. As an institution, it could have done so. For a long time it defended Joan's judges, and now it seeks to justify the one it once called a heretic. Yet many believers ask themselves: who, then, was the true culprit in that sad tragedy at Rouen?"

"Today, knowing perfectly well that she is a saint, the people have placed Joan among the protectors of the nation. But the Church has wanted to slip behind her pedestal, to substitute itself for her by placing her among its chosen ones. No one can deny it: Joan is more loved than the Church, and the Church, which once condemned her, cannot succeed in disfiguring her. But we cannot accept this beatification, which is a maneuver of the Church, for it is yet again one of those acts by which the Church has made itself too famous: a half-measure, born of calculation, where the desire for truth is masked by self-interest."

*Jerome of Prague*

**July 1909; through trance mediumship:**



"Love God above all. There lies the strength that will free you from this material world and enable you to endure the flames of suffering.

This love gave me all energy, all power.

I grieve to see the French quarrel over my soul.

I forgive the Church for everything—except its teaching. I cannot forgive it for spreading errors and terror in souls.

The Church is dying. Let us bless it for the good it has done. Let us pity it for the harm it has caused.

I am its guide, not its defender.

May France become once again conscious of her role, which is to spread ever greater lights throughout the world.

The times have come. The Spirit of Truth, promised by Christ, is near. He will be born among you. Christianity was not understood. It had come to lift the soul out of suffering and unconsciousness. Now, other, higher truths are about to shine."

*Joan*

# XVI
# JOAN OF ARC AND THE CELTIC IDEAL

*O land of granite, covered with oaks!*

*Brizeux*

One evening, the Spirit of J. Michelet, preceding and announcing that of Joan of Arc, spoke to us in these words during one of our study sessions:

"In her previous existences, Joan acquired the sense of the great duties she would one day have to fulfill. We met several times in those distant ages. That bond, established between her and us, draws her near. Just as she inspired me, she will inspire you. My book was only an echo of her passion for France and for truth. Now, she will descend among you to bring a fragment of the divine truth."

Joan's lives upon the earth have been numerous, like those of all souls who travel with us through the vast cycle of evolutions. Some were brilliant, lived upon the steps of a throne; others obscure, but all were beneficent for others and fruitful for her own advancement.

Her earliest earthly lives followed one another in the Celtic age, in the land of Armor. It was there that her personality was imbued with that particular genius—

made of idealism, fearlessness, and dreamy poetry—that we find again in her in the fifteenth century.

From her childhood in Domrémy, she loved to frequent the places where the druidic rites had once been performed: the groves of oaks, witnesses of ancient invocations of souls; the sacred springs; the rough stone monuments scattered here and there around her village. She loved to lose herself in the deep forest, to listen to its harmonies, when it shuddered and vibrated like a gigantic harp under the breath of the wind. With her seer's gaze, she discerned beneath its vaults the mysterious shades of those who once presided over evocations and sacrifices. Among her invisible guides, one might encounter the protective Spirits of Gaul, those very ones who, in every age, aided the sons of Arthur and of Merlin, granting to those who struggled for a noble cause the will and the love that lead to victory.



In vain the mistletoe has perished upon the branches, in vain the sacred flame has been extinguished in the hearths—faith in immortal lives and in higher worlds will always live in the heart of Joan. All historians who have analyzed and understood her character have recognized within her this double current—Celtic and Christian—which she herself will soon reveal to us. Henri Martin, in particular, observed it in the pages of his *History*. He first recalled in these terms the Celtic memories still alive in the time of the heroine:

"Near the house of Joan of Arc, a path climbed through clusters of currant bushes to the top of the hill; the wooded ridge was called the Bois Chesnu. Halfway up, under a great solitary beech, sprang a fountain, the object of a traditional cult. For time immemorial, those afflicted with fever had come to seek their cure in these pure waters... Mysterious beings, older among us than Christianity itself, and whom our peasants never consented to confuse with the infernal spirits of Christian legend—the spirits of waters, stones, and woods, the faerie ladies—haunted the ancient beech and the clear fountain. The beech was called the 'Fair May.' At the return of spring, under the may-tree, 'fair as lilies,' young girls would come to dance and to hang garlands upon its branches in honor of the fairies—garlands that, they said, vanished during the night."184

Henri Martin then described the impressions of the Lorraine maiden:

"The two great currents of Celtic sentiment and of Christian sentiment, which had once united to give birth to chivalric poetry, mingled again to form this predestined soul. The young shepherdess would sometimes dream at the foot of the may-tree or beneath the oaks... sometimes lose herself in the little church, rapt in ecstasy before the holy images that glowed in the stained glass... As for the fairies, she never saw them dance by moonlight around the fair May; but her godmother had seen them in years gone by, and Joan believed she sometimes glimpsed uncertain forms in the twilight mists: voices sobbed in the evening among the oak branches; the fairies danced no more—they wept; it was the lament of ancient Gaul expiring185!"

Finally, speaking of the trial of Rouen, the same author wrote186:



184 H. MARTIN, *Histoire de France*, t. VI, pp. 138, 139.
185 H. MARTIN, *Histoire de France*, t. VI, pp. 140.
186 H. MARTIN, *Histoire de France*, t. VI, pp. 302

"Joan knew how to oppose the free genius of Gaul to that Roman clergy which sought to pronounce the final word upon the very existence of France. Through her, the mystical genius claimed the rights of the human person with the same force as the philosophical genius; the same soul—the great soul of Gaul—born in the Sanctuary of the Oak, shone forth as well in the free will of Lérins and of the Paraclete, in the sovereign independence of Joan's inspiration, and in the 'I' of Descartes."

Joan herself, confirming these views, expressed herself in a message dictated in Paris in 1898[187]:

"Let us go back, for a moment, through the course of the ages, so that I may tell you what path I have traveled to prepare for that painful stage which you know.

"Numerous were the existences that contributed to my spiritual advancement. They unfolded in ancient Armorica, beneath the dome of great oaks centuries old, crowned with sacred mistletoe. It was there, slowly, that I turned toward the study of the laws of the spirit and the worship of the fatherland.



"O blessed hours above all, when the bard, through his songs of joy, stirred our hearts and opened our eyes to the light, allowing us to glimpse the wonders of infinity! He taught us then that the passage from death to the glorious resurrection of the Spirit in space was but a simple transformation—dark or luminous—according as man had followed here below the path of justice and love, or allowed himself to be ruled by the passionate forces of matter. He made us understand the laws of solidarity and self-denial; he taught us what prayer was

187 *Revue scientifique et morale du Spiritisme*, January1898.

and told us: 'To pray is to triumph. Prayer is the engine which thought uses to awaken the faculties of the Spirit, which are its tools in the infinite expanse. Prayer is the powerful magnet from which spiritual magnetic fluid emanates—fluid that not only can soothe and heal, but that also opens before the spirit endless horizons, and permits it to satisfy its yearning to know and to draw ever closer to that divine source from which all things flow. Prayer is the conductor that links the creature to the Creator and to His celestial messengers.'

"One day, penetrated by these truths, I fell asleep and had the following vision: First, I witnessed many battles—alas! impossible to avoid because of the free will of each individual, but above all because of the love of gold and of domination, those two scourges of humanity. Then I also clearly beheld the future greatness of France and her civilizing role to come. I resolved to devote myself to her especially.



"Immediately, a sympathetic throng surrounded me. Most of them wept and mourned my loss. Then poison, the gibbet, the stake slowly passed before me. I felt the flames consume my flesh, and I fainted!... but friendly voices recalled me to life, saying: 'Hope! The celestial phalanx charged with watching over this globe has chosen you to aid it in its task, and for your spiritual advancement. Mortify your flesh, so that its laws may not hinder your spirit. The trial will be short, but harsh. Pray, and strength will be given to you. You shall gather from your mission the blessings of all in the future. You shall assure the triumph of reasoned faith over error and superstition. Prepare yourself to do in all things the will of the Lord, so that, when the hour comes, you may have acquired enough moral strength to resist men and obey God! If you follow this counsel, celestial messengers will come to you—you will hear their voices, they will guide and counsel you. You need not fear, for they will not abandon you!'

"How can I describe the supreme impulse that took hold of me! I felt the spur of love pierce my whole being. I had but one aim left: to labor for the spiritual emancipation of that blessed land where I had tasted the bread of life and drunk from the cup of the strong. That vision was for my soul a celestial viaticum."

⚜

Far off, at the edge of the continent, like an immense citadel against which the sea and the storm wage eternal assault, rises a strange land—severe, solemn, given to study and profound meditation.

At its center, on a vast plateau, stretch, as far as the eye can see, heaths dotted with pink heather, golden broom, and prickly gorse. Then come the fields of buckwheat alternating with stunted apple trees; woods of oaks so dense that no ray of light penetrates beneath their boughs line the horizon.

This is Brittany, the sanctuary of Gaul, the sacred place where the Celtic soul slumbers in its heavy sleep of twenty centuries.

How many times have I wandered there, staff in hand, through its thickets, its wild ravines, its coves carved by the sea! How many times have I questioned the Ocean from atop its granite headlands! I know the folds and hollows of its coasts and valleys. I know the solitudes of its shadowy, murmuring forests: Kénécan,

Coatmeur, and above all Brocéliande—where Merlin sleeps, the Welsh bard with the golden harp, the enchanter enchanted by Viviane, the fair faery who symbolizes nature, matter, the flesh. But Merlin will awaken, for Radiance—his inspired soul, his immortal genius—keeps watch and, when the hour comes, will know how to draw him and his sons from the veils of sensualism that paralyze their action and arrest the flight of their thought.

Brittany resembles no other land. Beneath the dark branches of its oaks, upon its gray and desolate heaths where the sad lament of the wind resounds, upon its jagged coasts where foaming waves wage ceaseless battle against walls of rock—everywhere one feels a mysterious influence hovering; everywhere one senses the breath of the invisible passing. The land, the air, the waters—all are full of voices that whisper forgotten secrets to the soul of the dreamer. The poetry of Brittany has something austere about it that envelops and stirs you. It is virile and penetrating. Its teachings, when understood and applied, form great souls, heroic characters, proud and profound thinkers.



There still survive the last offshoots of that race; there still resound the accents of that sonorous tongue, whose phrases echo like the clash of swords and the shock of shields.

This is Armor! Ar-mor-ic—the land by the sea—where, behind the triple wall of forests, mountains, and reefs, lies hidden the deep soul, the melancholy and dreamy genius of Gaul. Only there can you rediscover in all its purity that valiant, tenacious, strong race that filled the world with the thunder of its exploits. There you will find it again under its two aspects: the Gallic, as Caesar described it in his Commentaries—lively, light, and changeable—and the Cymric, the more modern branch of the Celtic race, grave, sometimes sorrowful, faithful to its attachments, passionate for what is great, jealously guarding in the hidden folds of its soul the sacred ark of its memories.

This race—nothing has ever worn it down. It resisted two hundred years with arms, as Michelet said, and a thousand years with hope. Defeated, it still astonishes its conquerors. Yet it knew how to give itself, and it was through marriage that France assimilated it.

The Celtic soul has its sanctuary in Brittany, but the vibrations of its thought and its life extend far over all the region that was once Gaul—from the Scheldt to the Pyrenees, from the Ocean to the land of the Helvetii. It created, in every corner of the national soil, hidden retreats where the thought of the ages still lives, latent: the central plateau, Auvergne (Arvernia, the "high dwelling"), the Morvan, the rugged Cévennes, the forests of Lorraine where Joan heard her "voices."



And what, then, is the Celtic soul? It is the deep conscience of Gaul. Repressed by the Latin genius, oppressed by Frankish brutality, misunderstood, forgotten even by her own children, the Celtic soul nevertheless endures through the centuries.

It is she who reappears at the solemn hours of history, at times of disaster and collapse, to save the homeland in peril. She is the ancient mother who trembles each time the foot of the enemy defiles her resting place, and who rises from her sleep to call upon her sons and drive out the foreigner.

From her, too, come the mighty breaths, the irresistible impulses, the grand inspirations that have made France the champion of ideas and the inspirer of humanity.

Thus France cannot perish, despite her faults, her weaknesses, her decadence, and her falls. Each time the abyss has opened beneath her steps, from the depths of space a hand has been extended toward her to guide her. During the Hundred Years' War, as in the time of the Revolution, the Celtic soul reappears to rouse, to enflame the heroes. It is she who inspires the providential envoys and changes the course of events.

At times the Celtic soul grows silent; it slumbers, it sleeps. And then, when her voice is stilled, her people falter; they lose their virility, their greatness; they let themselves slip little by little down the slope of doubt, sensualism, indifference; they forget the virtues, the hidden powers within them. But the awakenings are resplendent. Sooner or later, the Celtic soul reappears—young, ardent, impetuous—to point out to her children the path toward the lofty summits and the source of high inspirations.



Such was the state of things in 1914. For a century the Celtic soul had been silent; the national genius had lost its brilliance. France was growing materialistic and degenerating—but the storm came. At the hour of peril, the soul of Gaul rose again, veiled in her long robes, and reminded her sons of the sublime goal, the sacred task. And after so many griefs and trials, behold! her finger, raised toward heaven, shows us the dawn, the renewal of the idea, the coming and final triumph of Celtic thought—freed at last from the shadows accumulated upon it by twenty centuries of oppression and foreign error.

Yet, here and there, certain manifestations of Celtic thought had already appeared. Even before the war, Rear Admiral Réveillère wrote to the Municipal Council of Paris regarding the broken menhir of Locmariaker that was to be erected on the Champ de Mars:

"Pan-Celticism must once again become a faith, a religion. The task of our age is twofold. First, it is the renewal of the Christian faith, grafted onto the Celtic doctrine of the transmigration of souls, just as the cross was grafted onto the menhir—the only doctrine capable of satisfying the intelligence, through the belief in the indefinite perfectibility of the human soul in a succession of successive existences. The second is the restoration of the Celtic fatherland and the reunion, in one body, of its now separated members. We are not Latins; we are Celts!"

Since then, this current of ideas has taken on a wide expansion. Each year, an assembly, or *eisteddfod*, gathers somewhere in Celtic lands the most illustrious representatives of the race. Every region sends its delegates: Scots, Irish, Welsh, Bretons of France, Cornishmen, islanders of Man, Celtic scholars from America, and even from Australia—for "wherever in the world they may be, the Celts are brothers." All unite under one common symbol, to honor their great ancestors and engage in contests of thought.

Even more numerous, at the present hour, are those who pursue the struggle in favor of a reborn Celticism, now under the form of modern spiritualism.

It is therefore useful to recall here, in succinct terms, what the beliefs of our forefathers were.

⚜

The works of eminent historians and erudite thinkers[188], by dispelling the prejudices sown in our minds by Latin authors and Catholic writers, have cast a bright light on the institutions and beliefs of the Gauls.

The philosophy of the druids, reconstructed in all its imposing grandeur, has been found to correspond to the aspirations of the new spiritualist schools. Like us, the druids affirmed the infinity of life, the successive existences of the soul, and the plurality of inhabited worlds.

It was in these virile doctrines, in the profound sense of immortality that flowed from them, that our fathers drew their spirit of liberty, their sense of social equality, and their heroism in the face of death.



A kind of vertigo seizes our thought when, looking back twenty centuries, we consider that the principles of this "new philosophy" were then spread throughout Gallic society, inspiring its institutions and nurturing its genius.

That great light, which once illuminated the land of Gaul, was suddenly extinguished. The brutal hand of Rome, in expelling the druids, gave place to the Christian priests. Then came the Barbarians, and night fell upon human thought—this night of the Middle

188 See: Gatien Arnoult, *Gaulish Philosophy*, vol. I; Henri Martin, vol. I of the *History of France*; Adolphe Pictet, *Library of Geneva*; Jean Reynaud, *The Spirit of Gaul.*

Ages, lasting ten centuries, so thick that the rays of truth seemed never destined to pierce it.

At last, after a long and painful gestation, the faith of our ancestors—renewed and enriched by the achievements of science, by the intellectual conquests of recent centuries, softened under the influence of Christianity—has been reborn in a new form. Sons of the Gauls, we take up again the work of our fathers. Armed with the philosophical tradition that made their greatness, enlightened as they were concerning the mysteries of life and death, we offer to modern society—overrun by material instincts—a teaching that brings, together with moral elevation, the means of establishing here below the reign of justice and true fraternity.

It is therefore important to recall what, in terms of beliefs and aspirations, was the legacy of our race. It is important to link the modern philosophical movement to these conceptions of our fathers, to the doctrines of the druids—so rational, based on the study of nature and on the observation of psychic forces—and to show in this spiritualist renewal a true resurrection of the genius of Gaul, a reconstitution of the national traditions which centuries of oppression and error may have veiled, but have never destroyed.



The essential foundation of druidism was the belief in the successive lives of the soul, in its ascension along the ladder of worlds. It is on this fundamental notion of destiny that I feel compelled to insist here.

I would wish to have the resources of eloquence and the persuasion of genius, in order to set forth this great law of the *Triads*[189]—to tell how, from the depths of the past, from the abysses of life, there ceaselessly spring forth, unfold, and rise the long processions of souls. The spiritual principle which animates us must descend into matter in order to individualize itself, and through its slow secular labor, form and develop its latent faculties and its conscious self. From degree to degree, it fashions for itself forms—organisms suited to the needs of its evolution—perishable forms which it abandons at the end of each existence like a worn garment, in order to seek others, more beautiful, better adapted to the necessities of its ever-expanding tasks.

Throughout the whole course of its ascent, it remains in solidarity with the environment it inhabits, linked to its fellows by mysterious affinities, contributing to their progress as they work toward its own. It descends again and again into life, into the ever wider and ever-changing crucible of humanity, in order to conquer new virtues, new knowledge, new qualities. And when it has gathered, from a given world, all that that world could offer of science and wisdom, it rises toward better societies, toward more favored spheres, carrying with it all those it loves.

Toward what end does it rise? What will be the ultimate goal of its efforts? The goal seems so distant! Is it not folly to dream of attaining it? The navigator who sails across the vast solitudes of the ocean chooses as the aim of his course the star whose light trembles far off on the horizon. How could he ever reach it? Impassable distances separate them! And yet, that star, lost in the

189 Cyfrinach Beirdd Inys Prydain: Mysteries of the Bards of the Isle of Britain, translated by Edward Williams, 1794.

depths of the heavens, he will one day know—in another time, under another form. So too shall the earthly human one day come to know the worlds of blessed and perfect life.

Perfection in the fullness of being—that is the goal. Always to learn, always to penetrate further into the divine mysteries. Infinity draws us. We spend eternity traversing immensity, tasting its splendors, its intoxicating beauties. Always to become better, always greater in intelligence and in heart; always to rise into harmonies more profound, into light more radiant; to draw upward with oneself all who suffer, all who are ignorant—this is the destiny assigned to every soul by divine law.

Is there not a lofty conception of life in this doctrine of the Triads? Man, artisan of his own destiny, by his acts prepares and builds his future. The true purpose of existence is elevation—through effort, through the accomplishment of duty, even through suffering. The more bitterness life contains, the more fruitful it is for the one who bears it bravely.



Life is like a tourney-field, where the valiant display their courage and win a higher rank; it is a crucible where misfortune and trial do for virtue what fire does for metals—refining and purifying them.

Through multiple lives and diverse conditions, man hastens his earthly journey, passing from one to another, after a time of rest and reflection in the spiritual world; ceaselessly, he advances along this path of ascension which has no end. Painful and grievous though most of these earthly existences may be, they are also fruitful; for it is through them that our souls grow, that strength and wisdom increase.

Such a doctrine can provide human societies with an incomparable incentive for good. It ennobles sentiments, refines morals; it distances us equally from the puerilities of mysticism and the aridities of positivism.

This doctrine is ours. The beliefs of our forefathers reappear, broadened and reinforced by an entire body of facts, revelations, and phenomena verified by modern science. They impose themselves upon the attention of every serious thinker.

⚜

Joan's former existences, like those of all souls, faded from her memory at each rebirth. Such is the common law. The body is a veil that extinguishes remembrance; the human brain, except in rare cases[190], can reproduce only the impressions it has itself registered. Yet our entire history remains engraved in our deeper consciousness. As soon as the spirit is released from its mortal covering, the chain of memories is reconstituted, with a clarity that grows in proportion to the soul's advancement, its light, its perfection. Despite the temporary forgetfulness, the past is always alive within us; it resurfaces in every earthly life, under the form of aptitudes, acquired faculties, natural inclinations, the traits of character and of mentality. It would suffice to study ourselves attentively to sketch the main lines of our own past.

So it was with Joan of Arc, in whom could be discerned the traces of her Celtic lives, as well as those less remote

190 See: *Life and Destiny*, chap. XIV.

existences of patrician ladies, fond of splendid attire and resplendent armor. Yet what persisted in her above all, from her earliest lives, was that distinctive strain of druidic and bardic mysticism: the direct intuition of the soul's realities, demanding personal revelation and rejecting imposed faith. Hers were the faculties of a seer—so characteristic of the Celtic race, so widespread at the dawn of our history, and still found today in certain ethnic groups, particularly in Scotland, Ireland, and Armorican Brittany. It was through the methodical exercise of these faculties that the druids acquired their deep knowledge of the invisible world and its laws. The feast of November 2nd—the commemoration of the dead—was of Gaulish origin. The evocation of the departed was practiced in circles of standing stones; druidesses and bards delivered oracles.

This teaching unveiled the stages of the soul in its ascent toward the good, through ever-renewed lives, increasingly radiant and blessed according to the merits gained. It established a living communion between the dwellers on earth and the departed—unseen, yet present.

Such instruction developed in minds lofty notions of progress and liberty. It is owing to this that the Celt introduced into the world that love of the ideal, which the Roman—more attached to practical realities—never knew. The Celt is drawn to great and generous deeds. In war, he loves glory rather than profit. His soul is magnanimous. He knows how to renounce, to scorn fear, to defy death. Hence his bearing in battle.

Study Joan of Arc carefully, and you will find in her all these same sentiments, these same inclinations. Joan is like a synthesis of the Celtic soul and the French soul, in what is purest and highest in both. That is why her memory will forever shine like a star in the darkened firmament of the fatherland. In every hour of national distress, France will instinctively turn to her, as to its living, protecting palladium.

A new Velléda, last blossom among the tufts of the sacred mistletoe, Joan personifies both the genius of Gaul and the soul of France.

All the marks, all the characteristic signs of the faculties once possessed by seers and druidesses are found in her; she is the medium par excellence, and the protecting spirits of Gaul—become France—made use of her to save the nation. And to save a people, one must be of the purest substance of its essence, bound to the living roots of its origins and its entire history. Joan was this in the highest degree; thus she incarnates within herself the double genius of Celtic Gaul and Christian France.



History furnishes parallels[191]. It recounts that Vercingetorix, beneath the dark branches of the forest, conversed with the souls of heroes fallen for their country. Like Joan, this other personification of Gaul, the young chief heard mysterious voices.

Another episode in Vercingetorix's life confirms that the Gauls invoked spirits in grave circumstances. At the extreme edge of the continent, where the harsh plateau of Cornouaille breaks off, high cliffs rise beneath a storm-laden sky. There the enraged waves wage eternal battle against the colossal rocks. Swift, foaming, like liquid walls, they surge from the open sea and hurl

---

191 V. BOSC et BONNEMERE, *Histoire nationale des Gaulois.*

themselves against the granite ramparts, which, gnawed by the waters, strew the shore with their fragments. On winter nights, the rolling of boulders and the immense clamor of the Ocean can be heard for leagues inland, awakening in hearts a superstitious dread.

A short distance from that sinister coast, amid reefs white with foam, lies an island once dotted with groves of oaks, beneath which rose altars of rough stone. This was Sein, ancient dwelling of the druidesses, Sein, sanctuary of mystery, where the foot of man never profaned the soil. Yet, before rousing Gaul against Caesar and, in one last supreme effort, striving to free the fatherland from foreign yoke, Vercingetorix went there, armed with a safe-conduct from the chief druid. There, amid the crashes of thunder, says the legend, the genius of Gaul appeared to him, foretelling his defeat and his martyrdom.



Certain facts of the great Gallic leader's life can only be explained by occult inspirations. For example, his surrender to Caesar at Alesia. Any other Celt would have taken his own life rather than fall into the hands of the victor and serve as a trophy in his triumph. Vercingetorix accepted humiliation as reparation for serious faults committed in previous lives, faults that had been revealed to him.

A part of our race has lost its distinct nationality, yet the Celtic soul survives within the French nation. It is, as we have said, her profound conscience; and just as the powers accumulated within us over the ages, dormant beneath the flesh, awaken with sudden brilliance, so too will the Celtic soul reappear in a splendid resurrection—not to save, as in former times, the material life of her people, but their compromised moral life. She will come to rekindle in weary souls the love of knowledge and the will to sacrifice.

She will speak to us again the consecrated words, the stirring calls that once made the shores resound and awakened the echoes of the forests. To hesitant spirits, tossed upon the ocean of uncertainty, she will restore the vision of horizons where all is calm and radiant.

What modern France lacked was the higher science of destiny, the divine hope, the serene confidence in the infinite future. Her educators have failed to provide her with these essential things, without which there can be no true greatness, no noble upliftings of the soul. Hence the relative sterility of our age, the absence of both ideal and genius. But here is the remedy.

At the very moment when the currents of democracy are leading us back to the political traditions of Gaul, experimental spiritualism is bringing us back to her philosophical traditions. Allan Kardec, inspired by the great Spirits, restored on a broader scale the beliefs of our ancestors. It is, in truth, the religious spirit of Gaul that awakens in this leader of a new school. Everything about him—his assumed name, wholly Celtic; the monument that, by his will, covers his mortal remains; his austere life, his grave and meditative character, his entire work—recalls the druid. Allan Kardec, prepared by his past existences for the great mission he has now accomplished, is nothing less than the reincarnation of an eminent Celt. He himself affirmed it in the following message, received in 1909:

"I was a priest, leader of the priestesses of the island of Sein, and I lived upon the shores of the raging sea, at the furthest point of what you call Brittany."

"Do not forget the great Spirit of life, the One who makes the mistletoe grow upon the oaks, and whom the ancient stones of your forefathers consecrate. I am happy to assure you that your fathers have always had faith; keep it as they did, for the Celtic spirit has not died in France—it has survived and will restore to the sons the will to believe and to draw closer to God."

"Do not forget your loved ones who surround you, like the stars in the sky that you cannot see in full daylight, though they are always there."

"The divine power is infinite; it radiates even to you through the mists of the earth, and you receive its rays, diffused and softened."

"Listen to the voice of your heart, when, standing before the ocean where furious waves chase one another, you feel yourself gripped with both fear and hope. It speaks loudly to those who wish to hear it. You must understand it, for you have already been given all the teachings of the earth combined."



"Love us—we, the ancient men of the earth. We need your remembrance, my beloved ones. May your souls come visit us during the sleep that God grants you!"

"You wish to know who I am: I will tell you my name, but what do names matter! On earth, with our body, we left behind the memory of names and of things, in order to remember only the will of God and the sentiments that draw us to Him, to know, above all, only His love and His glory. For in the infinite light, every flame seems to fade: the sun of God renders it less visible, blending it into an eternal radiance."

"The earth is but a place of passage, a vast and shadowed forest, where the echoes of the life of other worlds reach us only faint and muffled."

"We shall always be there—the great guides who lead suffering humanity toward that goal unknown to men, yet set by God; it shines for us through the night of time like a luminous torch."

"We await the moment when, at last liberated, you may return to us, to sing the eternal hymn that glorifies God."

"Souls of France, you are daughters of Gaul. Remember the faith of your ancestors, which is also yours. Lift up your thoughts at times to the pure sources of our origins, to the strong traditions and lofty heights of our history, so that you may find again your energy and your faith, revive your spirit, and warm your heart in the pure air and beauty of the heights, and in the infinite light."

*Allan Kardec*

# XVII
# JOAN OF ARC AND MODERN SPIRITUALISM. THE MISSIONS OF JOAN.

*When all seems darkened faith, morals, and laws*
*From Joan, on the horizon, rises the white star:*
*Let us know how to lift toward her both our eyes*
*and our voices.*

*Paul Allard.*

Gaul was not the only theater of manifestations from the Beyond. All antiquity knew the occult phenomena. They formed one of the principal elements of the Greek mysteries. The earliest times of Christianity are filled with visions, apparitions, voices, and premonitory dreams[192]. The initiates and the believers drew from them a moral strength, which imparted to their lives an incomparable impulse, and enabled them to face without faltering trials and torments.

Since the most remote times, the invisible humanity has always communicated with ours. Unceasingly, a current of spiritual life has spread over earthly humanity,

192 See: After Death and Christianity and Spiritism, passim.

through the intermediacy of prophets and mediums. It is this vital influx, coming from eternal sources, that gave birth to the great religions. All of them, at their origin, are steeped in those profound and regenerative waters. So long as they drink from them, they keep their youth, their prestige, their vitality. They weaken and die as soon as they turn away from them and disdain their hidden forces.

Such is the case with Catholicism. It has misunderstood, forgotten this great current of spiritual power, which fertilized the Christian idea at its cradle. It has burned by the thousands the agents of the invisible world, rejected its teachings, stifled its voices. The witchcraft trials, the stakes of the Inquisition have raised a barrier between the two worlds and suspended, for centuries, that spiritual communion which, far from being an accident, is on the contrary a fundamental law of nature.



The disastrous effects are felt around us. Religions are now only dried-up branches upon a trunk deprived of sap, because their roots no longer plunge into the living sources. They still speak to us of the survival of the being and of future life, but they are powerless to furnish the slightest sensible proof of it. It is the same with philosophical systems. If faith has become wavering, if materialism and atheism have made giant strides, if doubt, burning passions, and suicide wreak so much havoc, it is because the waves of the higher life no longer refresh human thought, because the idea of immortality lacks experimental demonstration.

The development of scientific studies and of the critical spirit has made man more and more demanding.

Mere affirmations no longer suffice for him today. What he demands are proofs and facts.

The importance is increasingly felt of a science, of a revelation, founded upon a body of phenomena and experiences, which bring us the positive demonstration of survival and, at the same time, the proof that the law of justice is not an empty word—each of us finding again in the Beyond a situation proportionate to our merits.

Now, this is precisely what modern spiritualism comes to offer us. It contains the seeds of a true revolution: a revolution in ideas, in beliefs, in opinions, and in morals. Hence the necessity of studying these facts, of classifying them, of analyzing them with method—both the facts themselves and the teaching which flows from them.

⚜

The moral situation of societies has become grave and troubling. Despite widespread instruction, criminality rises; thefts, murders, suicides multiply. Morals are corrupted. Hatred, disenchantment penetrate ever more deeply into the heart of people. The horizon is dark, and, in the distance, one hears muffled rumblings which seem to precede the storm. In almost all classes, sensualism has invaded characters and consciences. Every ideal has been extinguished in the soul of the people; they have been told: eat, drink, enrich yourself, all the rest is but chimera. There is no other god than money, no other goal in life than pleasures! — And passions, appetites, and covetous desires have been unleashed. The popular tide rises like an immense wave and threatens to submerge everything.

Yet, many good minds reflect and grieve. They feel well that matter is not everything. There are hours when humanity weeps for the lost ideal, when it feels the emptiness, the instability of earthly things. It has a presentiment that the teaching given has not said everything, that life is broader, the world vaster, the universe more marvelous than had been supposed. Humanity seeks, gropes, questions. It seeks not only an ideal, but rather a certainty which may sustain, console amid trials, struggles, and sufferings. One asks what is to succeed this time of transition which witnesses the death of a world of beliefs, of systems, of traditions, whose dust is scattered about us.

By its obstinacy in shutting itself up within the narrow circle of its dogmas, by its refusal to broaden its conception of human destiny and of the universe, religion has alienated from itself the elite of thinkers and scholars—almost all those whose opinion carries authority in the world. And the multitude has followed them. The gaze of humanity has turned toward science. For a long time it has asked of science the solution of the problem of existence. But science, that of yesterday, despite its magnificent conquests, was still too imbued with positivist theories to furnish humanity with a notion of being and of destiny which might exalt strength, warm the heart, inspire songs of faith and love to lull little children.

Now behold this invisible world, of which Joan was one of the interpreters, this world which the Church had fought, driven back into shadow during centuries, enters again into action; it manifests itself upon every point of the globe at once, under forms without number, and by the most varied means[193]1. It comes to show humanity the sure way, the straight way which must lead them toward the lofty summits.

In every milieu mediums are revealed, troubling phenomena occur, societies of study and reviews are founded, constituting so many centers from which, little by little, the new idea radiates. Already they are numerous enough, these societies, to form a network enveloping the entire planet. And through them, for sixty years, one has been able to see germinate at first, then prepare, accentuate, and afterward grow, the obscure, silent work of the blossoming of the century in which we live. This is what we call the new spiritualism, modern spiritualism, not a religion in the narrow sense of the word, but rather a science, a synthesis, a crowning of all the labors, of all the conquests of thought—a revelation which draws humanity forth from the paths and ways it has traveled until now, broadens its horizons, and makes it participate in the life of vast spaces, in universal, infinite life.



Modern spiritualism is the study of the human being, not in the corporeal and fleeting form, but in the spirit, in the imperishable reality, and in the evolution through the ages and the worlds. It is the study of the phenomena of transcendental thought and of deep consciousness, the solution of the questions of responsibility, of freedom, of justice, of duty, of all the problems of life and of death, of the here-below and the Beyond. It is the application of these problems to moral progress, to the good of all, to social harmony.

---

193 See: Into the Unseen; Spiritism and Mediumship.

Material life is but a passage, our present existence a moment in duration, our dwelling a point in immensity. The human being is a thinking and conscious atom upon the globe that carries them, and this globe itself is but an atom, rolling in the boundless universe. But our future is infinite like the universe, and the worlds which shine by night above our heads are our inheritance.

Modern spiritualism teaches us to step forth from the narrow circle of our daily occupations, and to embrace the vast field of labor, of activity, of elevation which is open to us. The great enigma dissolves, the divine plan reveals itself. Nature takes on a meaning; it becomes in our eyes the grandiose ladder of evolution, the theater of the soul's efforts to free itself from matter, from lower life, and ascend toward the light.

A communion of harmony links beings on all the degrees of the immense scale of ascension, and on all the planes of life. The human being is never alone when struggling and suffering for the good and for the truth. An invisible multitude assists and inspires, as it assisted Joan and the valiant ones who fought under her orders.



This solidarity is felt powerfully in the present time. In hours of crisis, when souls give way, when humanity hesitates upon the arduous road, the invisible world intervenes. The celestial Spirits, the messengers of space, set to work; they stimulate the march of events and that of ideas. At present, they labor to reestablish the broken link which united the two humanities. They themselves tell us this in these terms[194]:

194 Communication received in June 1909.

"Hear our voices, you who seek and weep! You are not abandoned! We have suffered in order to establish a communication between your world of forgetfulness and our world of remembrance. We have established a link, at first fragile, but which will become powerful: mediumship. Henceforth, it will no longer be despised, reviled, persecuted, and people will no longer be able to fail to recognize it. It is the only possible intermediary between the living and the dead, and the latter will not allow the outlet they opened to be closed again, so that the anxious person may learn to struggle by the light of the celestial radiances."

*John, disciple of Paul.*

It comes in its hour, the new revelation, and it takes on the character which the spirit of the time demands: the scientific and philosophical character. It does not come to destroy, but to edify. The teaching of the invisible world will illumine at once the depths of the past and those of the future; it will bring forth from the dust of centuries the slumbering beliefs, it will revive them by completing and fertilizing them. To the somber words of the Roman Church, words of fear and condemnation, saying: "You must die!" it comes to substitute these words of life: "You must be reborn!" Instead of the terrors inspired by the idea of nothingness or the dread of hell, it gives us the joy of the soul, blossoming in immense, radiant, solidary, infinite life. To all the despairing of the earth, to the weak, to the disenchanted, it comes to offer the cup of the strong, the generous wine of hope and immortality.

Let us return to Joan of Arc. It seems, at first sight, that the developments to which we have just given ourselves have led us far from our subject. Not so. These considerations will enable us better to understand the role and the missions of Joan. We say *missions*, for her present work, though less apparent, is of as much importance as that of the fifteenth century. Let us speak first of the latter:

What was Joan, in reality, when she appeared upon the great stage of history? Joan was a heavenly messenger and, following the expression of Henri Martin, a "messiah." How shall we define these terms? Let us leave that task to the Spirits themselves. Here is what one of our guides said to us, by mediumistic trance:

"When humanity is forgetful of duty, God sends a messenger, a helper, for the easier, but also more active, accomplishment of their task. These are the ones you may call the messiahs. At the grave hour when souls falter in cowardice, they have shown, through their inspired voice, the truth calling humanity. Remark, indeed, that they always appear in hours of crisis, when all seems to crumble beneath the ardent struggle of interests and passions. They act somewhat like the evening wind, which comes to pacify the surging, rebellious waves after the day's storm. Peace to you who seek your way, you who no longer have strength enough to turn to the Divine. Ask, and the divine aid shall be granted you, as our Master has promised. But do not reject the messenger: know how to understand them; respect their thought and their soul: they are envoys of God, their being is clothed with the light of divine truth, and thus you owe them your gratitude."

"Peoples do not always know how to discern, upon the brow of these superior beings, the superhuman and charitable radiance with which their soul shines. They perceive that the messiahs are other than beings of flesh, but they do not comprehend; and that is why, always, you will see the envoy of the Lord conclude their supreme teaching by signing their work with supreme sorrow. Seek and you will see that all those whom humanity has at last honored have died forgotten, or rather betrayed and sacrificed. It is because their teaching must also show the greatness of suffering, and their last word, which you find upon the lips of the Master and of all the great sufferers, has been: 'Forgive those who know not!' Suffering is still an act of love."

*John, disciple of Paul.*



Joan is one of those messiahs sent to save a people in agony, and yet awaited by great destinies. France was called to play a considerable role in the world. Her history has proved it. She had for that the necessary qualities. Certainly, one may say that among other nations there are those more serious, more reflective, more practical; yet none possesses those impulses of the heart, that somewhat adventurous generosity which has made France the apostle, the soldier of justice and liberty in the world. Nevertheless, this role to which she was predestined, France could only fulfill on condition of remaining free; and yet her faults had brought her to the very brink of ruin. It was believed, when Joan appeared, it was already said throughout all Europe, that the mission of France, of that great people who had distinguished itself by so many noble deeds, was finished. It was she above all who had given birth to chivalry, aroused the crusades, founded the arts of the Middle Ages. She had been the initiator of progress in the West. And now all human resources had become powerless to save our country. But what humanity can no longer do, a superior spirit is about to accomplish, with the aid of the invisible world.

Here a question presents itself. Why did God choose the hand of a woman to snatch France from the tomb? Was it, as Michelet thought, because France is woman, woman by the heart? Was it, as other writers have said, because woman is superior to man in sentiment, pity, tenderness, enthusiasm? Yes, doubtless, and therein lies the secret of woman's devotion, of her spirit of sacrifice.

In the fifteenth century, says Henri Martin, all the energies of the strong sex, the sex made for outward life, for action, were exhausted. The last reserve of France was in woman, sustained by divine power. That is why heaven delegated to us her whom the voices named "the daughter of God."

But to this choice there is a higher reason. If God, thus making sport of the strength of the strong and the prudence of the wise, willed to save France by the hand of a woman, of a young girl, almost a child, it was above all that, comparing the weakness of the instrument with the grandeur of the result, man should no longer doubt; it was that he might see clearly, in this work of salvation, the action of a superior will, the intervention of eternal power.

We shall be asked, doubtless: If Joan is a messenger from heaven, if her mission is providential, why so many vicissitudes, so many difficulties in the work of deliverance? Why those hesitations, those secret intrigues, those failures, those betrayals around her? When heaven intervenes, when God sends Its messiahs upon the earth, can there be resistances, obstacles to their action?

Here we touch the great problem. Before all, one must be deeply impressed with this: man is free, humanity is free and responsible. No responsibility without liberty. Humanity, free, undergoes the consequences of its acts through the ages. We have seen it: the same beings return from century to century, in history, to reap in a new life the sweet or bitter fruits, fruits of joy or of sorrow, which they have sown in their former lives. The forgetfulness of their past is only temporary, and proves nothing against the law.



Humanity is free; but liberty without wisdom, without reason, without light—liberty may lead it to abysses. "The blind person also is free, and yet, without a guide, of what use is that liberty? That is why humanity needs to be sustained, guided, protected, and inspired, in a certain measure, by Providence. But this support must not be too ostensible, for if superior power imposes itself openly, it becomes constraint; it diminishes, annihilates human liberty; the individual loses the merit of their initiative; they no longer rise by their own efforts; the divine goal is missed, the work of progress is compromised. Hence the difficulties of intervention in troubled times.

What then will the envoy from on high, the minister of the eternal wills, do? They will not impose themselves, they will offer themselves; they will not command, they will inspire; and the individual, the collectivity, humanity entire, will remain free in their determinations."

Thus are explained the mission of Joan, her triumphs and her reverses, her glory and her martyrdom. And thus also is explained the law of spiritual influences within humanity. The power that God sends acts in the world only in the measure in which it is accepted by the world. If it is welcomed, obeyed, sustained, it becomes active, fruitful, reformative. If it is repelled, it remains powerless. The envoy, the messiah, withdraws from the earth.

Humanity is on march through the centuries, to conquer for itself the supreme goods: truth, justice, love. These goods it must attain by its own free efforts. This is the law of its destiny, the very reason for its existence. But, in hours of trouble, of peril, of retreat, to the humanity that strays, forgets itself, is lost, heaven sends its missionaries.



Joan is of these. Like almost all the divine messengers, she descended among the poorest and most obscure. Her childhood has this in common with the childhood of Christ. It is a law of history and a lesson of God: that which is greatest springs from the lowest. Christ was the child of a humble carpenter; Joan of Arc a daughter of the countryside, sprung from the poor people of France. These two messiahs did not choose here below either science or riches. What would they have done with them? The sons of earth need material or scientific power in order to accomplish great things. These messiahs had no need of them. They possessed the power par excellence. Born and remaining humble, they were none the less superior to the noblest, to the most learned.

Joan had to fulfill a double mission, which she pursues still today upon the spiritual plane. To France, she brought salvation; to the whole earth, she brings the revelation of the invisible world and of the forces it contains; she brings the teaching, the words of life which must resound throughout the centuries.

This teaching, in the Middle Ages, humanity was neither apt to understand nor capable of applying. It was necessary, in order to render this revelation possible and profitable, that there be more than four centuries of labor and progress. That is why the Supreme Will permitted that the shadow should envelop for four hundred years the memory of Joan, and that a resplendent awakening should be made. Today this great figure emerges, radiant, from the obscurity of the ages. Human thought will penetrate this problem, and plunge into that world of Spirits, of which the life and the mission of Joan, of which her constant communion with the Beyond, are one of the affirmations, one of the most eloquent testimonies of history.

Joan had her protectors, her invisible guides; now, it is well to point out: in a lesser order, it is the same for each of us. Every human being has, near them, an invisible friend who sustains them, counsels them, directs them along the right path, if they consent to follow that inspiration. Most often, these are those we loved on earth: a father, a mother departed, a spouse who died prematurely. Several beings watch over us and strive to counter the instincts, the passions, the influences that urge us toward evil. And whether these are our familiar genii, as the Greeks called them, or the guardian angels of Catholicism, it matters little what name is given to them. In truth, we all have our guides, our hidden inspirers; we all have our voices.

But, while for Joan these voices were exterior, objective, perceived by the senses, in the greater part of us they are interior, intuitive, and resound only in the domain of conscience. Are there not among you, readers, those who have heard them, these voices? They speak in silence and in recollection; they tell of the struggles to be pursued, the efforts to be made to raise ourselves by raising others. Most certainly, you have all heard it, the voice which, in the sanctuary of the soul, exhorts us to duty and to sacrifice. And when you would hear it again, collect yourselves, elevate your thoughts. Ask, and you shall receive. Call upon the divine forces. Seek, study, meditate, so as to be initiated into the great mysteries, and, little by little, you will feel new powers awakening within you; an unknown light will descend in floods into your being; within you will blossom the delightful flower of hope, and you will be penetrated with that energy which comes from the certainty of the Beyond, from confidence in eternal justice.



Then, all will become easier for you. Your thought, instead of dragging itself painfully in the obscure labyrinth of earthly doubts and contradictions, will take its flight; it will be vivified, illumined by inspirations from on high. It must be remembered that within each of us lie dormant, useless, unproductive, infinite riches.

Hence our apparent indigence, our sadness, and, at times, even our disgust with life. But open your heart, let descend into it the ray, the regenerating breath, and then a life more intense and more beautiful will awaken within you. You will take delight in a thousand things which once were indifferent to you, and which will make the charm of your days. You will feel yourselves grow; you will walk through existence with a firmer, surer step, and your soul will become as a temple filled with light, with splendor, and with harmony.

⚜

Joan of Arc, we have said, was the messenger of the world of Spirits, one of the mediums of God. The faculties which she possessed are found only from age to age, in so eminent a degree, and one may say that she realized in our history the ideal of mediumship. Yet what she possessed as an exceptional gift may become the portion of a great number.

We have already cited elsewhere these prophetic words: *"When the times shall come, I will pour out my Spirit upon all flesh: your young men shall have visions, and your old men shall dream dreams*[195]*."*

All seems to indicate that these times are near. This word is verified little by little around us. What was, in the past, the privilege of a few, tends to become the common good of all. Already, everywhere, in the midst of the people, there are unknown missionaries; everywhere there are signs, indications which announce new times.

195 *Acts* II, 17.

Before long, all that constitutes the greatness and the beauty of human genius, all the glories of civilization, all shall be renewed, fertilized by that immense source of inspirations, which will open to the spirit of humanity a domain, a limitless field, where works shall arise that will eclipse all the marvels of the past. All the arts, philosophies, letters, sciences, music, poetry—all shall drink from these inexhaustible sources, all shall be transformed beneath the mighty breath of the Infinite.

The mission of the new spiritualism, like that of Joan, is a mission of struggle, crossed by hard trials. It is marked by signs, by omens, and bears the imprint of the divine seal. Its role is to fight, to drive out the enemy—and the enemy today is nihilism, pessimism, it is that cold and somber philosophy which knows how to make only either pleasure-seekers or the despairing.



First of all, it will have to follow the dolorous way. Such is the lot reserved for every new idea. At this moment, the hour of its trial has struck. Like Joan before her examiners at Poitiers, the new revelation stands upright before the beliefs and systems of the past, before the theologians, the representatives of narrow science and of the letter. Facing it stand all the authorities, the mandataries of the aged or incomplete idea, of the idea that has become insufficient and must give place to the new word, claiming its place in the world, beneath the great sun of life.

At the present hour, this solemn trial unfolds before the eyes of humanity, interested spectator and whose very future is in question. What will be the result, the judgment? No doubt is possible. Between the young and fruitful idea, full of life, which rises and advances, and old age, decrepit, weakened, which descends and collapses, how could one hesitate? Humanity has need to live, to prosper, to grow, and it is not amidst ruins that it will find an asylum for its reason and its heart.

The new spiritualism stands before the tribunal of opinion. It addresses itself to the Churches and to the earthly powers, and says to them: "You possess all the means of action which secular authority affords, and you can do nothing against materialism and pessimism, against crime and immorality, which spread like an immense plague. You are powerless to save humanity in peril. Do not then remain insensible to the appeals of the new spirit, for it brings you, with truth and life, the necessary resources to uplift and regenerate society. Appeal to what is great and beautiful in the soul of humanity, and with me say to them:

'Take flight, rise, human soul! Advance in the sentiment of the force which sustains you; advance with confidence toward your magnificent future. Infinite powers assist you; nature associates itself with your work; the stars, in their course, illumine your march!

'Go, human soul, strong with the help that upholds you! Go, like the Joan of battles, through the world of matter and the struggles of passions; at your voice, societies shall be transformed, aged forms shall disappear, to make room for new forms, for organizations richer in youth, in light, in life.'"

As for Joan, we have seen, her influence, her action persisted in the world after her departure. It was by her, first of all, that France was delivered from the English—not in a single campaign, not by a push like that of the waves of the Ocean sweeping the sands of the shore, as it would have been had men had as much confidence and faith as she herself, but through many vicissitudes, alternations of success and reverse. The soul of Joan, so full of love and of will for good, of devotion for her country, could not remain motionless in celestial beatitude. That is why she returns to us with another mission, to accomplish in a vaster domain, upon the spiritual and moral plane, what she did for France in the material order. She sustains, she inspires the servants, the spokesmen of the new faith, all those who bear in their heart an unshakable confidence in the future.

Know this: a revolution greater than all those which have been accomplished in the world has begun—a peaceful and regenerative revolution; it will tear human societies from their routines and their ruts, and will raise the gaze of man toward the splendid destinies which await him.



The great souls who have lived on earth reappear; their voices resound; they urge humanity to quicken its pace. And the soul of Joan is among the most powerful, in the multitude of those who influence the world and labor to prepare a new era for humankind. That is why truth has been revealed at this very hour concerning the character of Joan and her mission. Through her, through her support, with the aid of the great Spirits who have loved and served France and humanity, the hopes of those who will the good and seek justice shall be fulfilled.

The radiant legion of those Spirits, whose names mark, like so many centers of light, the stages of history—the great initiates of the past, the prophets of all peoples, the messengers of truth, all those who have fashioned humanity by centuries of labor, of meditation, of sacrifice—all are at work. And above them, Joan herself, Joan summoning us to labor, to effort. All cry to us:

*"Arise! no longer for the clash of swords, but for the fruitful struggles of thought. Arise! for the struggle against an invasion more redoubtable than that of the foreigner, the struggle against materialism, sensualism, and all their consequences: the abuse of pleasures, the ruin of every ideal; against all that slowly depresses us, enervates us, weakens us, prepares us for abasement, for the fall. Arise! work and struggle for the intellectual salvation and the uplifting of our race and of humanity!"*

⚜

The great soul whose poignant and glorious memory this book evokes hovers above us. On many occasions she has been able to make herself heard and to say what she thought of the movement of ideas that turns toward her, of so many diverse and contradictory appraisals of her role, and of the nature of the forces that sustained her. Yielding to our prayer, she consented to summarize all her thought in a message, which we consider it our duty to reproduce with scrupulous fidelity, as the most beautiful conclusion we can give to this chapter.

This message carries within it every desirable guarantee of authenticity. The Spirit who dictated it chose for interpreter a medium who had lived in the fifteenth century and who retains, in his "subconscious," memories and reminiscences of that age. That is what allowed him to lend to its language, to a certain extent, the forms of the time.

## MESSAGE FROM JOAN, 15 July 1909.

"Sweet is the communion with those who, like me, love our Lord and Father, and the vision of the past is not grievous to me, for it draws me near to you; the remembrance of my communications with the dead and the saints makes me sister and friend of all those to whom God granted the favor of knowing the secret of life and of death."

"I will give thanks to God for allowing me to share with you my belief and my faith, and still to say to those who know a little that the lives which the Lord gives us must be used saintly, in order to be in His grace. For us, every life must be sweet that permits us to fulfill the task assigned by the Almighty Judge and Father, and we must bless what we receive from His hand."

"God has always chosen the weak to accomplish His ways, for He knows how to give strength to the lamb, as He promised, but one must not go with the wolves, and the soul enamored of faith must beware of snares, and suffer with patience all trials and chastisements that it pleases the Lord to give."



"God brings us His truth under the most changeable forms, yet not all penetrate His will. Subject to His laws and seeking to respect them, I believed rather than understood. I knew that such sweet counsels could not be the work of the enemy, and the comfort they have always given me was a support and the sweetest of satisfactions. Never did I know what the distant will of the Lord was. God hid from me, by His messengers, the sorrowful end I should meet, having pity on my weakness and on my fear of suffering; but when the hour came, through them I had all strength and all courage."

"It is sweetest and most precious to me to return to the hours when I first heard my voices. I cannot say that I feared. I was greatly astonished and even a little surprised to find myself the object of divine mercy. I felt suddenly, before words had yet come to me, that they were servants of God, and I felt great sweetness in my heart which at last was calmed when the voice of the saint sounded in my ear. To tell you what was then within me is not possible, for I cannot put into words my peaceful and so great joy; yet I experienced such great peace that when they departed I felt myself an orphan of God and of heaven. I understood somewhat that their will must be mine, but though I greatly desired their visit, I was astonished at their commands and feared a little to see their desire fulfilled. It seemed to me indeed a noble work to become the safeguard of our France, but a maiden does not go among men-at-arms. At last, in their usual and gentle company, I came to have more confidence in myself, and the love I had always borne to God dictated my conduct, for it is not seemly to rebel against the will of a father."



"It was painful and yet a joy for me to obey, and I first of all fulfilled the will of God. Of this obedience I am happy, and therein I find also a reason to do what God wills: to forgive those who were instruments of my death, for I believe they had no hatred for my soul in giving it its liberty, but rather for the work I accomplished."

"This task had been blessed by God; therefore they were greatly guilty; but, like them, I hold no hatred for their souls. I am enemy to all that God reproves, to fault and to malice. It is their work that lies outside grace; they will always return to it, yet the memory of their past will not be effaced in them. I weep over the hatred they left among their brothers, over the bad seed they sowed within the Church, which brought to that mother—whom I so dearly cherished—more searching for faith than love of forgiveness. It grieves me, however, to see them amend and to see them partly acknowledge their error; but it was not at all as I would have wished, and my affection for the Church will detach more and more from that ancient mistress of souls, to give itself no longer than to our sweet and gracious Lord."

*Joan.*

# XVIII PORTRAIT AND CHARACTER OF JOAN OF ARC

*Long live labor!*

*Joan*

There is no subject that has stirred, as much as the person of Joan, the emulation of our poets, our artists, our orators. Poetry, music, and eloquence vie in brilliance and exalt themselves in singing her. Painting and statuary call upon inspiration and strive, without succeeding, to fix her image. Everywhere marble and bronze seek to reproduce her features, and soon her statue will rise in every city of our France. But alas, among the multitude of these fanciful reproductions, how many mediocre or frankly poor works!

In reality, we possess no authentic portrait of Joan. Among modern works, the physiognomy which appears the most resembling is that given to her by the sculptor Barrias in the monument of Bon-Secours, at Rouen. At least, this is what is affirmed by seers to whom she has appeared. Great artists sometimes have sure intuitions; they perceive gleams of truth and, from that point of view, they too are mediums.

Joan has made herself visible on several occasions, in circumstances which do not allow one to doubt the phenomenon. It is true that in this order of manifestations, errors and frauds abound. Many imaginary or fraudulent cases could be cited, where she has been made to intervene unduly. There is no psychic personality that has been more abused. In the exhibitions of a certain famous simulator, there was even a Joan of Arc. She had an English accent, that of the operator, and gave herself to eccentric demonstrations. In reality, her manifestations are rare. We know, however, some well-authenticated ones. We have mentioned them. Let us add that, in certain phenomena of trance, she reveals herself with impressive power and grandeur. I still see her suddenly invade the body of her favored medium, in the midst of a political discussion, rise up with a movement full of majesty, with a gesture of authority and a flash in her look, to protest against the theories of the without-country and the without-God. She is no less vehement in religious discussions. To a certain ecclesiastic, attending our séances by exception, she said:

"Never speak of eternal punishments! You make of God a tormentor. God is love; He cannot inflict sufferings without use, without profit. In speaking thus, you drive people away from God!"

When she intervenes, the voice of the medium is generally of a suave sweetness; it has melodious inflections which penetrate, move even the most insensitive. The manifestation is so impressive that one feels a desire to kneel. At the moment of appearing in séances, Joan is announced by a harmony that has nothing of the earthly, and which only mediums perceive. A great light shines forth, and for them she becomes visible. There is upon her brow and in her words something like a divine reflection, and the sound of wings beating in the air that surrounds her. None can resist her influence. She is truly the "daughter of God."

She is not the only one. There exists, high above us, a pure and superior region, where blossoms forth a whole angelic creation of which humanity are ignorant. From there come the messiahs, the divine agents upon whom fall the dolorous missions. They incarnate upon the worlds of matter and often mingle with us, to give to the sons of earth the example of love and sacrifice. One may encounter them among the ranks of the humble and the most obscure; but they are always recognizable by their noble sentiments, by their lofty virtues.

⚜



Of Joan, we have said, no contemporary image remains. Yet, during excavations carried out at Orléans for the opening of the Rue Jeanne-d'Arc, an ancient statuette of a helmeted woman was found, whose fine profile closely resembles the features of the statue by Barrias[196].

On the other hand, the historical documents containing descriptions of the Maid are few in number and not very precise. One must first cite a letter of the Counts Guy and André de Laval to their mother, written on 8 June 1429. They had seen her at Selles in Berry: "armed all in white, save the head, a small axe in hand,

196 Gothic Art, Encyclopedic Dictionary: Archaeological Museum of Orléans, by L. Gonse.

on a great black charger." And they add enthusiastically: "it seems something altogether divine, her bearing, to see her and to hear her[197]."

A Picard chronicler, drawing from the testimony of several people who had seen her, thus speaks of Joan as she journeyed between Reims and Soissons[198]:

"And she rode before the king, fully armed in complete harness, with standard unfurled. And when she was disarmed, then she had the appearance and dress of a knight: shoes laced off the foot, doublet and hose well fitted, and a hood upon the head, and she wore very noble garments of cloth of gold and silk, richly lined with fur."

According to the deposition of the knight Jean d'Aulon, "she was beautiful and well formed[199]"; "robust and tireless," said President Simon Charles[200]; "with at once a laughing countenance and an eye ready for tears," as related by Councillor-Chamberlain Perceval de Boulainvillers[201]. "She bore herself well under arms and had a noble chest," said her companion, the Duke of Alençon[202].

The debates of the trial teach us that her hair, painted blond by so many painters and flowing over her shoulders, "was black, cut short in a bowl-shape, so as to form upon her head a sort of cap, like a fabric of dark silk."



---

197 WALLON, *Jeanne d'Arc*, p. 100.
198 Picard Chronicle, Weekly Review, April 17, 1909.
199 J. Fabre, *Trial of Rehabilitation*, vol. I.
200 J. Fabre, *Trial of Rehabilitation*, vol. I.
201 Id., *Joan of Arc the Liberator*, p. 263.
202 Id., *Trial of Rehabilitation*, vol. I.

Colonel Biottot, summarizing the accounts of various chroniclers, thus describes the costume and bearing of the Maid[203]:

"The face of the heroine, in its regular features, was marked with gentleness and modesty. The body developed in full and harmonious lines. From the first days, the easy gestures of the child, her supple grace in every circumstance, and particularly under the garb of war, in the saddle, the lance or the banner in hand, astonished and charmed the eyes. Finally, over all, the candid radiance of her virginity and the flame of her inspiration shed 'a secret virtue which repelled carnal desire,' compelling even the coarsest to respect and regard."

According to all descriptions, there was upon this face, illumined by an inward thought, a sort of gentle radiance. The soul, to some degree, shapes the features of its covering. Thus we may form an idea of the beauty of this exceptional being, of the hidden fire within her, fire which lighted her countenance and shone through her actions. From her emanated a serenity, a radiance which spread over all who approached her, calming even the fiercest. In the tumult of battles and of camps, she preserved that imposing calm which is the privilege of superior souls. At Compiègne, in the thick of combat, when the Burgundians cut off her retreat and she was about to be taken, she was as though plunged into a dream, and said to the French who surrounded her in panic: *"Think only of striking!"*



203 Colonel Biottot, *The Great Inspired Ones before Science.*

Through the most varied documents, Joan appears to us like a flower of the fields of France, slender and robust, fresh and fragrant. It is lamentable, then, to see how most of our painters and sculptors have dressed her up, with no concern for truth or history. A certain critic spoke thus, not without reason, of the statue by Frémiet, erected in the Place des Pyramides, in the heart of Paris:

"He made of her a little boy, bored, dissatisfied, with long hair like a mane, a wooden arm, holding a long banner, a crown aloft!"

What wonder? he remarks: Frémiet is an animal sculptor, and so his Joan is "a hybrid being, of small stature, upon an enormous horse[204]." This statue is a parody, a shame for the French, above all in the place where it stands, exposed to the gaze of all foreigners.

That of Roulleau, at Chinon, is worse still, heavy, massive, as material as possible.



Other artists have succeeded better, without showing more scruples regarding respect for history. Charpentier represents her in prayer. The physiognomy is graceful and touching. But why this book fallen at her feet, when she did not know how to read, and at a time when printing had not yet been invented?

Painters are no more careful of historical truth: M. Jean-Paul Laurens signed the triptych that adorns one of the halls of the new Hôtel de Ville of Tours, reproducing three scenes of the heroine's life. The last panel shows us, beneath the night sky, the place where the execution took place. It is now empty, and from the pyre, finishing its extinction, a little smoke rises toward heaven. The

---

204 The Portrait of Joan of Arc by an Essene of the 19th Century.

last of the judges departs. M. J.-P. Laurens has not read. He ignores that the English, as soon as Joan was dead, had the fire extinguished, so that her poor charred body remained exposed for eight days to the gaze of the people, and that all could be assured she was no longer of this world. After a week, they rekindled the pyre until complete destruction, and had the ashes of the victim thrown into the Seine[205].

⚜

The study of certain souls draws the thinker's attention. That of Joan of Arc is captivating above all others. What most surprises in her is not her work of heroism—unique though it is in history—but her admirable character, where qualities seemingly the most contradictory unite and blend: strength and gentleness, energy and tenderness, foresight, sagacity, a lively, ingenious, penetrating spirit that knows, in few words, clear and precise, how to resolve the most difficult questions, the most ambiguous situations.

Thus, her life offers examples of every kind. Patriotic and French, in all circumstances she teaches us devotion carried even unto sacrifice. Profoundly religious, idealist and Christian, in an age when Christianity was the sole moral force of a still barbarous society, she displayed the elevated qualities, the lofty virtues of the believer, free from fanaticism and bigotry. In the intimate, family life, she appears endowed with the modest virtues that are the wealth of the humble: obedience, simplicity, love of labor. In a word, her whole existence is a lesson for

205 See H. Martin, *History of France*, vol. VI, pp. 304, 305.

those who know how to see and to understand. But what above all characterizes her is goodness—goodness without which there is no true moral beauty.

This harmonious alliance, this perfect balance of gifts which, at first glance, might seem mutually exclusive, make of Joan of Arc an enigma which we nevertheless claim to resolve.

It is a testimony rendered to her by all of her contemporaries who approached her: to a firm will that nothing, neither in warlike action nor in the midst of trials, could bend, she joined a great gentleness. The burghers of Orléans agreed in their depositions: *"It was a great consolation to have dealings with her*[206]*."* We have found these same traits of character in the Spirit who has often manifested under her name in our study circle. In her also the most varied virtues and sentiments blend into a perfect harmony.



To judge rightly this great figure, it is necessary to set her free from party quarrels, and to contemplate her in the pure light of her life and her thoughts. A ray from the Beyond crowns her beautiful and grave brow. She inspires an emotion mingled with reverence. Despite the skepticism of our age, one cannot defend oneself from the feeling that, above the ordinary conditions of human life, there exist chosen beings who are the honor of our race and the eternal splendor of history.

Like all great souls, she believed in herself, in her high mission, and she knew how to communicate her faith to others through all the radiations of her being. Always measured and wise, she united the humility of

---

206 J. Fabre, *Trial of Rehabilitation*, vol. I, p. 266.

the daughter of the fields with the pride of a queen, absolute purity with extreme audacity. Dressed as a man, she lived in the camps like an angel upon whom rests the gaze of God, and none thought to take scandal. The glory that surrounded her seemed to her so natural that she could not draw vanity from it. Had she not come to accomplish great things, and must not honor follow labor? Hence the ease she displayed in the midst of lords and noble ladies. Before God alone she bowed her head; she loved to make herself small among the little ones who offered her their homage: in church, it was among the children that she raised her soul most willingly toward heaven.

Joan is no less admirable in her words than in her deeds. In the midst of the most confused discussions, she always brings the right word, the precise argument. Beneath a certain Gallic naïveté, there pierces in her a profound sense of beings and things; and at decisive hours, she finds the accents which rekindle ardor in souls, powerful and generous sentiments in hearts.

How could one believe that a child of eighteen years could of herself find words such as those we have cited? How doubt that she was inspired by invisible spirits, as were before and after her so many other agents of the Beyond? Sublime words, as we have seen, abound in that short existence, and we shall not fail to reproduce some others still. Those eighteen-year-old lips uttered judgments worthy of taking their place beside the noblest precepts of antiquity.

*"She was very wise and little speaking*[207]*,"* said the Chronicle, but when she spoke, her voice had vibrations that penetrated to the deepest part of the hearer, awakening in him chords he did not know, that no power had until then been able to stir. That was the secret of her ascendency over so many rude, yet good, souls at bottom.

And these words did not profit only those who heard them. Gathered by history, they will go on, through the centuries, to console souls and warm hearts.

In all circumstances, she found the fitting expression, and the images she employed are full of relief and color. It is the same today, in the messages she dictates to a few rare mediums, some of which we have reproduced. These are for us so many proofs, so many revelations of her identity.



Let us recall some of her words, at once ingenuous and profound. They cannot be repeated too often, nor too much proposed as precepts and lessons to so many who, while honoring Joan, strive little to resemble her in character and virtues. We all have a personal interest in studying this life, in raising ourselves to the height of the teachings it contains, by the examples it offers of intimate life and of social life, of moral beauty and of greatness in simplicity.

*"From the moment I knew that I was to come into France, I gave myself little to games and to walks*[208]*."*

Carefreeness and lightness are habitual to childhood, and they persist in many even to an advanced age. Joan, on the contrary, had the care of the future, the constant

207 J. Fabre, *Trial of Rehabilitation*, vol. I, p. 135, note 1.
208 Third public interrogation.

preoccupation with the great mission that was hers, the weight of the charges that would fall upon her. She had been touched by the wing of angelic beings, and her life had received an impulse that would cease only with death. She perceived the mysterious call from above, and her conversations with the invisible had already imparted to her demeanor and her thoughts that gravity which was always to mingle in her person with grace and gentleness.

At the interrogation of Poitiers, Guillaume Aimery said to her: *"Joan, you ask for men-at-arms, and you say that it is God's pleasure that the English should depart. If that be so, there is no need of men-at-arms, for God alone suffices."* —*"In God's name!" she replied, "the men-at-arms will fight, and God will give them the victory*[209]*."*

These words contain a great teaching. Human beings are free. The supreme law requires that they themselves build their destiny across the ages, by means of their innumerable existences. Without this, what would be their merit, their claim to happiness, to power, to bliss? Such advantages, if they could acquire them without effort, would have little price in their eyes. They would not even understand their value. For human beings value things only in proportion to the labor they have cost them. But when obstacles become insurmountable, if their thought unites with the divine will, forces and help from on high descend to them, and they triumph over the greatest difficulties. That is the principle of divine intervention in history. The fruitful communion



209 Trial of Rehabilitation. Deposition of Brother Seguin.

of heaven and earth smooths our paths and furnishes to our souls, in desperate hours, the possibility of salvation.

Strange thing! Most human beings ignore or disdain what is most necessary to them. Without that help from above, and apart from the close solidarity which binds human weakness to the powers of heaven, how could we pursue, by our own resources, that immense ascent which raises us from the depths of life's abysses to God? The mere prospect of the immense road to travel would suffice to discourage and overwhelm us. The distance of the goal, the necessity of persistent effort, would paralyze our activity. That is why, upon the first rungs of the prodigious ladder, in the early stages, the distant goal is hidden from us, and our life-perspectives are restricted. But upon the rough path, at the perilous passages, invisible hands are stretched toward us to sustain us. We are free to repel them. If, on the contrary, we accept the aid offered us, the hardest undertakings may be accomplished. The work of beauty and greatness which our lives elaborate could not be achieved without the combined action of human beings and of their invisible brethren.



This is what Joan affirms again in these other words: *"Without the grace of God, I could do nothing."*

She always welcomed kindly the curious who came to see her, especially women. She spoke to them so gently and graciously, says the Chronicle, that she made them weep.

Nevertheless, simple and without pretension, she would have preferred to avoid the "adorations" of the crowd; she sensed their peril and said: *"In truth, I could not keep myself from such things, if God did not guard me*[210]*." "They kissed my hands as little as I could permit*[211]*,"* she declared at her trial. And when, in the city of Bourges, women of the people brought her small objects that she might touch them, Joan, laughing, said: *"Touch them yourselves. They will be just as good by your touch as by mine."*

One particularly painful fact: in her short political career, those who most owed her support, gratitude, love, were those who made her suffer the most.

Her character, however, was not embittered. She conceived no resentment. When she had to endure some bitter disappointment, she showed unshakable constancy and had recourse to prayer: *"When I am contradicted in any way," she said, "I withdraw apart and I pray to God, complaining to Him that those to whom I speak do not readily believe me. My prayer to God ended, I hear a voice that says to me: 'Daughter of God, go, go, I shall be your help, go*[212]*!'"*



She was accused of having wished to commit suicide at the castle of Beaurevoir. It was a falsehood. It is true that, captive of John of Luxembourg, she attempted to escape, considering that such is the right of every prisoner. Far from wishing to destroy herself, as they tried to insinuate at the trial, she had, she said, "the hope of saving my body and of going to aid so many good people who were in peril[213]." These were the besieged of Compiègne, whose fate lay so close to her heart. She reflected, matured her project at length, and did not leap

210 J. FABRE, Trial of Rehabilitation, vol. I.

211 Sixth public interrogation.

212 Trial of Rehabilitation. Deposition of Dunois.

213 Sixth private interrogation.

foolishly into the void, as is generally believed. A rope which she fastened to the window of her cell allowed her to let herself down along the tower; but, too short, or broken under the strain, it could not prevent her from falling heavily upon the rock. Half-dead, she was raised up and brought back to her prison[214].

It is above all at Rouen, before her wily and astute judges, that her sharp and spontaneous replies shine forth—her brief, incisive, fiery retorts. Guido Görres records it in terms worth citing:

"At each question Joan had the hardest of battles to sustain. Yet the simple young girl, who had learned from her parents only the *Pater*, the *Ave*, and the *Credo*, fixed upon her enemies a firm and tranquil gaze; and more than once she made them lower their eyes and filled them with confusion, suddenly tearing apart the web of their perfidy, and appearing before them in all the radiance of her innocence. If, but lately, the bravest knights had admired her heroic courage in the midst of battles, she showed a far greater courage now, when, laden with chains and in face of a horrible death, she bore witness even to her enemies of the truth of her divine mission, and prophesied before that tribunal, ready to condemn her in the name of the King of England, the complete downfall of English power in France and the triumph of the national cause."

"Do you know," she is asked, "if Saints Catherine and Margaret hate the English?"

—"They love what God loves and they hate what God hates[215]."



214 . FABRE, Trial of Rehabilitation, vol. II, p. 142, note 2.
215 Eighth private interrogation.

And the judge is silenced. Another questions her: "Was Saint Michael naked?"

—"Do you think that God has nothing with which to clothe him?"

—"Did he have hair?"

—"Why should it have been cut[216]?"

She foils their traps with a single word. They ask her if she is in a state of grace:

—"If I am not, may God put me there; if I am, may God keep me there[217]."

Let us recall again the dignified and proud reply she made when reproached for having unfurled her banner at the coronation at Reims:

—"It had been at the toil; it was well reason that it should be at the honor."

One of the inquisitors seems to mock her about her captivity and the punishment that awaits her. She replies without hesitation:



—"Those who would take me from this world may well go before me."

The Bishop of Beauvais, anxious, tormented by his conscience, asks her:

—"Do your voices ever speak to you of your judges?"

—"I have often, through my voices, news of you, my lord of Beauvais."

—"What do they say to you of me?"

—"I will tell you, to you alone."

And with these simple words, a prelate is recalled to the sentiment of his dignity by the very one whose ruin he had resolved.

---

216 Fifth public interrogation.
217 Third public interrogation.

# Joan of Arc
# Medium

How shall we explain, in Joan of Arc, the contrasts which lend to that great figure such powerful brilliance: the purity of a virgin and the intrepidity of a captain; the recollection of temple and prayer, and the joyful cheer of the camps; the simplicity of a peasant girl and the refined tastes of a great lady; grace and kindness joined to audacity, strength, and genius? What are we to think of this complexity of traits, which make of our heroine a physiognomy without precedent in history?

We shall explain it in three ways: first, by her nature and her origin. Her soul, as we have said, came from on high. What proves it is that, deprived of all earthly culture, her intelligence rose to the most sublime conceptions. Next, by the inspirations of her guides. And thirdly, by the treasures accumulated within her during the course of her previous lives, lives which she herself revealed.

Joan was a missionary, a messenger, a medium of God. And, as with all the messengers of Heaven for the salvation of nations, three great things are found in her: inspiration, action, and finally passion—the suffering which is the crowning, the apotheosis of every noble existence.

Domrémy, Orléans, Rouen: these were the three chosen stages for the birth, the development, and the consummation of this marvelous destiny.

This life offers striking analogies with that of Christ. Like Him, Joan was born among the humble of the earth. The youth of Nazareth replied to the doctors of the law in the Sanhedrin; likewise, she confounded those at Poitiers when responding to their insidious questions. When she drove the prostitutes from the camp, we recognize the gesture of Jesus expelling the merchants from the Temple. And is not the Passion at Rouen the counterpart of that on Golgotha? Can not the death of Joan of Arc be compared to the tragic end of the son of Mary? Like Him, she is denied and sold. The price of the victim rings in the hand of Jean de Luxembourg as once in that of Judas. And as Peter in the praetorium, so the king Charles and his counselors turned away their heads and seemed no longer to know her when they were told that Joan was in the hands of the English and threatened with a dreadful death. Nor is even the scene at Saint-Ouen without analogies with that of the Garden of Olives.

We have spoken at length of the missions of Joan of Arc. Let us not be mistaken about the meaning of that word. It is fitting to say here, in truth, that every soul has its mission in this world. Most are allotted humble, obscure, hidden missions; others have higher tasks, proportioned to their aptitudes, to the qualities acquired in their evolution through the centuries. To noble souls alone are reserved the great missions, crowned by martyrdom.

Every earthly existence, we know, is the resultant of an immense past of labor and trials. This law of ascension through time and space, which we have already set forth[218], Joan had no need to know in the fifteenth century in order to accomplish her work; for

218 See above, Chapter XVI, and *Life and Destiny*, passim.

it was not within the views of her age. The conception of destiny was then very limited; the vast perspectives of evolution would have troubled, to no purpose, the thought of men too backward still to understand and comprehend the magnificent designs of God for them.

And yet, in that superior spirit of Joan, which, like all others during earthly incarnation, underwent the law of forgetfulness, a grand past still reveals itself: virtues, faculties, intuition—all prove that this soul had traversed a vast cycle and was ripe for providential missions. One can even, as we have seen, recognize in her more particularly a Celtic spirit, steeped in the qualities of that enthusiastic and generous race, passionate for justice, ever ready to devote itself to noble causes. Familiar from the dawn of history with the great problems, that race has always abounded in mediums. Joan appears to us, in the midst of the dark Middle Ages, as a rebirth of some ancient seeress, at once warrior and prophetess.



But what dominates in her, in all times and environments where she has lived, is the spirit of sacrifice, of kindness, of forgiveness, of charity. In all the tasks entrusted to her, she has shown herself what Henri Martin so aptly defined in a single phrase: *"the girl with the great heart."*

These tasks, in her eyes, have not ended. She still considers herself bound toward those whom God has placed under her protection. Her love for France is as ardent today as it was in the fifteenth century, and those who, at that time, were the objects of her solicitude, are still her protégés in the present hour. Among those who took part in her heroic life, whether for good or ill, several live again today upon the earth in very different conditions. Charles VII, reincarnated as an obscure townsman weighed down with infirmities, has often received the visit of the "maid of God." Initiated into spiritualist doctrines, he was able to communicate with her, to receive her counsels and encouragements. She never allowed him to hear more than one word of reproach: *"It is you,"* she once said to him, *"that I had the greatest difficulty in forgiving."*

By means and with the help of influences which it would be superfluous to indicate here, she had succeeded, some years ago, in gathering together at one point those who had been her enemies—even her executioners—and, through her ascendancy, she sought to lead them toward the light, to make of them defenders and propagators of the new faith. It was then a moving spectacle for anyone who, knowing those personalities of another age, could understand her sublime way of avenging herself—by striving to transform them into agents of renewal.



Why must truth oblige me to say that the results were mediocre? All of them, no doubt, listened to her with admiring deference, feeling well that in her there was a spirit of lofty worth. But the weight of worldly cares, of selfish interests, of preoccupations of vanity, fell back heavily upon these souls. The breath from on high, which for an instant had made them tremble, was extinguished. Joan revealed herself only to a few. The rest could not divine her. Very few could understand her. Her language was too lofty; the summits where she wished to draw them were too high. These stigmatized ones of history, who ignore themselves, were not ripe for such a role. Yet what she did not succeed in doing in the course of this existence, she will obtain in those to come, for nothing can weary her patience or her kindness. And souls always find one another again upon the pathways of destiny.

# XIX
# MILITARY GENIUS OF JOAN OF ARC

*The principal merit of the victory belonged to the Maid.*

*Colonel E. Collet*

The detractors of Joan of Arc—Anatole France, Thalamas, H. Bérenger, Jules Soury, and others—concur in denying her military talents. Anatole France, in particular, neglects no opportunity to belittle her role, to diminish her participation in the work of deliverance. He pays little regard to the depositions of her companions-in-arms at the trial of rehabilitation, on the pretext that these testimonies are mingled with those of an "honest widow." He ridicules historians who have seen in her "the patroness of officers and non-commissioned officers, the inimitable model of the cadets of Saint-Cyr, the inspired national guard, the patriotic gunneress[219]." And further, he writes:

*"She had but one tactic, which was to prevent men from blaspheming and from keeping company with harlots... To*

219 ANATOLE FRANCE, *Life of Joan of Arc.* Preface, p. XXXVIII.

*lead men-at-arms to confession, that was her whole military art*[220]*."*

What, then, are we to make of such judgments? To what extent are professors, novelists, or journalists—who may never have borne arms—competent to evaluate the military operations of the Maid?

In his work *Joan of Arc, History and Legend*, Mr. Thalamas advises us, wisely enough, to hold to direct testimonies and to neglect the rest. This counsel seems to us especially applicable to the question before us. The testimonies concerning Joan's military aptitude are explicit. They emanate from men who saw her closely, shared her dangers, and fought at her side. The Duke of Alençon expressed himself thus[221]:

*"In the matter of war, she was most expert, both in wielding the lance and in assembling an army, or in ordering a combat and arranging artillery. All marveled to see that, in military affairs, she acted with as much wisdom and foresight as if she had been a captain with twenty or thirty years of warfare. It was above all in the handling of artillery that she excelled."*



Another captain, Thibauld d'Armagnac, sire of Termes, said in turn:

*"In all these assaults (at the siege of Orléans), she was so valiant and conducted herself in such a manner that it would not be possible for any man whatsoever to have borne himself better in the matter of war. All the captains marveled at her valor and activity, and at the pains and labors she endured... In the matter of war, for leading and arranging troops, for ordering battle and animating the*

220 ANATOLE FRANCE, *Life of Joan of Arc*, vol. I, p. 309.

221 J. FABRE, *Trial of Rehabilitation*, vol. I.

*soldiers, she bore herself as though she had been the most skillful captain in the world, trained at war in every age*[222]*."*

Among contemporary writers who have studied Joan of Arc, the most competent to assess her military role are evidently those who have practiced the profession of arms, commanded troops, directed operations of war. And all are unanimous in recognizing Joan's talents in the art of combat, her instinct for tactics, her skill in the use of artillery.

The Loire campaign remains, for them, a model of the kind. The Russian general Dragomirov summarized it thus:

*"Only on June 10 was she permitted to march with the army of the Duke of Alençon, to clear the points which the English continued to occupy on the Loire. On June 14, she stormed Jargeau; on the 15th, the bridge of Meung; on the 17th, she occupied Beaugency; on the 18th, she defeated Talbot and Fastolf in a pitched battle. Result for the five days: two assaults and one battle. That would not have disgraced the glory of Napoleon himself, and that is what Joan was capable of when she was not hindered*[223]*!"*

What must be remarked in this lightning action is the ardor, tempered with prudence, that inspired and directed it. These rapid movements had for their aim to strike the enemy at the height of his power, without leaving him time to recover—according to the method of the great modern captains.

It was again Joan's strategic sense that dictated the march on Reims and then urged the king toward Paris. The great city would have been taken, had it not been

222 J. FABRE, *Trial of Rehabilitation*, vol. I.

223 DRAGOMIROW, *Joan of Arc*, p. 37.

for the disgraceful abandonment of the siege ordered by Charles VII.

Add to this her heroic courage and her constant self-sacrifice. She knew neither fear nor fatigue, sleeping fully armed and contenting herself with the most frugal nourishment. Above all, she had a marvelous gift for inspiring the troops. At Troyes, according to the testimony of Dunois, she displayed more energy and resource in organizing an assault against the city's walls than could have been done by the best generals of all Europe combined. Marshal de Gaucourt, veteran of the Hundred Years' War, agreed with Dunois in his praise of Joan's admirable conduct on that occasion, in which he himself took part.

Her concern for discipline was constant, and her solicitude for the soldier reveals a profound understanding of military life. At the Tourelles, though wounded, she ordered that the troops refresh themselves before returning to the assault. Regarding her aversion to pillagers and harlots, her desire that the soldiers abstain from debauchery, sacrilege, and brigandage, it may be easy for Anatole France to mock her "beguine" prudery; let us nonetheless admit that this was the only way to restore order and discipline—conditions essential to success.

"*She concerned herself,*" says Andrew Lang, "*as much with the souls as with the bodies of her men, which today seems childish and absurd to the scientific mind of M. France's school; but let us remember that she was a woman of her time, and that her method was that of Cromwell, that of the greatest leaders of men in all past history.*"

Her understanding, her foresight, her discernment of political matters were no less remarkable. M. Anatole France sometimes seems to regard her as a sort of simpleton. Let him recall her reception of the constable of Richemont, clumsily repelled by the king, and whose eight hundred lances largely contributed to the victory of Patay; then, the stratagems she employed to deceive the enemy concerning her messages, in cases where they might fall into hostile hands. Nor let us forget with what subtlety she discerned—long before the most sagacious politicians—the falsity of the negotiations opened by the Duke of Burgundy after the coronation of Charles VII. She then declared: *"No peace will be found with the Burgundians, save by the point of the lance*[224]*."*

Joseph Fabre vigorously underscores this gift of penetration she possessed:

*"Forcing success by the strength of her faith, with what proud instinct she tears through the cobwebs of diplomacy to hurl herself into action without reserve! She is a bird of high flight who victoriously disconcerts the politicians crawling upon the earth, cowardly promoters of peace at any price*[225]*."*



Let us now consult the military writers who seem to us to have studied Joan's role with the most sagacity and conscience. General Canonge expresses himself thus[226]:

*"Joan imparted to the operations around Orléans an activity until then unknown and, after nine days, the siege, which had lasted six months, ended to our advantage.*

224 J. FABRE, *Trial of Condemnation*, 6th interrogation.

225 J. FABRE, *The National Feast of Joan of Arc.*

226 General F. CANONGE, *Joan of Arc, War Leader. Le Journal*, April 15, 1909.

*"Conducted offensively, the Loire campaign succeeded with unforeseen rapidity; the day of Patay, June 18, brought it to a close. Vainly has it been attempted to deny, against all truth, the part Joan took in that decisive victory: she had done what was necessary so that contact with the English was not lost, she announced the battle, and while providing the formula of pursuit, she gave the victory.*

*"During the march to Reims, from June 29 to July 16, before Troyes, Joan's moral force intervened effectively at the very moment when the royal entourage was thinking of nothing less than retreating the army back upon the Loire. As is known, the pitiful liberty of action grudgingly granted to the Maid was quickly followed by the fall of Troyes.*

*"From the coronation onward, Joan was neglected. Yet it is proven that she opposed the wavering march upon Paris and, well-inspired in every respect, she advocated a direct advance.*

*"As for the failure before Paris, it cannot be imputed to her. Had the weak Charles VII listened to her instead of reducing her to powerlessness, the setback of September 8 would quickly have been repaired.*



*"On the upper Loire, during the sieges of Saint-Pierre-le-Moutier and La Charité, Joan, placed in a subordinate role, acted only by her marvelous example—as a captain.*

*"Finally, in her last campaign, so brutally cut short, Joan played the role of a leader of partisans.*

*"At the moment when she was taken prisoner, she was scarcely eighteen years and five months old; her military role had therefore lasted but thirteen months.*

*"It is unnecessary to dwell on demonstrating that the complete liberation of France did not coincide with the disappearance of the Maid. Yet it is undeniable that, thanks*

*to Joan, the indolent monarch had recovered the greater part of the country lying between Orléans and the Meuse, that confidence had returned, and that the final deliverance resulted from the prodigious patriotic impetus she had communicated.*

*"The military role of Joan of Arc may be viewed in two ways:"*

*"The 'soldier' distinguished herself by a combination of qualities whose conjunction is rare. "In any loyal observer not disposed to deny even the evidence, the 'war leader' provokes a genuine astonishment. "It is, further, a set of qualities that are found among the few victors whose names history has recorded. In Joan, in fact, conception and execution go hand in hand. Her conception leads to an audacious, tenacious offensive, of the kind which, admitted since Napoleon, holds the enemy fast, gives him no time to recover himself, and succeeds in breaking him materially and morally. "Execution is impetuous but tempered, when needful, by prudence. "It will suffice to enumerate the other qualities which enabled her to wrest victory: mastery of timing, foresight, uncommon good sense, unshakable faith in success, an example both inspiring and heartening, great power of work, persistence seconded by an indomitable will, knowledge of the human heart—whence a moral influence which only a few great captains have possessed, with time, in the same degree. "The character of war in the fifteenth century did not furnish Joan the occasion to do the work of a strategist. For example, it is certain that all her contemporaries recognized in her a remarkable and formidable tactician. "The origin, the ignorance and inexperience of the things of*

*war, the sex and youth of Joan have confounded many minds.*

*"If it cannot be a question either of comparing our heroine with this or that great captain, or even of assigning her a rank in the glorious phalanx of men of war, it is just, for an excellent reason, to place her there: the talents she displayed are those which, in every age, have procured victory.*

*"Let us now approach the search for the reason of Joan's sudden initiation into the most delicate secrets of the art of war.*

*"In truth, this search would be useless if it were true, as has been very lightly asserted, that the military art did not exist in the fifteenth century, that it then sufficed merely to mount a horse, and finally, that—so far as Joan is concerned—her military art was reduced to leading men-at-arms to confession. Here, let us speak plainly.*

*"The first negation proceeds, without a doubt, from complete ignorance of the question. The second is stupefying: Dunois and certain other captains added, in fact, to experience and knowledge, an equestrian skill more than sufficient to conquer; yet success failed them until the arrival of Joan. As for the last allegation—moreover in complete disagreement with the facts—it is at the very least singular.*

*"Let us then come to the objections formulated by historians who are serious and worthy of all regard, because they have sought the solution with unquestionable loyalty. However, this examination shall be brief.*

*"To deny the incomprehensible in the military role of the Maid is to make light of the difficulties of the problem.*

*"'Good sense,' that master quality which has been invoked, was powerless to give, from one day to the next, the technical knowledge necessary to conduct operations.*

*"Could the ardent faith reigning in the fifteenth century provide Joan with a sufficient lever? Doubt is permissible.*

*"Obedience has also been invoked; yet it really came only after the deliverance of Orléans.*

*"To say that Joan realized the unity of action which, until her, was lacking, is to acknowledge a fact; it is not to render it intelligible.*

*"Dunois is a witness with whom one had to reckon. Nevertheless, he showed himself quite the small boy in the face of the Maid on 7 May 1429, at the attack on the bastion of the Tourelles. One knows with what impetuosity she attacked. The procedure was the same at Jargeau, at Patay, and before Troyes and Saint-Pierre-le-Moutier.*

*"Finally, people have thought themselves entitled to attribute 'solely to a feeling of patriotic revolt' Joan's successes. Certainly, patriotism can, whether collectively or individually, engender miracles; but it is powerless to transform into a commander of armies, from one day to the next, an ignorant young girl under eighteen years of age. Joan constitutes a true phenomenon, unique in her kind; on that ground, she occupies an exceptional place in France and in the history of all peoples. The following comparison is worthy of reflection. In 1429, the patriotism whose development Joan hastened was only beginning to be born. Why in 1870–1871, when it was more enlightened, more ardent, and more widespread, was it manifestly powerless to save France, reduced then to extremity?*

*"In sum, it seems that none of the human reasons adduced provides the key to victories won by employing—consciously or not—the principles applied, on theaters of operations more or less vast, by great captains.*

*"As a soldier, I declare myself incapable, humanly speaking, of resolving the military problem of Joan of Arc."*

And General Canonge, in concluding, adopts the solution that Joan herself furnished, pointing out as the origin of her principal acts "the help of God."

To these considerations from a writer whose authority in such matters cannot be contested, we shall add the following citations, borrowed from the work of Colonel E. Collet[227], vice-president of the Society for Psychic Studies of Nancy, which answer point by point the criticisms of Anatole France and Mr. Thalamas concerning the raising of the siege of Orléans—a success which, according to them, should be attributed far more to the besieged than to Joan herself. The author enumerates the events of the siege, then adds:

*"It is therefore well established that the Maid, from the first day, showed a military sense infinitely superior to that of the best captains of the army, by disciplining the troops and by wishing immediately to march upon the point where the English had their principal forces. The captains of lofty or upright spirit, like the Bastard of Orléans, Florent d'Illiers, La Hire, etc., and the men-at-arms who were neither proud nor jealous, were not long in recognizing it.*

*"The communal militia recognized her on the spot as its true chief and was persuaded that it would be invincible under her orders. — This is a fact of military psychology which is easily explained in this case, but whose cause is more mysterious in many other cases of which history makes mention. By what instinct of just discernment has the ignorant crowd of soldiers often recognized, without any apparent sign, the one who was truly capable of guiding it and procuring success for it? — In fact, it contributed*

227 Colonel E. COLLET, *Military Life of Joan of Arc. Considerations on the Siege of Orléans.*

*more than the paid troops to the taking of the Tourelles, and showed all the worth and strength of those who fight for the defense of their homes and their liberty; this is what gave the Maid the first idea of a permanent national army, instituted later by King Charles VII, become wiser and more patriotic.*

*"We have already spoken of the intuitive reasons which determined her to continue the attack on the works on the left bank, despite the contrary decision of the captains, which seemed based on prudence; the event proved that those reasons of a psychological order were sound. When, wounded during the action, she overcame her suffering—encouraged by her voices—and ran to the Bastard of Orléans to prevent him from ordering the retreat and then to direct herself the decisive assault, she obeyed still the same intuition of military psychology and the most rational principle of a sound offensive in tactics, that of perseverance.*

*"One may therefore affirm, with complete certainty, that the principal merit of the victory belonged to the Maid, well seconded by the valiant captains and men-at-arms who followed her on the left bank, and powerfully aided by the Orléanais, acting with as much skill as vigor in the attack on the Tourelles by the bridge of the Loire: without her, the attack would not have taken place or would have failed.*



*"It must be recalled that, as early as May 3, Joan had announced that the siege would be raised within five days. (Deposition of Brother Jean Pasquerel and admission of Jean de Wavrin du Forestel, chronicler of the English party.)*

*"Mr. Anatole France distrusts the testimony of Brother Pasquerel, although it is corroborated by another testimony. The Maid's predictions seem suspect to him, and to justify his skepticism he cites this one: "'Before the day of Saint John the Baptist arrives (in '29),*

*there shall not be an Englishman, however strong and valiant he may be, who will allow himself to be seen in France, either in the field or in battle.' Source cited: Clerk of the Chamber of Accounts of Brabant in Procès, vol. IV, p. 426 (Vie de Jeanne d'Arc, vol. I, p. 402)."*

*"Now we have sought this supposed prediction in the cited document (Procès, vol. IV, p. 426), and we have not found it there. On the contrary, one sees that Joan's prediction regarding the deliverance of Orléans, her wound, and the coronation at Reims was perfectly fulfilled. And such deceptions abound in the book of Mr. France: history could not be more ignobly sabotaged."*

Let us add further this picture, full of vigor and color, which Colonel Collet draws of the Maid's role at the siege of Troyes:

*"The Maid, on horseback, a staff in her hand, at once hastened through the encampments to have the engines and the materials necessary for a storming assault on the place prepared in all haste. She quickly communicated her ardor to the troops, and each man pressed to the task assigned him: knights, squires, archers, men of all conditions applied themselves with prodigious activity to arranging, at well-chosen points, the few cannon and bombards the army possessed, to transporting fascines, beams, planks, doors, shutters, etc., and to constructing shelters and approaches in view of an imminent and terrible assault.*[228]

*"Joan encouraged the workers, stimulated their zeal, oversaw everything, and, says Dunois in his deposition, showed such marvelous diligence that two or three seasoned captains could not have done more.*



228 Chronicle of the Maid.

*"And this took place in the middle of the night, which lent a fantastic aspect to these extraordinary preparations: movements of men, horses, and wagons, in the smoky light of torches, in a deafening din of cries, calls, neighing, blows of axe and hammer, crashes and collapses, grinding axles, jolts, and so forth.*

*"The spectacle was by no means commonplace, assuredly, for the men-at-arms of the garrison, watching from behind the battlements, and for the townspeople, perched atop the highest houses and public monuments; and we can easily imagine their astonishment and terror. What change, then, had come over the rather discouraged French camp? What meant this strange agitation, this terrifying tumult? A mystery foreboding nothing good: a formidable catastrophe hung over the city, that was certain!*

*"The most sinister rumors circulated among the terrified townsfolk; they crowded into churches; they lamented; they cried out that they must submit to the king and to the Maid, as Brother Richard urged in his preachings. The bishop and the notable burghers were in cruel perplexity: they had pledged to resist unto death, yet they began to glimpse the advantages of submission. As for the lords and men-at-arms of the garrison, they were little reassured as to the outcome of the struggle, if the terrible Maid were to assail them.*

*"Meanwhile, the frightful tumult gradually ceased in the French camp; the torches went out one after another, and the night seemed blacker still. The anxious besieged saw only dark and shapeless masses, which seemed to swell and move on certain points near the ditches; they heard nothing but a vague murmur of muffled voices, of clashing arms, of uncertain steps, of rustling branches, and so forth—a sinister growl, precursor of the storm.*

*"But at dawn, everything took clearer shape before the troubled eyes of the people of Troyes; the fantastic little by little gave place to a reality no less menacing, namely: the complete disposition of an assault which could only be furious, obstinate, implacable!*

*"The French army, equipped with its materials for approach and attack, was drawn up in perfect order on the most favorable points, for the Maid, as was her custom, had made good use of time to reconnoiter the place; the three or four pieces of artillery, well-placed and well-protected, were preparing to open fire and to make up in speed and accuracy for what they lacked in number; the groups of carriers with fascines and ladders, the archers and crossbowmen hidden behind the defenses, the assault columns and the reserves, silent and intent, awaited the signal—and the Maid, standing at the edge of the ditch, her standard in hand, cast a satisfied glance upon that imposing array before calling forward the trumpeters to sound the attack: it was a scene most striking."*



Our history is rich in great captains: noblemen or sons of the people, all valiant with the sword. Joan of Arc, as one sees, equals them, and in certain respects surpasses them. She possesses all their military qualities, and she has more besides: skill in preparation, and audacity, irresistible ardor in execution. She knows by instinct that the French soldier excels in the offensive, that *furia* is one of the privileges of our race. Thus, five days suffice her to raise the siege of Orléans, eight days to clear the Loire valley, fifteen to conquer Champagne: in all, scarcely two months to lift up fallen France. In vain would one seek a comparable fact in history. The most illustrious warriors may bow before this young girl of eighteen years, whose brow is illumined with the prestige of such victories!

Not a single moment of physical or moral weakness is to be met with in this astonishing career, but everywhere and always endurance, intrepidity in combat, indifference to danger and to death, greatness of soul in suffering. Unceasingly, the love of country vibrates and throbs in Joan, and in desperate hours it bursts forth in brief, burning words that carry all before them.

In short, without the intervention of occult causes, one certainly could not explain in this child the conjunction of military aptitudes and technical knowledge which only experience and long practice in the trade of arms can provide.

France has possessed thousands of valiant soldiers and skillful generals; she has had but one Joan of Arc!



Returned to the life of space, Joan has not on that account forgotten France. In difficult hours, this great soul hovers above us to inspire all with resolve in trial, with courage in adversity.

As we have explained in another book[229], her role in the last war was considerable—whether in the "councils" of Spirits where measures to be taken and maneuvers to be provoked were deliberated upon, then suggested to the generals; or in the ardent struggle when she sustained and inspired our defenders—everywhere her influence was felt and powerfully contributed to the final success, to victory.

---

229 *The Invisible World and the War* (Leymarie, publisher).

Even now she often leaves the higher world where she dwells to descend again to this land of France that she so greatly loved, and there to spread her beneficent fluids. As soon as she appears, the dead of the war—the innumerable throng of those whom duty and sacrifice have crowned—hasten and gather around her to form her escort. Having reached the earthly goal, they slip in everywhere, penetrate all circles where there is misfortune to relieve, sorrow to console.

At times, with other missionary Spirits, Joan receives from on high the task of taking part in the councils of statesmen, in the assemblies where the destinies of nations are debated, and of influencing them in the direction of right and justice. Certainly, they do not always succeed, for human beings are free and their passions carry them away; but how many iniquities have these generous Spirits succeeded in preventing!

For, though unknown to us, a close collaboration is continually at work between earth and space, between the visible and invisible worlds, through which the action of the great Spirits unfolds for the fulfillment of the divine plan and the advancement of humanity.

# XX
# JOAN OF ARC IN THE TWENTIETH CENTURY; HER ADMIRERS; HER DETRACTORS.

*I grieve to see the French disputing over my soul.*

*Joan.*

The second half of the nineteenth century and the beginning of the twentieth saw the rise, in favor of the Maid of Lorraine, of a powerful current of opinion—both secular and religious. Weakly founded reputations rarely withstand the test of time. The figure of the heroine, on the contrary, grows greater with the centuries and shines with ever brighter splendor.

This current of opinion has two sources. On the one hand, it arose from the numerous works of history and scholarship published by J. Michelet, Quicherat, H. Martin, Wallon, Siméon Luce, J. Fabre, and others. In this field, no subject has provoked such an imposing body of research. On the other hand, it derived from the inquiries and trial conducted by the Catholic Church with a view to the canonization of Joan of Arc.

From both sides, the heroine's memory has found sincere admirers and generous defenders. After a long period of silence and neglect, there came a renewal of enthusiasm, as if one were reliving the days following the deliverance of Orléans. As the research advanced, the light became more complete. This great figure emerged from the narrow confines in which the past had imprisoned her. She appeared in all her beauty, as the purest incarnation of the idea of country, as a true national messiah. This magnificent surge of sympathy, despite the efforts of certain detractors of whom we shall speak later, has never ceased to grow stronger; today, the Maid is on the verge of becoming the most popular historical figure of our land.

As early as 1884, the political cabinet presided over by M. Dupuy took the initiative of a national feast in honor of Joan of Arc. A first proposal was presented to the Chamber on June 30. It bore the signatures of 252 deputies and opened with the following statement of reasons:



"A great movement of opinion has just taken place in favor of instituting a national feast of Joan of Arc, which would be the feast of patriotism. The Republic of the United States, besides its feast of Independence, has its feast of Washington. The French Republic, besides its feast of Liberty, would have its feast of Joan of Arc. On that day, all French people would unite in a beneficent communion of enthusiasm."

The Committee of Initiative concluded in favor of consideration. But as the legislature ended, the proposal was suspended, then taken up again by the Senate, at the request of 120 republican senators.

In his report presented to the high assembly, Senator Joseph Fabre of Aveyron expressed himself as follows:

"Neither the Orient with all its legends, nor Greece with all its poems, has conceived anything comparable to this Joan of Arc whom history has given us." (…) Is it not timely to oppose this great memory to the dangerous declarations of all the pontiffs of cosmopolitanism, who would try to persuade us that not even the one religion remains which admits no atheists—the religion of country?"

The bill was voted by the Senate and referred to the Chamber. After lying dormant for a long time in the files, and following an energetic petition by the Women of France, the project was finally taken up again and voted on July 10, 1920, in the following terms: *"The second Sunday of May of each year is hereby declared the national feast of Joan of Arc."*

What consideration, then, held back our skeptical politicians of the Chamber for so long? Probably the "voices" of Joan of Arc and the spiritual character of her mission. Yet those voices did exist; the invisible world did intervene. The solidarity linking living beings extends beyond the physical world, embracing two humanities and revealing itself through facts. The entities of space saved France in the fifteenth century through the mediation of the heroine. Whether it pleases some or not, history cannot be forgotten. France and the world are in the hands of God, even when it is materialists and atheists who govern. The Revolution itself was a gesture of the invisible powers; but it was not understood in the original idea that inspired it.

One may combat clericalism and its abuses; but as for the spiritual and religious ideal, it will never be destroyed. It dominates times and empires, transforming with them to assume an ever broader and loftier character.

It must be noted that Joan has every claim to the affection of democrats. Indeed, her work is not only an affirmation of the Beyond, it is also the glorification of the people from whom she sprang, of womanhood, of the rights of nations, and above all the affirmation of the inviolability of conscience.

The men of '89 and '48 already had a very high conception of this ideal figure. All bowed before Joan's memory, and Barbès wrote that "she would one day have her statue even in our smallest hamlets."

On the Catholic side, the current of opinion in favor of the Liberator followed a steady and continuous course. The bishop of Orléans, Mgr Dupanloup, was the first to conceive the project of canonization. On May 8, 1869, he addressed to Pope Pius IX a petition signed by many bishops, to obtain that the "Maid, proclaimed saint, might receive in the temples the homage and prayers of the faithful." The events of 1870 and the fall of temporal power delayed the effects of this first petition. But shortly afterward, the matter was again examined, and the "informative process," ordered in 1874, was concluded in 1876.



On October 11, 1888, thirty-two French cardinals, archbishops, and bishops addressed to Leo XIII "their supplications that Joan of Arc might soon be placed upon the altars."

Finally, the canonization was celebrated with great pomp on May 16, 1920, at St. Peter's in Rome, by

Pope Pius X, in the presence of 30,000 French pilgrims, including 65 bishops. The crowd overflowed the steps and covered the square up to Bernini's colonnade.

We do not in any way intend to blame the solemn manifestations that took place in Rome and throughout France. All French people have the right to honor the Liberator as they see fit. We regret only that in the Catholic movement in favor of Joan of Arc, the interest of caste appears so evident. It seems that one wishes to exploit the heroine's memory, and distorts her by sanctifying her. Is there not an attempt to make her a trophy, a rallying symbol for semi-political, semi-religious struggles?

The Maid of Lorraine seems little touched by these tributes. To noisy ceremonies, she prefers the affection of so many modest and humble souls who know how to love her in silence. Their thoughts rise toward her like the discreet perfume of violets, in the calm and recollection of prayer. And this moves her more than the splendor of festivals and the thunder of organs or cannons.

⚜

The Catholic movement provoked an opposing reaction. One saw, with astonishment mingled with dismay, a campaign of denigration arise against Joan of Arc. While all nations envy her, while the Germans glorify her through the work of Schiller, and even the English honor her as one of the noblest examples offered to humanity, it was in France itself that one heard criticism, belittling, and disparagement of one of the purest glories of our nation.

A whole category of freethinking writers hurled themselves against Joan's renown.

Did they yield to the unhealthy need to pull down every form of superiority—a trait of certain minds—like that newspaper director in Paris and that professor of the University who gained a special notoriety by distorting Joan's work? Or did they obey another motive equally unavowable? Whatever the case, one can only deplore the attitude of these two men, whose intellectual culture ought to have shielded them from such degradation.

Let us read what M. Bérenger, director of the journal *L'Action*, wrote about the great soul whose life we have just studied:

"Sickly, hysterical, ignorant—Joan of Arc, even though burned by priests and betrayed by her king, does not deserve our sympathies. None of the ideals, none of the sentiments that inspire humanity today guided the mystical hallucinated girl of Domremy. In supporting a Valois against a Plantagenet, what did she accomplish that was heroic, or even praiseworthy? More than anyone else, she contributed to creating, between France and England, the miserable antagonism from which we struggle to free ourselves six centuries later."



What can be said of this heap of insanities, where almost every word is an insult, every thought a challenge to history and to common sense?

And M. Thalamas, that professor of a Paris lycée, striving, through his lessons to fifteen-year-old children, to implant in their young minds doubts about the true character of the Maid! From what source did he draw his so-called erudition?

Jaurès, the great socialist orator, who on December 1, 1904, rose in the Chamber of Deputies to defend this singular professor of history, was more skillful. He saved his client from disciplinary measures that might have been decreed against him, by drawing upon his own school memories to fashion a sort of panegyric of the great maligned one. In his speech, Joan is no longer the hallucinated figure described to his pupils by the professor of the Lycée Condorcet; the orator is compelled to concede her "a marvelous height of moral inspiration; a marvelous subtlety and refinement of spirit," linking her "to the ancient Gallic core of our race."

In his newspaper articles, conferences, and pamphlet, M. Thalamas seems as alien to the patriotism and noble sentiments woven throughout the history of the Maid as he is to the psychic notions and military knowledge necessary to understand her, let alone to describe her accurately. Leafing through his little work *Joan of Arc, History and Legend*, one is at once struck by the lightness with which he presumes to lecture historians such as Michelet, H. Martin, and others, who read the texts, understood them, and interpreted them logically from their psychological, patriotic, and human perspective, in noble language. While here and there he grants justice to Joan's "splendid conviction" and even to her "heroism," under his pen the physiognomy of the Maid of Lorraine fades, pales, her memory diminishes, her role is narrowed. She becomes a secondary or even tertiary character.

At times, his tactic is to compare or to set against Joan other visionaries: Catherine de La Rochelle and Perrinaïc the Bretonne. But in the lives of these poor women, one would search in vain for a deed, an act, or a word comparable to those found in abundance in Joan's life. There is here a deliberate bias, a clear desire to diminish the heroine.

In his conferences across France, M. Thalamas expressed the opinion that the besieged people of Orléans could have managed on their own; in his pamphlet, however, he takes quite the opposite stance. The capture of Orléans, he writes (p. 34), within a more or less short time, despite the poor conduct of the siege, was nonetheless inevitable.

But the Parisians, in 1870, might also have expelled the Germans; neither men, nor money, nor courage were lacking to them—as the length of their resistance proved. What they lacked was a leader possessing the communicative faith and the military talents required. That leader, Orléans found, and through her, it was saved!



Among the writers who disparage Joan of Arc, Anatole France secured a considerable place with the publication, in 1908, of two large octavo volumes. But his work, however imposing in appearance through its scope and documentation, loses much of its value when subjected to careful analysis. What dominates in it is perfidious irony and subtle mockery. There is none of the brutal crudity of the Bérengers and other critics. The clever academician proceeds by insinuation. Everything in these pages conspires to belittle the heroine, and often to render her ridiculous.

If in certain cases he consents to render her justice, most often he drags her down to the lowest rank and attributes to her the role of a foolish girl. Thus, when

Loyseleur came to visit her, many times, in her prison—sometimes disguised as a cobbler, sometimes as a cleric—she is said not to have realized she was dealing with one and the same man.

The first volume of A. France was notable for its style and coordination of ideas. One recognized the subtle man of letters. The second was incoherent, written in a slack style, full of amusing or tragic anecdotes, curious facts sometimes foreign to the subject. These tales, however, made the reading entertaining and ensured its success. But in vain would one seek throughout the work any elevated sentiment, any grandeur. These qualities are unknown to the author. And what deliberate errors!

These errors were among the first to be signaled by M. Achille Luchaire, professor at the Sorbonne, one of the uncontested masters of medieval studies. Here is one example: Robert de Baudricourt, for M. Anatole France, is a "simple and jovial" man. To support this claim, he cites (*Procès*, vol. III, p. 86)—a page where this character is not mentioned at all (*Grande Revue*, March 25, 1908, p. 231, note). France even attributes to Baudricourt the opinion that "Joan would make a fine strumpet, and that she would be a dainty morsel for the men-at-arms." But, says Luchaire, the *Procès* (vol. III, p. 85), to which France refers in this matter, speaks only of the meeting at Chinon and the siege of Orléans, and not at all of the captain of Vaucouleurs (*Grande Revue*, March 25, 1908, p. 230, note)[230].

M. Luchaire provides other examples. Identical observations were made by M. Salomon Reinach in



---

230 See *Revue Hebdomadaire*, July 4, 1908.

the *Revue critique*. A. France writes: "She heard the voice that said to her: 'There he is!'" with a reference note to *Procès* (vol. II, p. 456), where nothing of the sort is found (*Revue critique*, March 19, 1908, p. 214). Likewise, M. Andrew Lang, in the *Fortnightly Review*. Concerning supposed prophecies that priests are said to have revealed to certain devotees, among them to Joan of Arc, M. Lang observed: "In support of his claim, M. France cites a passage from the trial which proves exactly the opposite of what he has just asserted." Elsewhere, it concerns the journeys Joan is supposed to have made to Toul, to appear before the ecclesiastical tribunal under the charge of breaking a promise of marriage. M. Lang objects: "In support of his claim, M. France cites three pages of the *Procès* (vols. I and II). One of the three (vol. II, p. 476) does not exist; the other two in no way confirm what he asserts, and one of the following pages contradicts him."



In a bibliographic article published in the *Revue hebdomadaire*, M. F[231]unck-Brentano rightly underscores these grave flaws in M. France's work:

"The inaccuracies recur constantly. They are surprising in an author who, in the course of his preface, is so severe toward his predecessors; but, after all, these are only venial sins, though they repeat often. One becomes more perplexed about the historical value of France's work when one finds that the texts themselves bear a meaning quite different from that which he attributes to them. When a historian forces his thought in the direction of preconceived ideas, it is regrettable; but what is to be

231 *Revue Hebdomadaire*, July 4, 1908.

said if he bends the documents themselves arbitrarily? The various critics who have dealt with the resounding work of M. France, this *Life of Joan of Arc* that made such noise even before appearing, have been surprised to find, in many places, that the texts to which the author referred as the foundation of his narrative or opinions were not only inaccurately reproduced or commented upon, but contained nothing that bore even the slightest connection to what M. France made them say. "Common sense," says France, "is rarely the sense of what is just and true" (vol. I, p. 327). Accordingly, common sense has been scrupulously excluded from his book. In its place, for the reader's entertainment, picturesque and unexpected tales (vol. I, p. 532)—such as the supposed gift attributed to our ancient kings of curing scrofula. Our charming historian adds that, in old France, virgins possessed the same gift, provided they were entirely naked and invoked Apollo. This, at least, is unexpected! The citation refers to Leber (*Des Cérémonies du sacre*). M. Salomon Reinach verified it: it is, in fact, a borrowing by a medieval cleric from Pliny, who lived in the first century!"



In the same article, M. Funck-Brentano also cites the opinion of Andrew Lang, author of a well-regarded work on Joan of Arc published in English:

"M. Lang points out the eternal and disagreeable snicker with which A. France fairly overwhelms his readers. The word 'snicker' is doubtless a little harsh. A. France does not snicker. It is the fine smile of an amiable ironist. But irony is not history. The ironist mocks, whereas the historian must explain. What is history? The explanation of the facts of the past.

But let us return to M. Lang, who says: 'The first quality of the true historian is sympathetic imagination, which alone permits him to understand the age of which he speaks, to know its thoughts and sentiments, and to live again, in some sort, the life of men of old. Anatole France lacks this essential gift to a quite astonishing degree.' 'A. France is an admirable sophist—in the true sense of the word.'"

Finally, M. Funck-Brentano comments on an article by the German critic Max Nordau concerning Anatole France's *Jeanne d'Arc*. He began with these words, borrowed from Schiller with regard to the Maid of Orléans: "The world likes to tarnish what shines; it likes to drag in the dust what has risen." The conclusion of the article answered this opening:

"After Anatole France's work, it will be difficult for us to pass by the equestrian statue of the Maid of Orléans without a shrug. Without brutality, with the deft, gentle, caressing hand of a soubrette, he has stripped her of her legend; and now, deprived of that rich adornment of tales and traditions, Joan of Arc inspires only pity; there can no longer be any question of admiration for her, nor even of sympathy."

These lines clearly bring out the perfidious and harmful character of the work of a so-called rationalist writer who, understanding nothing of effects, nevertheless presumes to indicate their causes, and does not fear to torture texts in order to mislead opinion.

From certain points of view, Anatole France's work is a grave error and a bad action. One could apply to him Mme de Staël's remark about Voltaire's *Pucelle*: "It is a crime of lèse-nation!"

To these diatribes we shall oppose the opinion of illustrious contemporaries who did not let themselves be blinded by political hatred. Toward the end of the last century, a journalist, Ivan de Woestyne, having conceived the idea of asking members of the Académie française for their views on Joan of Arc, gathered a set of testimonies constituting the most magnificent eulogy of the inspired heroine[232]. These representatives—the most refined in talent and esprit in our country—deemed it an honor to lay at the heroine's feet the tribute of their admiration and their gratitude.

Pasteur wrote:

"The greatness of human actions is measured by the inspiration that gives them birth: the life of Joan of Arc is the sublime proof of it."

Gaston Boissier in turn said:

"We recognize her; she is of our race and of our blood indeed: French by the qualities of her mind as much as by her love for France."



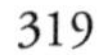

Léon Say added:

"When the homeland is unhappy, the French still have a consolation. They remember that a Joan of Arc was born, and that history begins again."

Finally, Alexandre Dumas expressed in a brief formula the sentiments of the entire country:

"I believe that in France everyone thinks of Joan of Arc what I think of her myself. I admire her, I miss her, and I hope in her!"

---

232 See *Le Figaro* supplement of August 13, 1887.

Many other thinkers and statesmen associated themselves with this demonstration. In a speech delivered at the American Circus, Gambetta exclaimed[233]:

"We must put an end to historical quarrels. One must passionately admire the figure of the Lorraine girl who appeared in the fifteenth century to humble the foreigner and to give us back our country."

For his part, Jules Favre pronounced at Antwerp a panegyric of Joan of Arc that ended thus:

"Joan, Maid of Orléans—she is France! beloved France, to which one must devote oneself all the more because she is unhappy; she is more still—she is duty, she is sacrifice, she is the heroism of virtue! The grateful centuries will never have blessings enough for her. Happy if her example can raise souls, fill them with passion for the good, and spread over the whole homeland the fruitful seeds of noble inspirations and disinterested devotions!"



Before Jules Favre, Eugène Pelletan had admired in Joan the patroness of democracy. He said also[234]:

"O noble girl! you were to pay with your blood for the most sublime glory that has crowned a human brow. Your martyrdom was to divinize your mission yet more. You have been the greatest woman who has walked upon this earth of the living. You are now the purest star that shines on the horizon of history."

On the other hand, certain journals—*Le Monde* and *L'Univers*, among others—vigorously attacked the institution of a feast of Joan of Arc by the Republic, and

233 See J. Fabre, *The National Festival of Joan of Arc.*

234 See J. Fabre, *The National Festival of Joan of Arc.*

maintained that it belonged to Catholics and royalists alone to celebrate the Maid[235].

Numerous political demonstrations were produced in the same sense in various parts of France, where Joan's name became a kind of trophy, an instrument of combat.

Exalted by some, disparaged by others in a spirit of systematic opposition, her prestige has not diminished. The pure and noble image of the Maid of Lorraine remains engraved in the heart of the people, who, for their part, know how to love her for herself, without ulterior motive. Nothing could efface it. The name of Joan of Arc is still the only one capable of rallying all the French in the cult of country. Deep divisions still separate the parties. The violent claims of some, the selfishness and resentment of others, contribute to weakening the French family. Great sentiments grow rare; appetites, covetousness, passions reign as masters.

Let us lift our souls above the contradictions of the present hour. Let us learn, by the example and the words of the heroine, to love our country as she knew how to love it, to serve it with disinterestedness and with a spirit of sacrifice. Let us proclaim aloud that Joan belongs neither to a political party nor to any Church whatsoever. Joan belongs to France—to all the French!

No criticism, no controversy can tarnish the chaste halo that surrounds her. Thanks to an irresistible national movement, this great figure rises ever higher in the firmament of calm thought, recollected, freed from selfish preoccupations. She appears no longer as

235 See J. Fabre, *The National Festival of Joan of Arc.*

a leading personality, but as the realized ideal of moral beauty. History offers us brilliant constellations of beings of genius, of thinkers, and of saints. It names but one Joan of Arc!

A soul made wholly of poetry, of patriotic passion, and of heavenly faith, she stands forth in splendor from among the fairest of human lives.

She reveals herself unveiled to our skeptical and disenchanted century, as a pure emanation of that higher world—the source of all strength, of all consolation, of all light—that world we have too greatly forgotten, and toward which our gaze must now be turned.

Joan of Arc returns among us, not only in memory, but by a real presence and in a sovereign action. She calls us to place our trust in the future and in God. Under her aegis, the communion of the two worlds, united in the same thought of love and of faith, may once more be realized—for the regeneration of expiring moral life, for the renewal of the thought and the conscience of humanity!

# XXI
# JOAN OF ARC ABROAD

*We in England think that Joan is the greatest heroine the world has ever seen, and we regret what was done and ill done.*

*Edward Clarke*

The life and work of Joan of Arc have inspired the admiration of all our neighbors. The Maid of Lorraine, sometimes criticized and disparaged in France, encounters abroad nothing but universal respect and sympathy.

Domremy has become the goal of international pilgrimages. The English, whether in groups or alone, flock there. One also meets Americans, Italians, Russians, Dutch, Belgians, Germans, and others.

All England has been seized with enthusiasm for the great inspired one, and her sons never miss an opportunity to glorify her. At the Norman festivals celebrated each May in Rouen, English delegations appear every year, crossing the Channel to solemnly honor the memory of the Maid. Already in 1909, one such delegation, led by Mr. Edward Clarke, mayor of Hastings, presented itself in full ceremonial, preceded by the two traditional mace-bearers, to lay down a wrought-iron lily branch upon the very place where Joan was martyred. The mayor of Hastings pronounced the moving words that serve as the epigraph to this chapter.[236]

In 1885, when a fifteenth-century memorandum on the "miracles" accomplished by Joan was discovered in the Vatican archives, a commission was established to examine and verify the document. The designated president was an English cardinal, the eminent Howard, of illustrious birth. He expressed himself nobly: "It is not with a bloodstained hand that I shall turn the pages of this sublime history; it is with a repentant hand."

England had already repudiated Bedford's crime on the day Queen Victoria wished to keep before her eyes the image of our Joan and had her portrait painted. Catholic England had not sought to intimidate Rome at the time of the trial of rehabilitation; become Protestant, she did her utmost to aid the beatification. A touching spectacle indeed: the leopard lies down at the feet of the Maid of Domremy and implores her pardon!



Is there not here a lesson for the French? An invitation to weave the fairest of crowns for their heroine, and, like our neighbors across the Channel, to make amends before her against whom all parties were guilty? Yes indeed, guilty! It was French Catholics who condemned her, at the very moment when the royalists abandoned her to her cruel fate, and the free-thinkers have hardly acted better toward her: one of their masters, Voltaire, profaned her, and even today it is among them that all her detractors are to be found.

⚜

236 See *Le Journal*, May 31, 1909.

Let us examine how the memory of Joan gradually conquered public opinion in England and in Germany. In this inquiry, we will be guided especially by the work of Mr. James Darmesteter: *Nouvelles Études anglaises*, and by the interesting brochure of Mr. Georges Goyau: *Jeanne d'Arc devant l'opinion allemande*.

First, concerning English opinion, let us cite Mr. J. Darmesteter:

"The life of Joan of Arc in England, from her death until our own days, is divided into three periods: witch – heroine – saint; at first two centuries of insult and hatred, then a century of human justice; finally, in 1793, there opens an era of adoration and apotheosis."

To the first period belong the chronicles of Caxton and Holinshed, and the *Henry VI* attributed to Shakespeare. The wave of hatred and slander raised by the work of Joan of Arc halts there. In 1679, Dr. Howell already notes that "the famous shepherdess Joan of Lorraine accomplished very great things."



In 1747, the conservative historian William Guthrie writes, concerning the trial of the Maid: "Like gold, she came forth purer with each ordeal."

In 1796 appears the celebrated work of Southey: *Joan of Arc*, an epic poem full of gaps and errors, yet animated by a generous spirit. This work accentuated the reversal of opinion in favor of Joan.

Certain English critics, however, found it insufficient. Thomas de Quincey, one of the most erudite and esteemed writers of his time, reproached the poet for stopping the heroine's career at the coronation of Reims and for evading her Passion. He says on this subject:

"All that she had to do was accomplished; what remained for her was to suffer. Never, since the foundations of the earth were laid, was there such a trial as hers, if one could unfold it in all its beauty of defense, in all its infernal horror of attack. O child of France, shepherdess, young peasant girl trampled under the feet of all who surround you!"

For a century now, England has not ceased to render to the memory of Joan the warmest homage. Richard Green considers her as "the figure of purity standing forth from the midst of the greed, the lust, the selfishness, the unbelief of her time." Biographies of the heroine, apologies, multiply. Let us also recall these words of Carlyle:

"Joan of Arc must have been a creature of dreams full of shadows and profound lights, of indescribable feelings, of thoughts wandering through eternity. Who can tell the trials and the triumphs, the splendors and the terrors of which that simple soul was the scene?"



The more recent work of the Scottish writer Andrew Lang on Joan of Arc[237] constitutes a magnificent plea in favor of the heroine, whom the author defends with humor and sagacity against the insidious attacks of Anatole France. He writes, among other things:

"From the middle of the eighteenth century, when David Hume, thanks to the Scottish chroniclers, could acquire certainty of the iniquity of Joan's condemnation, everyone in England was enlightened on that historical event. Since then, her martyrdom has been glorified in

237 ANDREW LANG, *The Maid of France*. Longmans, Green.

many ways. Every child knows her story, a story without equal."

In the days of trial during the Great War, when our two nations were united in a supreme effort and the memory of Joan was awakened more intensely, English manifestations in her honor took on a touching character. For example, in 1915, English parliamentarians, come in large numbers to Paris, laid at the statue in the Place des Pyramides a palm branch bearing the following inscription:

"The representatives of the British Parliament lay this palm at the feet of Joan of Arc as the symbol of the complete reconciliation of the two countries, at the hour when the two peoples, united in the same sentiment of veneration for the heroine of old France, together defend the freedom of the world.[238]"

Finally, we had the satisfaction in 1924 of seeing the eminent English writer Sir Arthur Conan Doyle himself translate and publish in its essential parts the present work under the title *The Mystery of Joan of Arc*[239]. His talent and his knowledge of psychic matters assured in advance the success of a work that the entire English press welcomed with favor.



Sir Arthur Conan Doyle, in presenting this book to the public across the Channel, wrote a preface from which we extract only the following lines:

"If we set aside the divinity of Christ, we shall find a great analogy between these two characters if we compare them from a purely human point of view. Both belonged to the humble and laboring class; both

238 See also my book *The Invisible World and the War*, p. 32 ff.

239 J. Murray, publisher. Albemarle Street, W. London.

affirmed and accomplished a mission. Both suffered martyrdom while still young. Both were acclaimed by the people and betrayed and despised by the great. Both inspired the fiercest hatred in the Church of their time, whose high priests plotted the death of one and of the other. Finally, both expressed themselves in clear and simple phrases, strong and concise.

"The mission of Joan was apparently warlike, but in reality it had as its result the ending of a century of war. Her love and her charity were so immense that they can only be compared to the words of Him who, upon the cross, prayed for his executioners."

⚜

In Germany, the exploits of Joan of Arc, says Mr. Georges Goyau[240], were known and followed day by day. Written proof remains, for example, in the *Memorial* of Eberhard von Windecke, historiographer of Emperor Sigismund.



A century later, toward the end of the reign of Francis I, at the very moment when Du Maillan, the official chronicler of the Valois, defamed the Maid, and when Étienne Pasquier noted with sorrow the discredit into which her memory had fallen in our country, a young Prussian, Eustache von Knobelsdorf, improvised a pathetic eulogy of the great inspired one.

In 1800, Schiller, whom the Convention had honored with the title of French citizen, avenged Joan of Arc in a soaring tragic poem from the inanities of Voltaire. This poem was staged and obtained throughout Germany an

240 G. Goyau, *Joan of Arc in the Eyes of German Opinion.*

extraordinary success. From 1801 to 1843, the *Maid of Orléans* had no fewer than 241 performances on the Berlin stage alone; the public never tired of applauding her.

Goethe wrote to Schiller[241]: "Your play is so good and so beautiful that I see nothing to compare with it." This work, however, is far from perfect. The author rightly saw in Joan a soul inflamed with patriotism, but in his drama he often distorted history. Nevertheless, this drama has passed into posterity, for it bears witness to the noble ideal of its author, with verses sometimes incisive, which engrave themselves like maxims upon the memory, sometimes so moving, so deeply human, that the soul retains a lasting impression.

An eminent critic, A.-W. Schlegel, expressed his admiration in these words for the character of Joan of Arc in Schiller's work[242]: "The high mission of which she is conscious, and which imposes respect on all who approach her, produces an effect extraordinary and full of grandeur."



The literary odyssey of the Maid in Germany does not end there. In the aftermath of 1815, a Bavarian publicist, Friedrich Gottlob Wetzel, wrote a tragedy on Joan of Arc. The Baron de la Motte-Fouqué, descendant of Protestant refugees, to celebrate the heroine, became a translator. He adapted to German taste Lebrun des Charmettes' *History of Joan of Arc.*

But the most rigorously historical work consecrated beyond the Rhine to the memory of our Joan is that of

241 *Correspondence between Goethe and Schiller*, translation by Saint-René-Taillandier, vol. II, p. 229.

242 *Course of Dramatic Literature*, vol. III, pp. 309–310.

Guido Görres. Joseph Görres and his son Guido wrote a book in which "they laid at the feet of the French Maid the homage of Germany." Joan of Arc is the envoy of God for the salvation of France: such is the thesis sustained by Joseph Görres in the preface with which he introduces his son's book. He writes:

"It was the destiny of the French to become, in the hands of God, in later ages, a scourge and a goad for other peoples, and France could not have fulfilled this providential role if she had not been delivered from foreign domination and had not preserved her individuality.[243]"

According to Joseph Görres, Joan belonged to two worlds, that of earth and that of heaven; she was called to act in one as the envoy of the other; thus, she would belong to all peoples—by blood to the French, by her noble deeds to others.



It was not by much that Guido Görres did not precede Quicherat in his research. Montalembert had the intention of approaching this great subject, but the work of Guido Görres seemed to him sufficiently important to make him renounce it, and he wrote as much to the author's father. Guido stayed at Orléans, came to Paris, to the National Library, and was projecting a new book on the Maid, more documented than the first, when he was recalled to Germany and diverted to other labors.

Since that time, a whole host of scholars, historians, and writers of every rank have, beyond the Rhine, set themselves to comment on the epic of the Maid of Lorraine. Through the pens of the two Görres, German

243 GUIDO GOERRES, *Joan of Arc*, translation by Léon Boré.

Catholicism had rendered homage to the Maid; Charles Hase, in 1850, brought her the homage of Protestantism[244].

One of Joan's German biographers, Professor Hermann Semmig, dared to write in 1883: "In France, outside of Orléans, the Maid is not everywhere as dear to the French people as she is to the German people.[245]"

"Germany," writes again G. Goyau[246], "seems to affect a sort of coquetry toward the Maid; and this coquetry, at times, in the expression it assumes, becomes almost offensive for us. If France could be accused of forgetting Joan, Germany would be there to celebrate her; if some Frenchman defames Joan, the German springs forth as her knight. It would seem that literary and scholarly Germany, always enamored of the ancient Velléda, bears some envy toward the French."

⚜



Italy offers us, on the same subject, the *General Chronicle of Venice* or *Diario* of Antonio Morosini, recently translated and published[247].

A. Morosini, a noble Venetian and ship-owning merchant of real distinction, composed under this title a "journal," kept without interruption from 1404 to 1434, which the *Revue Hebdomadaire* comments on in these terms:

244 *Heilige und Propheten*, Part Two (3rd edition, 1893).

245 *Die Gartenlaube*, 1883, no. 18, p. 291.

246 G. GOYAU, *Joan of Arc before German Opinion*, pp. 76–77.

247 Chronicle of ANTONIO MOROSINI. Commentary and translation by Léon Dorez.

"A prudent and discerning observer, he (Morosini) knew how to intercalate into his text twenty-five letters or groups of letters recounting, step by step, the progress of the actions of the Maid. Thus is composed, spontaneously, the most genuine of collections, the most captivating 'series' of notions, impressions, and sensations, written not only from week to week but almost from day to day.

These correspondences, for the most part, come from Bruges, the great commercial hub of Flanders, center of trade, business, and information. They themselves often summarize letters of multiple origins—Burgundy, Paris, Brittany. Others reach Venice directly from Avignon, Marseille, Genoa, Milan, Montferrat. Their principal author is the Venetian Pancrazio Giustiniani, residing in Bruges. Beside him appears Giovanni de Molino, established in Avignon.



In very few days—perhaps as early as May 10—with truly astonishing rapidity, the news of the Battle of the Tourelles, fought on the 7th, along with the prediction of the immediate lifting of the siege, traveled from Orléans to Flanders. By ordinary mail, the 'valise' that ran between Bruges and the City of the Doges, Giustiniani almost immediately forwarded it to Venice, to his father. That very day, June 18, Antonio Morosini transcribed the letter, preserved it, and thus saved it.

From then on, at more or less regular intervals, he records, copies, or summarizes continuous missives. The English retreat, Patay, the coronation, the march on Paris—all are announced, observed, transmitted, with the reflection of the astonishment and enthusiasm stirred up by these incomprehensible realities. Even after the dreadful return to the Loire, after the disaster of Compiègne, sympathies persisted. Down to the mourning of Rouen, the drama was followed with an emotion that never faltered.[248]"

⚜

Through this brief study, one can see how Joan, glorified everywhere abroad—even by her former enemies—has met with detractors only in the very country that she made free and victorious. Is not the reverence with which she is held abroad enough to strike those who, while calling themselves internationalists, persist in disparaging her? It is only in France that Joan has been maligned by writers who may have had merit, but who were incapable of understanding her, because in her the human and the divine are blended and harmonized into an ideal figure that surpasses us all.

Her life is like a reflection of that of Christ. Like him, she was born among the humble; like him, she endured the injustice and cruelty of men. Dying young, her short and painful existence is illuminated, as his was, by the rays of the invisible world. To this is even added a further element of poetry: she was a woman—and among women, one of the most sensitive and tender. Singular and moving is the fact that this warrior bore the gift of pacifying and uniting. She drew all toward herself. The English, who once sacrificed her, are today her most ardent supporters; and in France itself, for all those whose souls have not been dried up by the winds



248 G. LEFEVRE-PONTALIS, *Joan of Arc and Her Contemporaries. Revue hebdomadaire*, April 17, 1909, p. 313.

of skepticism, differences of opinion concerning her fade and vanish into a shared veneration.

We speak of dried-up souls—and they are many in our country. For a century, skepticism has done its work. It tends more and more to impoverish the sources of life and thought. Far from being a strength or a virtue, it is rather a disease of the mind. It destroys, it annihilates the confidence we should have in ourselves, in our hidden resources, in the possibilities of developing, growing, and rising—through sustained effort—onto the magnificent planes of the universe; the confidence in that supreme law that draws the being from the depths of life's abysses and opens, to its initiative and its flight, the infinite perspectives of time and the vast theater of worlds.

Skepticism gradually loosens the springs of the soul, softens character, extinguishes fruitful and creative action. Powerful for destruction, it has never given birth to anything great. If it grows unchecked, it may become a scourge, a cause of decline and death for a people.



Criticism is a product of the skeptical spirit of our time. It has carried out a slow work of disintegration; it has reduced to dust all that once made the strength and grandeur of the human spirit. Literature is its principal medium of influence. The new generation allows itself to be seduced by the elegance of language and the magic of expression in its predecessors, and also by that morbid notion that it is easier to criticize and mock than to study a subject thoroughly and conclude logically. Thus, little by little, people renounce all conviction, all lofty faith, preferring instead to wallow in a kind of vague and sterile dilettantism.

It has become fashionable to strike a pose of disillusion, to consider effort vain, truth inaccessible, and to dismiss all arduous labor, contenting oneself with comparing opinions and ideas only to treat them with irony and turn them into ridicule.

Such a method is as impoverished as it is fatal, for it weakens intelligence and judgment. Over time, it leads to a palpable lessening of the virile qualities of our race, to indifference toward the great duties of existence, to ignorance of life's purpose. These spread from one to another, penetrating even into the heart of the people, and tend to dry up the sources of national energy.

The advance of skepticism can be explained by the fact that, among us, the forms of faith no longer meet the demands of the modern mind and of the law of evolution. Religion lacks the rational foundations on which a strong conviction can be built. Experimental spiritualism comes to fill this void and offers to the contemporary soul a field of observation, a body of proofs and facts, which constitute a firm support for the beliefs of the future.

As in the times of Joan and of Christ, the breath of the invisible passes over the world. It will rekindle failing courage; it will awaken souls that seemed dead. One must never despair of the future of our race. The seed of resurrection lies within us, within our minds, within our hearts. Enlightened faith, confidence, and love are the levers of the soul; when they inspire it, sustain it, carry it forward, there is no summit it cannot reach!

# CONCLUSIONS

From the life of Joan of Arc, three great lessons shine forth in lines of light. They are these:

Humanity, in its hours of crisis and trial, is not abandoned to itself; but from above, aid, strength, and inspiration come to sustain it and guide it on its path. When evil triumphs, when adversity rages against a people, God intervenes through His messengers. The life of Joan is one of the most resplendent manifestations of Providence in history.



A powerful communion binds together all planes of life, visible and invisible. For sensitive and evolved souls, whose inner senses and psychic faculties are sufficiently developed, this communion is established even here below, in the midst of earthly life. It is all the closer and more fruitful as these souls are purer, detached from lower influences, and better prepared for the missions entrusted to them. Such is the case with most mediums. Among them, Joan of Arc was one of the greatest.

This communion between the living and the dead, between the inhabitants of the earth and those of space, is one in which each of us is called to participate in the future, through psychic evolution and moral perfection, until both humanities, earthly and celestial, form but one vast family, united in the thought of God.

Even now, bonds endure between the living and the departed. All souls that have encountered one another on earth remain linked by mysterious threads. The present is bound to the past and to the future, and the destiny of beings unfolds in an ascending spiral, from our humble planet to the depths of the starry heavens.

From there, from those heights, descend the messiahs, the providential messengers. Their appearance among us constitutes a revelation. In studying them, in learning to know them, we lift a corner of the veil that hides from us the higher and divine worlds to which they belong—worlds that people scarcely suspect, burdened as they are, for the most part, beneath the heavy chrysalis of matter.

On the great pages of history, God offers such lives as examples and lessons to humanity. It is toward these figures of heroes and martyrs that the gaze of those who doubt, of those who suffer, must be turned. Among them, none is sweeter than that of Joan of Arc. Her actions, her words, are at once ingenuous and sublime. This existence, so short yet so marvelous, is one of the most beautiful gifts God has given to France, and it will remain one of the glories of the nineteenth century—amid so many errors and faults—to have restored to light this noble profile of a virgin. No nation possesses in its annals a fact comparable to this life. As Etienne Pasquier wrote, she is truly "a prodigy of the hand of God."

Her action in the past was the signal for a national renewal; in the present, she is the signal for a religious renewal, different from those that have preceded it, but even better adapted to the necessities of our evolution. When we say religious, it would be more accurate to say scientific and philosophical. Be that as it may, humanity's beliefs are about to be renewed. Will the religious sentiment perish on that account? No, certainly not; it will only transform itself, to take on new forms. Faith cannot be extinguished in the heart of man. It disappears for a moment only to give place to a higher faith. Must not our sun pass beneath the horizon for the stars of night to be kindled, for the immensity of the heavens to be revealed to our eyes? When the day fades, it seems as though the universe were veiled and life about to end. And yet, without the extinction of daylight, could we behold the swarming of the stars in the depths of the skies? It is the same with the present forms of religion and belief. They die only in appearance, so that they may be reborn larger and more beautiful.

The action of Joan and of the great souls from space prepares this rebirth, to which, for our part and on the earthly plane, we have long been working without respite, under the guidance of the glorious inspirer, whose counsels and instructions have never failed us.

Thus it is with a feeling of ardent sympathy for her, of tender veneration and deep gratitude, that I have written this book. It was conceived in hours of meditation, far from the agitations of this world. As the course of my life hastens on, the aspect of things grows sadder and the shadows thicken around me. But a ray from above illumines my whole being, and this ray emanates from the spirit of Joan. It is she who has enlightened me, guided me in my task.

For half a century, much has been written, argued, and debated concerning the Maid of Lorraine. Violent controversies and noisy manifestations have taken place on every side; battles have almost been fought in her name. Amid these contradictions, these struggles, which she followed with saddened gaze, she has wished to make her voice heard. She has deigned to communicate with us, as with a devoted servant of the cause she protects today. These pages are the faithful expression of her thought, of her views. It is on this account, in all personal humility, that I present them to those who, in this world, honor Joan and love France.

**THE END**

www.ingramcontent.com/pod-product-compliance
Lightning Source LLC
LaVergne TN
LVHW051223080426
835513LV00016B/1377

* 9 7 8 1 9 4 8 1 0 9 4 7 5 *